READY FOR
SCHOOL!

READY FOR SCHOOL!

A PARENT'S GUIDE *to* PLAYFUL LEARNING *for* CHILDREN AGES 2 TO 5

ROSEMARIE T. TRUGLIO, PhD

with Pamela Thomas

Foreword by Kyle D. Pruett, MD

RUNNING PRESS
PHILADELPHIA

To Joan Ganz Cooney & Lloyd Morrisett, Co-founders of *Sesame Street*,
For their Vision & Dedication to Preschool Education

Hachette Book Group supports the right to free expression and the value of copyright.
The purpose of copyright is to encourage writers and artists to produce
the creative works that enrich our culture.

The scanning, uploading, and distribution of this book without permission is a theft
of the author's intellectual property. If you would like permission to use material from the
book (other than for review purposes), please contact permissions@hbgusa.com.
Thank you for your support of the author's rights.

Running Press
Hachette Book Group
1290 Avenue of the Americas, New York, NY 10104
www.runningpress.com
@Running_Press

Printed in China

First Edition: September 2019

Published by Running Press, an imprint of Perseus Books, LLC,
a subsidiary of Hachette Book Group, Inc. The Running Press name and
logo is a trademark of the Hachette Book Group.

The Hachette Speakers Bureau provides a wide range of authors for speaking events.
To find out more, go to www.hachettespeakersbureau.com or call (866) 376-6591.

The publisher is not responsible for websites (or their content)
that are not owned by the publisher.

Print book cover and interior design by Frances J. Soo Ping Chow.

Library of Congress Control Number: 2019938751

ISBNs: 978-0-7624-6607-8 (paperback), 978-0-7624-6606-1 (ebook)

1010

10 9 8 7 6 5 4 3 2 1

Stock Photo Credits:
Getty Images © front cover (top left), pages 8, 12, 30, 64, 104,
176, 185, 210, and 246; Shutterstock © page 146

CONTENTS

FOREWORD

Sesame Street, the longest, safest, and most interesting street on the planet, opened for foot traffic fifty years ago. Because of regular repair and upgrade, it continues to delight, intrigue, and educate preschool children and their parents today. A survivor from the late 1960s—a time of chaos, opportunity, creativity, and Great Society promises—this now-iconic television show embodies a promise kept. And what was that promise? To give young children the support and skills they need when they are very young so they will thrive intellectually and socially in school and beyond, with an appetite for learning, competence, and enough curiosity to last a lifetime.

As a former board member for Sesame Workshop, I had the opportunity (of a lifetime) to know many of Sesame Street's creators, critics, artists, musicians, writers, educators, researchers, producers, and puppeteers. Over time, I began to understand that their approach to preschool programming is a unique recipe indeed. That recipe is a pot full of delicious and nutritious, fun and spicy ingredients, about which young kids care deeply: relationships, security, play, language, food, making stuff, making stuff up, loss, animals, numbers, feelings good and bad—the whole human experience. Working from a research base, Sesame Street's content combines humor, surprise, and clever adult hooks to entertain tapped-out parents, while great music and engaging dialogue between characters (both puppet and human) encourage young minds to explore beyond what they already know.

These same qualities run cover to cover through Ready for School! For those who know Sesame Street well, this book will feel very familiar: no preachy or clichéd advice, just the stuff that matters. Expertly guided by Rosemarie Truglio, Senior Vice President of Curriculum and Content, this book will make you feel like the authors almost know you and your child. Dr. Truglio and her Sesame Workshop colleagues have been at their work for many years, and it shows.

This book couldn't have come at a better time. Most of the parents I know these days, regardless of economic or educational security, are hungry for meaningful, relevant suggestions about how to do the best they can for their children, despite being crazy-busy and worried about how to keep their kids happily and safely engaged with the world around them. In my decades of working with families, I have found no more savvy travel guide than *Sesame Street.*

Ready for School! covers all the subjects that make up Sesame Workshop's Whole Child Curriculum, offered as accessible text along with lots of quick and easy extras, like "Oops and Ahas" (personal parenting moments that illustrate how we all learn when making mistakes) and "Play & Learn" (suggestions for playful learning experiences parents and children can share). My favorites? As a child psychiatrist, I went first to Chapter 6 "Celebrate You/Celebrate Me," Chapter 5 "Thinking It Through!" and Chapter 1 "Words and More Words!" I felt plenty of "Ah-Has," despite my long experience with young children and their families. As a physician, I then went to Chapter 7 "Happy Healthy Monsters!" and left with a ton of ideas about how to help parents appreciate their children's drive to be grown-up, but not too fast. The parent in me went to the remaining chapters in no particular order, but I would loved to have had Chapter 3 "How Many Blocks All Together?" on my nightstand when we were raising our first.

And I love the charts! They are like those "quick reference guides" that come with complex electronics. In each chapter, the charts highlight the important stuff you want to understand about *where* your kids are on the scale of developmental learning, and—more important—about *what* comes next, without the anxiety-provoking emphasis on *when* it comes.

Woven throughout this book are *Sesame Street*'s signature guidelines for helping children and their parents face the big and little issues in their lives with courage and respect. Over the years, *Sesame Street* has helped kids deal with everything from homelessness to Mr. Hooper's death, being bullied, racism, and natural disasters. Real-life experience as well as research tells us that *Sesame Street* has helped explain these issues to preschoolers time and time again. Often, parents feel helpless when facing some of the bewildering events that shape our lives and our communities. *Ready for School!* is informed by the tradition of finding a way to help kids and those who love them understand they are not alone, that they have the stuff in them to figure it out, and help is never too far away, even when things—for now—are bad, scary, or beyond understanding.

The other signature *Sesame Street* touch, obvious from the first pages of *Ready for School!,* is the ability to instill a sense of delight and playfulness into the learning process of being ready to learn in school. The repetitive, rote drudge of so many "flash-card" learning approaches is nowhere to be found in this book. *Sesame Street* has known for fifty years that such approaches don't work for learning that endures. Instead, *Ready for School!* encourages even the most reluctant "I-don't-know-how-to-play" parent to use bits of "guided play" with preschoolers to build skills and self-regard, which ultimately culminate in precious "I DID IT!" moments.

The creators of *Sesame Street*—and *Ready for School!*—clearly understand that raising a preschooler, physically and emotionally, is an exhausting, never-ending, 24/7 commitment. They know that even when you are not with them, your children are in your minds or not far from it. They respect what you're trying to give to your family, what you're up against in doing it, and that raising kids is a lifelong adventure.

This empathic tone for parents' challenges pervades *Ready for School!* Mothers and fathers, grandparents, aunts, uncles, older siblings and other extended family members, partners and other caregivers were all in the minds of the writers as they created the content for this gem of a book. You will appreciate having this guidebook to playful learning nearby as you proceed on your singular child-raising journey. Indeed, the iconic question "How do you get to *Sesame Street*?" finally has an answer.

Kyle D. Pruett, M.D.
Emeritus Member, Sesame Workshop Board of Directors
Clinical Professor of Child Psychiatry, Yale School of Medicine
Author (with Marsha Kline Pruett) of Partnership Parenting

INTRODUCTION

About *Sesame Street* & This Book

by Rosemarie T. Truglio, PhD
Senior Vice President of Curriculum and
Content at Sesame Workshop

Welcome to your child's amazing preschool years! It is a time of wonder, imagination, curiosity, experimentation, relationships (especially the one between you and your child), challenges, and, most important, joy—both in your life and in your child's!

I have written this book in celebration of parenthood during these years, when your child's brain is undergoing its most rapid growth and development, with neural connections forming across all regions. As a developmental/child psychologist at Sesame Workshop, I have learned a great deal about preparing children for preschool. Writing this book provided the opportunity to pass on this knowledge to help you get your young child ready for school.

What is Sesame Workshop & How Does It Work?

Before talking about *Ready for School!*, I believe it's important to give you an over-view of Sesame Workshop, the nonprofit educational organization behind *Sesame Street*. Launched on PBS on November 10, 1969, *Sesame Street* was designed as an educational experiment to assess how to harness the power of television to teach children, especially those who were disadvantaged, school-readiness skills so they would be better prepared for kindergarten. The experiment was hugely successful and soon after co-productions of *Sesame Street* began to grow glob-ally, ultimately reaching over 150 countries, making *Sesame Street* the longest street in the world. More than 1,000 academic studies attest to its powerful edu-cational impact.

Sesame Workshop's mission is to help kids grow SMARTER, STRONGER, AND KINDER by delivering research-based, curriculum-directed content that addresses critical educational needs of young children. *Smarter* involves not only teaching academic skills, (literacy, mathematics, and science), but includes the cognitive skills necessary for children to learn how to process and apply information effectively. *Stronger* addresses children's physical health as well as their ability to manage their emotions and build resiliency. *Kinder* refers to all the social skills so imperative to the development of an emotionally healthy child: sharing, taking turns, empathy, compassion, friendship, as well as celebrating physical and cultural differences and similarities.

To ensure the educational integrity of *Sesame Street* content, the Workshop's co-founders, Joan Ganz Cooney and Lloyd Morrisett, PhD, established the Sesame Workshop model, which has been implemented by numerous heads of research and education, including myself, throughout the history of the Workshop. The model is made up of three distinct disciplines, which are represented by experts in each area: Research (headed by developmental/child psychologists who study how children learn); Education (led by educators, who develop and implement curriculum); and Creative (including writers, producers, animators, and songwriters). Experts in these three areas work collaboratively to develop the television show, as well as all other Sesame Workshop–related educational products (books, toys, digital games) and themed entertainment experiences.

At the core of all media content is *Sesame Street*'s whole-child curriculum, which encompasses all aspects of child development: academic, social, emotional, and physical. This comprehensive curriculum was established in 1968, and every year since then has changed and evolved, based on current research, to ensure that *Sesame Street* continues to address the critical educational and societal needs of preschoolers and their families. Toward that end, each new season of *Sesame Street* focuses on a specific component of school readiness, such as literacy, math, health, resiliency, self-regulation, and kindness.

The production phase begins with an annual curriculum seminar. Having identified a critical educational need, we invite leading academic researchers and educators in the field to advise us about best practices in early childhood education. Although these content experts are invaluable, the *real* experts are the children themselves. Before we produce the show's episodes, we kid-test story scripts, new show formats, digital games, and other media products to make sure the content is engaging and the intended lessons and messages are understood.

About This Book

Ready for School! is based on *Sesame Street's* whole-child curriculum, and represents the Workshop's 50 years of research and development in early childhood education. It is composed of eight content areas that, together, provide a comprehensive approach to school readiness: Language, Literacy, Mathematics, Science, Approaches to Learning (including logic and reasoning), Social and Emotional Development, Health, and the Arts. Across these areas, we highlight specific learning objectives, and provide "learning progressions" for neurotypical developing children, ages two to five. We included these progressions to help you gain a better understanding about what is developmentally appropriate; however, it is important to note that these progressions are meant to serve only as guideposts, as all children develop in their own ways. As parents, it is important to acknowledge the process through which your child is learning and not judge the end product based on your expectation of what is best.

    Ready for School! is written and designed for super-busy, 21st-century parents,

and expresses Sesame Workshop's approach to parenting and school readiness, which is grounded in three core principles:

1. **PARENTS ARE ESSENTIAL TO SCHOOL READINESS.** You know your child best, and that makes you uniquely equipped to nurture in your child a lifelong love of learning and curiosity about the world.

2. **OPPORTUNITIES FOR LEARNING ARE EVERYWHERE!** At the kitchen table, on the bus, or in the grocery store, children develop skills and build their understanding of the world through everyday moments and daily routines.

3. **LEARNING THROUGH PLAY IS CRITICALLY IMPORTANT.** With the right support and encouragement, all parents can engage in playful activities to help their children get ready for school and for a happy, healthy, and successful life!

With these principles in mind, we've created a book that will allow you to access the essential information you need quickly and easily. *Ready for School!* is not meant to be read front to back; instead, it is structured so that you can dip into any topic that interests you or that is immediately relevant to you and your child. Each chapter includes a chart that outlines the developmental learning progressions, providing a quick and easy way for you to gather information, depending on the age of your child. Peppered throughout are strategies, activities, hints, tips, and other resources for you to use with your child to discover and develop essential school-readiness skills.

The Importance of Play

Among the most important elements in the book are a series of activities we've called "Play & Learn." We have learned from our advisors that today's children are often stressed, overscheduled, and, at times, pressured to perform beyond what is developmentally appropriate. Coupled with these findings is the strong indication that today's families are so super-busy balancing myriad demands that there has been a decline in children's play and families playing together. This decline is troubling because it is through play that children learn a range of important school-readiness skills.

When children are engaged in play that is meaningful, joyful, and socially interactive, they are learning academic skills, physical skills (both fine- and gross-motor), social skills (communication, conflict resolution, cooperation, and turn-taking), emotional skills (empathy, regulating feelings, and self-confidence), reasoning, and creativity. Play is also beneficial for the whole family. A global research study, commissioned by the LEGO Foundation in 2018, showed that families who spend more than five hours a week playing together—be it outdoors, engaging in pretend play, making things together, playing games of all kinds, including digital ones—consider themselves to be happy, and parents feel more relaxed, energized, and creative.

Children's learning is also enhanced when parents and other adults (caregivers, aunts, uncles, teachers) follow their child's lead and guide their play. Guided play involves enriching your child's play by making comments, encouraging your child to ask questions, and extending your child's interests. For example, you can use math language when building with blocks (words such as "tall," "short," "wide," "measure") or count items and set the table for the specific number of "customers" when playing restaurant. You can also set up a play activity with a learning goal in mind, such as acting out *The Little Engine That Could* with a train set to build literacy skills. By joining your child's play (without taking control of the play), you strengthen your relationship with your child and infuse learning experiences with school-readiness skills.

Parenting & School Readiness

School readiness goes well beyond teaching literacy and mathematics. It means providing a toolbox of skills for your child so that he or she will approach learning positively. This includes taking safe risks and not avoiding failure; persevering after making a mistake; calming down when frustrated, angry, or disappointed;

focusing attention on a task, or being able to shift attention to find another solution; delaying gratification of a desired item; taking the perspective of another; and being empathic, compassionate, respectful, and kind to others.

Parenting is not about perfection or a list of "musts" or "shoulds." Nor is it a time to expedite your child's learning to leapfrog to the head of the class. Parenting is about taking the time to listen, identifying and encouraging your child's interests, providing space to try things out and solve problems (which encourages independence and autonomy), and engaging in playful activities to support your child's learning. It is through everyday experiences and play that your child not only learns academic skills, but also builds confidence as a learner, and character as an empathic, compassionate, and respectful person.

During my almost 30 years as a developmental/child psychologist, I have learned so much from the children in my life, including children associated with my professional experiences, my nieces and nephew, and, ultimately, my son.

In 2004, my son, Lucas Albert, was born, giving me the opportunity to put into practice what I had preached for years. Of course, like all parents, my husband and I had a lot to learn. We had to adjust to Lucas's temperament (shy, slow to warm up); figure out how to follow his interests (his love of nature, including worms and bugs, which was not a particular passion of mine!); model strategies for how to be resilient in times of transition or error; and indicate on a daily basis how to be kind and respectful to others. A big lesson I learned from his kindergarten teacher was to spill more milk at home. "What?" I said to her. "Why would I do that?" Her response: "Lucas needs to see how you react when you make a mistake!"

I encourage you to adopt a positive—and playful!—approach to parenting, build on your child's strengths, understand your child as a learner, and better understand what to expect, based on your child's age. Be sure to spend time together, one-on-one, and as a family. Most important, take the time to notice and see the world through your child's eyes.

Remember, these magical years go by too quickly! Enjoy the wonder!

1. WORDS, WORDS & MORE WORDS!

Listening & Speaking

I n 2006, the producers of *Sesame Street* introduced a new female character, Abby Cadabby. As always, about a year before this new season, the Education Department at Sesame Workshop arranged for a daylong seminar to introduce the show's producers and writers to the upcoming curriculum—in this case, literacy with an emphasis on vocabulary. We decided that one of Abby's defining characteristics would be WORDS, especially rhyming words, as she learned to do her magic as a fairy-in-training.

In her first appearance on *Sesame Street*, Abby Cadabby introduced herself by saying, "I know I'm just a little fairy, but I've got a big vocabulary." She then burst into a song, that, in part, went like this:

> *Words, words, and more words,*
> *How I adore words.*
> *I love words more than I can say.*
> *Short words and long words,*
> *singing-a-song words*
> *I like words better every day.*
> *Words, and words, and more words,*
> *How I adore words,*

Words help me mean just what I say,
Story-to-tell words
Magical spell words
I try a new word every day!

The next year, Murray Monster also made his debut on *Sesame Street*, as host of a newly created segment called "Word on the Street." He played the role of a roving street reporter, interviewing children and adults who defined each episode's vocabulary word through actions, visuals, and verbal descriptions. After Murray introduced the episode's featured word ("pumpernickel," "jealous," "cheer," "octagon," and "soggy" are a few examples), the word was repeated in the episode's "Street Story," and then reinforced in a subsequent segment that featured a celebrity and a puppet character. Celebrities were invited not only to pique the interest of the adult co-viewers, but also to show adults how to extend the learning of these words into the child's daily life experiences.

In order for a child to understand a new word and use it appropriately, she needs to be exposed to the word repeatedly and across different contexts. This is why it is so important to talk, sing, and read to your child throughout the day. Television, as an audiovisual medium, also provides a wonderful opportunity for preschoolers to hear a word while simultaneously seeing a visual depiction of it. And on *Sesame Street*, we make a concerted effort to highlight a broad range of words, and repeat them throughout the program.

QUICK TIP

As you talk, sing, or read to your child, think of your language-rich exchange as a two-way conversation. Allow your child to respond, first with coos, then babbles, and finally with real words. Leave a space or pause for a few seconds after you have asked your child a question: "Look at the big blue bus! Where do you think it's going?" "How does the bunny's fur feel?" "Do you feel warm and snuggly in your new jacket?"

The development of children's vocabulary and oral language comprehension during the preschool years plays an essential role in their readiness for kindergarten, and is also a predictor of their long-term academic success. From the moment of birth, it is important to expose your child to rich language in a variety of contexts.

Developing Language:
Listening & Speaking

During their first five years, children experience the most significant brain development of their lives. Neural networks and pathways explode as children interact with and learn from their environment. And the most important aspect of a child's cognitive growth is the development of language and literacy.

Language development is divided into two areas, receptive language (listening) and expressive language (speaking). RECEPTIVE LANGUAGE includes understanding spoken words and the ability to follow directions. EXPRESSIVE LANGUAGE refers to how words are used to communicate ideas, feelings, and an understanding of concepts.

GOOD STUFF!
"FIRST WORD" BOOKS

"First Word" books are illustrated books showing everyday objects together with the word that describes the object. It may be a simple noun (such as a photograph of an apple together with the word "apple") or it may be an adjective (a picture of a blue bicycle with the word "blue" next to it). More complex word books involve detailed illustrations, such as a city street, with various words called out next to objects, such as "tree," "car," "window," "police officer," or other objects or people included in the picture. "First Word" books serve as excellent early introductions to language and literacy.

For very young children, start with simple board books, ideally books with photos of brightly colored objects; small board books are easier for little hands to hold and can withstand rough treatment. For slightly older children, check out "category" books, such as animals, transportation, dinosaurs, and other subjects of interest to your child. "Look-and-Find" books, illustrated books, often with flaps that direct the reader to "look-and-find" various items in a scene, are a delight for many children and can be excellent tools for learning first words.

EVERYDAY ADVENTURES WITH WORDS

Encourage your child, no matter what age, to look at all the things and actions in his environment and then name them. These can involve the most mundane activities: getting dressed ("shirt," "button," "zipper," "collar," "elastic"); bathing ("hot water," "cold water," "foamy soap," "squishy washcloth"); cooking ("mixing bowl," "chop," "peel," "spread," "stir," "measuring spoons," "measuring cups"), going to the supermarket (label specific vegetables, fruits, breads, dairy products). Every object and every activity at every age offer an opportunity for language development.

Point out various objects to your child and label them. For example, when you're out walking or riding in your car or on a bus with your child, indicate familiar things in your neighborhood: trees, birds, flowers, squirrels, dogs, buses, bicycles, trucks, a school, the supermarket, the library, the mail carrier, the delivery person, and any other people, places, or things your child sees frequently.

Don't be afraid to use more complex words or descriptions. For example, instead of just saying "Look at the bird!," try using a specific name, such as "sparrow," "pigeon," or "robin," or a more complicated description, such as "Look at the pretty red bird, It's called a cardinal.'"

Also, ask lots of questions. "What color is the bus?" "I see two squirrels. How many do you see?" Think about "word webs," and encourage your child to think along those lines. For example, as your child enjoys a glass of milk, ask her if she knows where the milk comes from: "cows." Then allow the word "cow" to lead to other related words, such as "farm," "barn," "farmer," "tractor," as well as other farm animals. Not only does this sort of word web build vocabulary, but it enhances the child's conceptual knowledge about the word.

Strong language skills, especially a wide and deep vocabulary, help children understand the world around them and express what they know, which is important for school achievement, but critical for managing their emotions and building relationships. Expanding vocabulary in the early years is an important step—perhaps the most important step—toward future reading success. By simply talking, singing, and reading with you, children get to hear new words in action.

To build their vocabulary (in any language), children need to:

- **BE EXPOSED TO WORDS OF ALL KINDS**, from simple ones to more complex (from "happy" to "ecstatic"; from "bird" to "pigeon"; from "red" to "scarlet").

- **HEAR NEW WORDS MULTIPLE TIMES** and in different situations to understand their meaning. ("Remember when you were trying hard to open that box of crackers and it wouldn't open? You felt frustrated. Mommy's having a hard time finding the house keys. I'm feeling so frustrated!")

- **SHARE EXPERIENCES** that show the meaning of words ("What transportation should we take to get to the doctor's office? Should we take the bus, a car, a subway, a taxi, or a bike?") and how they are related to words children already know. ("Transportation is what we use to get from one place to another—like cars, trains, or buses.")

- **BE ENCOURAGED TO USE NEW WORDS** they are learning. ("There are lots of birds at the park today. I see a cardinal. A cardinal is a bird with beautiful red feathers. Let's look together and tell me when you see a cardinal.")

QUICK TIP

Put your phone down and *play* with your child! It's no secret that cell phones, digital tablets, and all forms of social media are "disruptors," and are linked to the fact that parents are spending less time interacting with their children. Instead of talking on your cell phone, checking your texts, or wandering through social media, take time to notice how your child is engaging with his world. Then, start to consider vocabulary associated with his interests—whether it's trains, dinosaurs, or ballerinas—and introduce those words into your conversations with him.

Language is also the key to building positive relationships. Communicating feelings in appropriate ways and understanding how to take turns during conversations are essential skills for positive interactions with both grown-ups and other children.

17

Understanding Language (Receptive Language)

As children build their understanding of language, they start to comprehend different kinds of words we use in everyday situations, from common words to more complicated and unfamiliar words and directives. For example, as children mature, they learn:

- **BASIC WORDS**, or words that they encounter through their everyday experiences (usually nouns and verbs), such as "rain," "bus," "ball," "run," "jump," and "dance."

GOOD STUFF!
CHAPTER BOOKS

Introducing chapter books (books in which the story evolves over several chapters) can add extra interest and variety to your everyday reading routine. If you often read together at bedtime, you can read a new chapter each night, giving your child something to look forward to at bedtime. It also encourages her to think about the story during the day, and to hold onto the story line, which develops memory and reading comprehension. Also, the ever-evolving story gives you something to discuss ("What happened in the last chapter?" "What do you think might happen now?") when you start to read each night.

Classic, beloved chapter books include:

- *Magic Tree House* series by Mary Pope Osborne and Sal Murdocca

- *Nate the Great* by Marjorie Weinman Sharmot, illustrated by Marc Simont

- *Pippi Longstocking* by Astrid Lindgren, illustrated by Michael Chesworth

- *Stuart Little* by E. B. White, illustrated by Garth Williams

- *The Trumpet of the Swan* by E. B. White, illustrated Garth Williams

- *Amelia Bedelia* chapter books by Herman Parish, illustrated by Lynne Avril

- *Winnie-the-Pooh* by A. A. Milne, illustrated by Ernest H. Shepard

- CONTENT WORDS, or words that are linked to math, science, emotions, or health topics, that need more explaining from trusted grown-ups, books, or other media; that is, words like "octagon," "calendar," and "alive."

- RARE WORDS, or words that are used in special situations, like a "prescription" at the pharmacy, a "receipt" from the supermarket, or a "bill" from a restaurant.

- CONNECTING WORDS, or words that join thoughts or ideas ("about," "than," "because"), as well as words that are used across all learning or across a broad range of activities, whether it is math, science, art, or sports ("plan," "compare," "check," "speed").

- CATEGORY WORDS, or words that connect to other words your child already knows, as well as group-related words, including synonyms ("big," "large," "huge," "gigantic") and superordinate words, words that designate general categories. For example, snakes, lizards, and turtles are all "reptiles"; refrigerators, stoves, and blenders are all "appliances"; and cars, trains, boats, bikes, and airplanes are all modes of "transportation"; thus, "reptiles," "appliances," and "transportation" are all superordinate or category words.

- TO FOLLOW DIRECTIONS. When children learn to follow directions, it shows that they are hearing and understanding new language. ("Please speak softly when we're inside the library.")

- TO RESPOND TO VERBAL REQUESTS AND QUESTIONS. Children show us they understand a request or question when they respond appropriately with their actions. ("Please put your shoes by the door.")

What to Expect From Your Preschooler

AGE 2

At two years old, your child is probably very interested in the conversation around her, especially familiar voices. She looks when people are speaking to her or her name is called. She also looks at an object when it is named and pointed to ("Look, kitty is playing with the ball").

At age two, she will connect words with familiar people and things. She points to a dog in a picture when you ask, "Where's the dog?" And she walks (or runs!) toward the door when you say, "Daddy's home!"

Her vocabulary is mostly made up of common objects that are part of her world, people (parents, siblings), actions (walking, eating), and describing words (pretty, red). She probably groups things together into very general categories, such as pointing to other birds when asked to find the "duck."

She also responds when you make a simple request, especially if the request is modeled. For example, your child imitates you when you say and wave, "Bye-bye" and smiles for the camera when you grin and say, "Smile!"

Finally, as she nears three years old, she starts to understand simple one-step directions by words alone. You may see this when your child gets her shoes from the closet or puts away large puzzle pieces inside a box when asked.

AGE 3

At three years old, your child probably understands and can respond to simple words, sentences, stories, and questions. For example, he finds his favorite stuffed animal when asked or makes motor sounds when a favorite story mentions a big truck.

He understands more words. This includes a person, place, or thing ("cousin," "playground," "basketball"), action words or verbs ("hop," "spin," "chew"), and describing words or adjectives ("shiny," "hot," "rough"). He is also learning connecting words ("because," "about") and content words (describing basic shapes and feelings).

He also knows some category words ("animals," "clothes," or "transportation") and is beginning to understand how a word is related to other similar words ("huge," "gigantic") and falls into a category ("size"). You may see this when your child correctly points to or even names "a duck," "a chicken," and "a goose" when asked, "What birds are in this picture?"

He's also able to follows directions of two or more steps related to something familiar or routine. You may see this when he responds, for example, to your request to put his jacket away and then wash his hands.

PLAYING IN MORE THAN
ONE LANGUAGE

Learning to understand and speak more than one language can play an important role in your child's intellectual and social development. If you speak a language other than English in your home, don't hesitate to keep on using that language as much as possible. If you are an English speaker, but simply enjoy speaking, reading, and writing in other languages, introduce this pleasure to your children.

• MULTILINGUAL PLAY. Don't worry: Exposing children to more than one language at a time is not confusing to your child. As you talk and play with your child throughout the day, move back and forth between your native language and English. Introduce multiple languages in all facets of everyday life, from playing with puzzles and blocks to shopping for groceries or getting ready for bed. Approach multilingual skills as an easy and fun—even playful—way to communicate.

• SHARING STORIES IN YOUR NATIVE LANGUAGE. If you or other family members were born in another country, share funny moments of that life—either from your own childhood or from your relatives' lives, and tell them in your native language. Not only will you be exposing your child to your cultural heritage, but you will also be sharing with her a rich oral tradition. Cuddle up as you tell your stories; the experience will prove educational and provide warm memories for you both.

• SINGING SONGS IN YOUR NATIVE LANGUAGE. If your native language is not English, teach your child to sing songs and recite poems in your native language. Even if your native language is English, introduce children's songs ("Frère Jacques" in French, "Los Politos Dicen" in Spanish, or "Two Tigers" in Chinese, for example) and poems in other languages to your child.

AGE 4

At four years old, your child is most likely beginning to understand more challenging words, sentences, questions, stories, and requests. For example, she can act out a familiar story that has been read to her. You may also observe that she listens more carefully when grown-ups are having a conversation and may be curious about what is being discussed.

At four, she has an understanding of how words are related and fall into basic categories. She recognizes that bananas and apples are fruits, broccoli and carrots are vegetables, and these all are foods she can eat.

She is starting to understand words related to time ("tomorrow," "yesterday," "later") and to more complex feelings ("frustrated," "worried," "excited"), as well as more content words and rare words used in special situations (an "invitation" to a birthday party; a "thermometer" to take your "temperature" to "check" if you have a "fever").

At four, she follows more detailed directions. For example, she helps set the table by placing a place mat, plate, and cup for each person, and she knows that her bedtime routine includes taking a bath, brushing her teeth, reading, and getting a hug good-night.

AGE 5

By the time your child turns five, he probably understands and responds to more challenging and complex words, sentences, questions, stories, and requests. For example, he can answer the question, "What is your favorite game? Why is it your favorite game to play?" and is able to follow longer stories you read to her. This is a good time to introduce short chapter books, such as *Magic Tree House* by Mary Pope Osborne or even classics such as *The Trumpet of the Swan* by E. B. White.

At five, he has a deeper understanding of how words are related to each other and fall into more complex categories. For example, he connects "winter" to a variety of words, such as "snow," "mittens," "sled," and "holidays," and he comprehends that winter, spring, summer, and fall are all seasons.

At age five, he also understands many content words, some rare words used in special circumstances, and a growing number of words that help us as we learn (like "plan," "observe," "describe").

Also, he follows more detailed, multistep directions. You may see this when your child is able to help with several steps of a recipe you read out loud, or is able to play a new game following instructions you give.

Using Words (Expressive Language)

As children develop their speaking skills and learn to use language to express their ideas, they start to:

- **USE NEW WORDS TO TALK ABOUT WHAT THEY SEE.** Young children like to use words to name and express their thoughts, actions, observations, feelings, and needs. As their vocabulary develops, they use a greater mix of basic words, useful content words, and rare words.

- **CONNECT WORDS THAT ARE RELATED AND NAME THE CATEGORY THEY BELONG TO.** Children learn to play word games by relating or replacing similar words as they speak (. . . or sing!) familiar poems and songs. With familiar songs like "Old MacDonald Had a Farm," children enjoy substituting baby farm animals for grown ones (dog/puppy; pig/piglet; sheep/lamb); with "The Wheels on the Bus," they substitute more unusual parts of the bus and what they do ("The wipers go whish, whish, whish") and people's behaviors ("People go up and down"). Children also learn to use a category to name a group of words. For example, they understand that a hammer, a screwdriver, and a wrench are all tools.

QUICK TIP

You remember "Jack and Jill Went Up the Hill," "Mary Had a Little Lamb" and all the wonderful songs and poems that are now simply a part of you. Begin to recite or sing nursery rhymes to your child from her earliest days and she will never forget them. As your child grows just slightly older, introduce "action" songs with finger play and movement, including "Where is Thumbkin?," "Five Little Ducks," "I'm a Little Tea Pot," and "If You're Happy and You Know It."

If your memory needs jogging, check out a book of nursery rhymes, such as *My Very First Mother Goose*, edited by Iona Opie and illustrated by Rosemary Wells; a collection of simple songs, such as *Sesame Beginnings: My First Songs*; or a story that features movement to emphasize the meaning of action words, such as *Barnyard Dance* by Sandra Boynton.

23

"ABBY SAYS"

Do you remember playing "Simon Says" as a child? This old-fashioned game remains as much fun for children today as it was when we were kids. It is also an excellent way to teach "receptive" language, including understanding basic words and responding to verbal directions, as well as other important school-readiness skills, such as listening, focusing attention, and controlling impulses.

For this version of this game, use "Abby" instead of Simon. For example, for very young kids, "Abby says, touch your nose" or "Abby says, jump up and down." For slightly older children, try more complicated directives, such as "Abby says, pull on your ear, wiggle your toes," or "Abby says, hop *three times*." Gradually build up to more complex routines, even encouraging your child to hop on one foot, run in place, pat your head while rubbing your tummy, or, just for fun, add silly directives, such as "Make a silly face." Finally, other phrases to add to the game are: Abby says, "Freeze," or Abby says, "Melt," or Abby says, "Stop," or Abby says, "Go."

Don't forget to drop "Abby says" every now and then! The whole point of the game is to NOT do something unless Abby tells you to!

OOPS & AHA!

I planned to recycle a number of large boxes I had received in the mail (Oops!) until my kids, ages three and five, insisted that I keep them. They ended up playing with them for hours, turning the boxes into trains and houses. My son and daughter took turns being the "conductor" and the "passenger" on their trains. When they turned the boxes into houses, they compared which one was "sturdier" and more "spacious." I saw firsthand (Aha!) how everyday objects can ignite children's creativity while building language skills.

—Jennifer, educator & mom

- **USE WORDS TO NAME AND EXPRESS THEIR THOUGHTS, ACTIONS, OBSERVATIONS, FEELINGS, AND NEEDS.** As their vocabulary develops, they use a greater mix of basic words, useful content words, and rare or unusual words.

- **BEGIN CONVERSATIONS, TAKING TURNS SPEAKING AND LISTENING.** As their language skills get stronger, children feel more comfortable starting conversations and asking questions that are on their minds. This supports both their social and academic growth. They learn to stay on the top of the conversation and take turns speaking and listening. Remember to pause and give your child time to process what you are saying and the time she needs to put her thoughts together to respond. As she matures, encourage her to do the same to people she is conversing with.

- **TELL STORIES ABOUT ANOTHER TIME OR PLACE.** Children begin to talk about the past, present, and future. ("Yesterday, I went to the park. Today I'm going to play with my friend, Charlie, from school. Tomorrow, my grandmother is coming for a visit.") They also learn to talk about ideas and events from their imaginations.

What to Expect from Your Preschooler

AGE 2

At two years old, your child can probably speak in sentences of two or more words and take turns in a conversation listening and speaking (up to two times). He responds with an enthusiastic, "Yes!" when asked if he wants to go outside, then asks, "Mama, play soccer?"

Although he makes grammatical errors as he talks ("I go zoo" or "No like carrots"), he is beginning to talk. He names familiar people, places, and things in his world, even when they are not present ("Mama working" or "Doggie go bye-bye"). He may overstretch or misuse some words (calling a toolshed a "house" or an ambulance a "fire truck"), but it is clear that he understands the word's meaning.

AGE 3

At three years old, your child probably can say longer sentences with several words and fewer errors in grammar but, for example, she may still use pronouns incorrectly ("Her came over to play today"). She joins in longer conversations, taking turns listening and speaking (up to three times).

At age three, she tells simple stories about recent events but probably leaves out details and may tell the events out of order ("I went down the slide. Me and Daddy went to the park.")

She also talks about and describes familiar items. ("This is a toothbrush. I clean my teeth with it." "Soap takes dirt away.") She may be able to list items in a category ("What fruits can we get at the supermarket?" "What colors do you see in the rainbow?") and uses more basic words and content words.

AGE 4

At four years old, your child can probably speak in full sentences and join in even longer conversations, taking turns listening and speaking (up to four times). He can talk about past and future events with correct grammar. ("We went to the playground today. Tomorrow we see Grandma.") He can begin to tell stories

GOOD STUFF!
AUDIOBOOKS

Although reading with your child, one-on-one, remains the best way to develop strong literacy skills, allowing your child to listen to audiobooks (recordings on CDs or other digital devices) offers a fun way for your child to become familiar with stories and songs on his own during play, and to learn new words, even in a second language. Hundreds of popular storybooks, as well as delightful musical collections, are available digitally, and can be found in libraries, stores, and online.

26

MAKING STORIES FROM WORDS

Introduce the notion to your child that stories are made up of words. Ask your child to come up with four or five of her favorite words, such as "park," "swing," "pizza," "dog," or "bicycle," and include the names of a sibling, friend, or pet. Write the words down on a piece of paper in large, block letters. Then, start the story using her selected words; for example, "What happened when Marty Dog went to the park?" Once the story gets started, ask your child to embellish it. You might even encourage her to use a few rhyming words. Have fun exploring ideas and following your child's lead as the story comes from her imagination and probably will get very silly! Print aspects of the story on separate pieces of paper, highlighting the special words, and ask your child to draw a picture on each page, referencing that word. When you're finished, staple the pages together to create a "book."

Brought to you by "The Letter L"! Each day on *Sesame Street*, one letter of the alphabet is featured, which we've learned is an effective way to teach letters and words. Try this at home. Ask your child to pick a favorite letter—maybe the first initial of his name, like "L" for "Lucas"—then use that letter to plan activities for that day. For "L," you might go to the "library," call cousin "Lucy," and make "lasagna" for supper. Think of as may activities as you can. Also, write down your "L" words on a piece of paper, show it to your child, and ask him to say the words back to you.

about recent events in the right order. ("I went to the park with Daddy. I went down the slide three times!")

He continues to talk about and describe the use of familiar items. ("Daddy uses oven mitts because the cookie sheet is hot.") He can list more items in a category and name more categories. ("Drums and trumpets are musical instruments.") His vocabulary is growing with content words (like "seed," "sprout," "roots"), and some rare words that he has picked up in specific situations (like "camouflage," "harvest").

AGE 5

At five years old, your child probably speaks in full sentences and joins in longer conversations, taking turns listening and speaking (up to five times). She uses new words that she's learning, including technical words (less familiar words that are used in special situations), like "graph," "scale," and "illustrator."

She tells detailed stories about recent events. For example, she is able to share details about an afternoon spent with an aunt, including where they went, how they got there, who they saw, and what they did.

At age five, she can explain how things are related to each other within a category. ("Trees, flowers, and grass are all plants. They all need water, soil, and sunlight to grow.")

Conclusions

The development of language during a child's first years—both receptive and expressive language—is one of the most important aspects of a child's growth. The expansion of your child's vocabulary, his understanding of a broad range of words, and his ability to express them verbally is of paramount importance. With them, he can move with pleasure to his next area of development: reading and writing.

UNDERSTANDING LANGUAGE

AGE 2	AGE 3	AGE 4	AGE 5
Is very interested in ambient conversation, especially familiar voices.	Understands and can respond to simple words, sentences, stories, and questions.	Is beginning to understand more challenging words, sentences, questions, stories, and requests.	Understands and responds to more challenging words, sentences, questions, stories, and requests.
Connects words with familiar people and things.	Understands more words, including nouns, verbs, adjectives, connecting words, content words.	Is starting to understand words related to time, content/concepts, and to more complex feelings.	Understands more complex words, needed to help with special circumstances or learning situations.
Responds when you make a simple request.	Knows some category words, such as animals, foods, types of play, etc.	Understands in greater depth how words are related and fall into basic categories, such as seasons, clothing, holidays, and other things that are related.	Has a still deeper understanding of how words are related to each other and fall into more complex categories.
Starts to understand simple one-step directions by words alone.	Follows directions of two or more steps.	Follows more detailed directions.	Follows more detailed, multistep directions.

USING WORDS

AGE 2	AGE 3	AGE 4	AGE 5
Can say sentences with two or more words.	Can say longer sentences with several words.	Can speak in full sentences, and join in longer conversations.	Speaks in full sentences, and joins in still longer conversations.
Makes grammatical errors when talking.	Makes fewer grammatical errors.	Uses grammar correctly.	Uses newly learned words when having a conversation.
Names familiar people, places, and things, even when they are not present.	Tells simple stories about recent events.	Can talk about past and future events.	Tells detailed stories about recent events.
	Talks about and describes familiar items.	Continues to talk about and describe the use of familiar items.	Can explain how things are related to each other within a category.

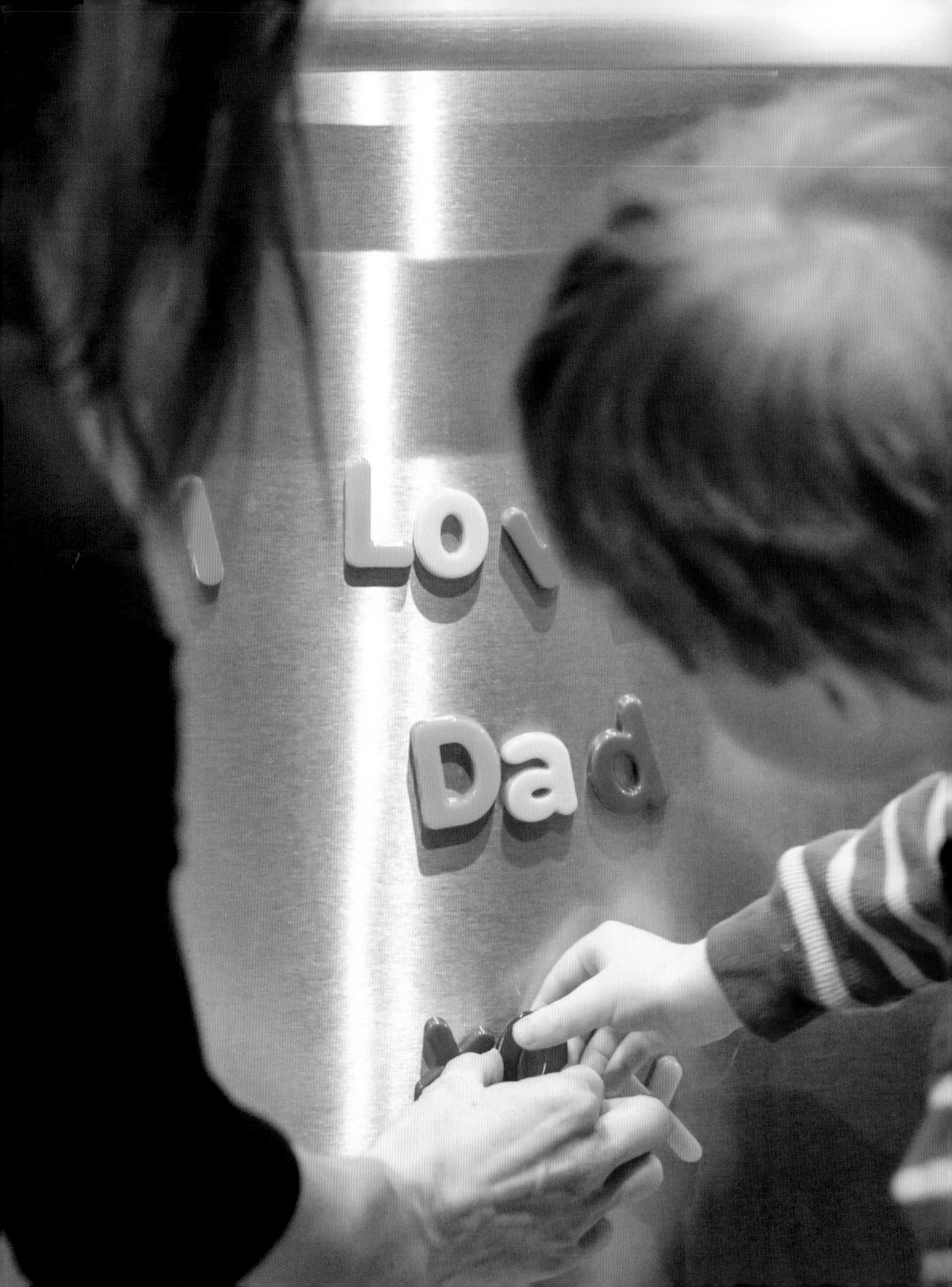
Dad

2. SIGHTS, SOUNDS & SCRIBBLES

Early Reading & Writing

On a classic *Sesame Street* episode, one focusing on the joys of literacy, Elmo asks his friend Maria to read his favorite book to him—over and over again. The title of the book is *Lucy the Lazy Lizard*, and the story emphasizes alliteration (when the same first letter sound occurs repeatedly in a series of words). It also features descriptive vocabulary, suspense, and a perfect example of how a child can extend the story into imaginative play with a friend.

The story stars Lucy, a lazy lizard. As the tale begins, Lucy is lounging lazily on her lovely little log when a long, loud train comes lumbering down the tracks going to Lackawanna. Lucy looks up and sees the looming long, loud train getting closer, but is too lazy to move. Luckily, Lucy is the strongest lizard in Lackawanna, and she lifts up the tracks over her head at the last minute so that the train passes right over her. Then, Lucy lazily returns to lounging on her lovely little log.

QUICK TIP

It's never too early to begin reading to your child. If possible, choose a book that was a favorite of yours, such as *The Tale of Peter Rabbit* by Beatrix Potter or *Green Eggs and Ham* by Dr. Seuss. By the time he is two, some of your favorite books may become his favorite books, too. And, together, as your child develops his own interests, you'll create a list of favorites, not only for you and your child, but also for your entire family.

After Maria reads the book several times and explains to Elmo that she must go back to work, Elmo, a typical three-year-old, wants to hear the story yet again, and goes to find someone else to read it to him. He encounters Telly, who is playing with his train set. Telly explains that he can't read the book now because the Triangle Express has to get triangles to Tuscaloosa. (More alliteration, but this time with the letter "T.") But wait . . . the triangles have already gone to Tuscaloosa! This gives Elmo an idea! Maybe the triangles could go to Lackawanna instead. Telly loves this idea because who doesn't need triangles in Lackawanna? Elmo goes on to tell his favorite story about Lucy as Telly excitedly acts it out with his train set. It turns out to be the greatest train adventure ever! Telly can't wait to read this book now. Luckily, Elmo knows it by heart.

The Basics of Literacy

Reading together with your child opens doors to new and exciting experiences and adventures. Nurturing an early love of reading helps children build vocabulary, comprehension, alphabet knowledge, letter sounds, writing skills, and content knowledge. By reading to your child and engaging in literacy-rich playful moments, parents help their children build essential early literacy skills and a passion for reading and writing. These fundamental literacy skills prepare preschoolers to succeed in school and to become joyful readers and writers throughout their lives.

Before children are able to read and write, they must learn the fundamentals of literacy, including the ability to:

- UNDERSTAND THE BASICS OF THE PRINTED WORD. For example, they need to understand that text carries meaning, is made up of individual words and letters, and is read from left to right in the English language.

- RECOGNIZE AND NAME THE LETTERS OF THE ALPHABET, both uppercase and lowercase.

- MAKE THE SOUND OR SOUNDS ASSOCIATED WITH EACH LETTER, including the sound each letter makes alone, when blended together (putting the letters "s-a-t" together to make "sat"), or when broken into

READING & WRITING IN
MORE THAN ONE LANGUAGE

Developing literacy skills in more than one language offers countless benefits for your child's intellectual and social capabilities. If your native language is not English, make an effort to speak, read, and write in your native language as well as in English in your home. Here are a few tips:

- **READING IN YOUR NATIVE LANGUAGE.** If books are difficult to find in your native language, approach written language by pointing out signs (if you live in a multiethnic neighborhood), food labels, newspapers, magazines, and other print items to your child in your native language. Highlight words your child knows.

- **WRITING IN YOUR NATIVE LANGUAGE.** As your child begins to write in English, don't hesitate to help write those words in your native language at the same time.

- **LEARNING MATH AND SCIENCE IN YOUR LANGUAGE.** Math and science skills are the same in every language, so, when talking about math or science subjects with your child, speak in the language with which you are most comfortable.

GOOD STUFF!
BILINGUAL STORYBOOKS

Many children's books are available in both Spanish and English. Here are a few suggestions for delightful Spanish language (or bilingual Spanish/English) books for parents or caregivers who want to introduce the Spanish language to their children.

– *La Madre Goose: Nursery Rhymes for Los Niños* by Susan Middleton Elya, illustrated by Juana Martinez-Neal

    In this book, Mother Goose rhymes are laced with important Spanish words. A wonderful way for a child to learn both Spanish and English vocabulary.

– *La Princesa and the Pea* by Susan Middleton Elya, illustrated by Juana Martinez-Neal

    Here a classic fairy tale is told in English, interwoven with important Spanish words.

– *De la cabeza a los pies* (*From Head to Toe*, Spanish edition), written and illustrated by Eric Carle

    This is the Spanish-language version of the famous Eric Carle book, *From Head to Toe*. Many other iconic Eric Carle books are also available in Spanish.

– *Diez Deditos and Other Play Rhymes and Action Songs* by José-Luis Orozco, illustrated by Elisa Kleven

    This book is for bilingual parents who want to keep the traditions of finger play and songs in their native Spanish language alive with their children. The songs are also translated. The book includes a CD.

– *Mis colores, mi mundo* by Maya Christina Gonzalez

    A bilingual, Spanish/English introduction to the subject of colors for younger children, ages two to three.

34

syllables in a word ("ba-na-na"). When helping children make letter sounds, it is important not to use the "uh" sound at the end of the letter (for example, "puh" for the letter "p"). The letter sounds should be as short and clear as possible.

- **EXPERIMENT WITH SIMPLE FORMS OF WRITTEN COMMUNICATION,** including both drawing and writing.

Developing Literacy

Literacy skills can be developed in a number of simple and playful ways. Pre-schoolers love books with rhyme, rhythm, and repeated phrases. In fact, as these stories are read over and over again, children learn the sequence of the story and master their "reading" skills as they pretend to read the stories back to you (often with the help of pictures). Children may also enjoy other aspects of story-telling, such as making up or retelling favorite stories using dolls, stuffed animals, or puppets; singing songs; playing rhyming games; drawing pictures; and even writing simple words under their pictures to express ideas.

Literacy skills can also be developed through joyful and meaningful play. For example, you might engage your child in a game of "restaurant," and, while making a menu or restaurant signs together, you can introduce all the words associated with a restaurant, from foods ("eggs," "pizza," "milk") to other aspects of a restaurant ("table," "chairs," "plate," "bowl," "spoon"). While delighting in the game together, you'll create a strong learning experience with and for your child.

The most effective way for children to develop language and literacy skills during their early years is through simple everyday experiences. You can help your child build her literacy skills by narrating experiences throughout the day. For example, actively point to and label things in the environment as you are walking down the street or riding on a bus or in a car. During these shared-attention moments, your child can learn simple nouns ("dog," "cat," "car," "light"), as well as descriptive words to highlight color ("red bird," "blue coat"), relational concepts ("tall building," "fast bicycle"), quantity ("three bowls, "two hats"), and spatial relations ("under," "over," "in front of," "behind").

DEEP DIVE
READING TIME & DIGITAL MEDIA

Digital media have become an important part of our daily lives, but experts worry about exposing young children to too much technology. When used with discretion, however, apps and ebooks can provide engaging, playful literacy moments for you and your child to share. If you're using digital media, it is important to consider the age of your child, as well as the content he is being exposed to. And remember, whether you're using digital media or a good old-fashioned print book, young children learn best when a parent and child engage in the experience together.

Tips for identifying high-quality educational apps:

- **ACTIVE PARTICIPATION.** Avoid apps that simply grab her attention through mindless activities, such as pressing a "hot spot" to hear a funny sound or make a character move. Instead, look for apps that require a child to think, participate ("minds-on"), and succeed at the task. Choose apps that guide your child to discover new information that she will find interesting. For example, the app "Elmo Loves ABCs" teaches the English alphabet by exploring what letters look like, the sounds they make, and words that begin with each specific letter.

- **SUSTAINED ENGAGEMENT.** Choose digital ebooks and apps that keep the child's attention on the story or activity itself, and not on extraneous "bells and whistles" features, which tend to distract young readers. Studies have shown that such distracting features are related to parents' use of negative talk during reading time ("Stop pressing the buttons!" "Don't turn the page!"), compared to more positive parent-child interactions when reading printed books. If possible, select apps that provide "lock-in" narration and "lock-out" interactivity for the first "read" of the story. "Cookie Monster's Challenge" is an excellent example of an app that sustains a child's interest in a playful way.

- **MEANINGFUL CONNECTIONS.** Select apps and ebooks that help your child make meaningful connections between new information and information she already knows and/or that relates to subjects of interest to her, such as kittens and cats or sports. For example, *Sesame Street*'s "Breathe, Think, Do" app features engaging stories of typical everyday experiences, but teaches children how to practice mindfulness strategies in similar real-life situations. In addition, interactivity and gaming moments should be directly tied to the story line or the learning goal, as they are in "Elmo's Birthday Bash," an app featuring a delightful situation all kids can appreciate.

- **SOCIALLY INTERACTIVE.** While children may enjoy apps and ebooks independently, they should also be encouraged to share these experiences with others. Look for apps that allow multiple users to share the same experience. For example, PBS Kids "Scratch Jr." (a free app) is designed to allow several users to create an interactive story, in this case featuring popular characters from various PBS television shows. It also teaches elementary coding, digital literacy, STEM (science, technology, engineering, mathematics) skills, and problem solving.

- **QUESTIONS TO ASK WHEN SELECTING APPS OR EBOOKS FOR YOUR CHILDREN:**
    - What are the curriculum goals? (*Note*: Goals are usually stated in the product description.)
    - Is the content age-appropriate, usable, and easy to navigate?
    - Does it offer customization so parents can turn features ON and OFF?
    - Does it include two modes: READ TO ME and READ ON MY OWN?
    - Can readers highlight words, one at a time, as they are spoken in the READ TO ME mode?
    - Does it take into account a child's possibly limited dexterity—and resulting frustration—when interacting with "hot spots" or selecting a response?
    - Does it provide any assessment or learning trackers to consult when the child completes the book?
    - Does it offer "Parent Tips" to extend the learning?
    - Can access to promotional materials and in-app purchases be easily disengaged or avoided?

This "Deep Dive" is based on the following article: Hirsh-Pasek, Kathy; Zosh, Jennifer M.; Michnick Golinkoff, Roberta; Gray, James H.; Robb, Michael B.; Kaufman, Jordy. "Putting Education in 'Educational' Apps: Lessons from the Science of Learning." *Psychology Science in the Public Interest* (Volume 16, Number 1, 2015.) © The Authors 2015. Reprints and permissions: Sagepub.com/journalsPermissions.nav DOI: 10.1177/1529100615569721 pspi.sagepub.com

You can also encourage literacy skills by asking questions while reading your child a story. For example, stop and ask: "What do you think will happen next?" or "Can you find the mouse on the page?" and thus advance his verbal knowledge as well as his creative observation and retention.

By asking your child to retell or narrate the events of his day in sequence ("What happened after you woke up?," "What did you have for breakfast?," "What did you do after lunch?"), you not only promote verbal development, but you can discover a lot about your child's perceptions of the world around him.

Early writing skills can also be encouraged through drawing, such as asking your child to draw a picture of his favorite TV character or a special family occasion. These fun interactions not only help strengthen your child's memory, but can also give you an interesting glimpse into how your child perceives his everyday routine, while pointing you toward his natural interests. Then, finding books on these topics of interest will motivate your child to read more.

Other ways you can encourage literacy include:

- **READING ALOUD TOGETHER EVERY DAY.** Finding a regular time, such as bedtime, helps reading become a part of your child's daily routine.

- **ENCOURAGING TWO-WAY CONVERSATIONS.** For example, taking turns talking and listening. Look for opportunities to have these conversations during daily routines, such as while you're cooking dinner, at mealtime, while shopping, at bath time, and at bedtime.

- **POINTING TO, NAMING, AND TALKING ABOUT EVERYDAY THINGS.** Think of yourself as your child's life "sportscaster," giving your child the play-by-play of your daily experiences together.

- **WRITING DOWN YOUR CHILD'S WORDS.** Ask her to dictate a note to a relative or describe what's happening in a drawing. Then, write out the note or add some of her words to the drawing.

- **RETELLING STORIES WITH PICTURES OR PROPS.** Use photos or pictures from books to tell a story. Or act out a story using everyday items, such as a paper plate, while pretending that it is the steering wheel of a car.

QUICK TIP Help your child enhance literacy skills by engaging in language-rich conversations. Remember: Keep the conversation moving; don't lecture. Volley back and forth, and allow for pauses to give your child time to process and respond.

● EXPLORING TOPICS OF SPECIAL INTEREST THROUGH BOOKS, STORIES, PICTURES, AND DRAWINGS. This helps inspire curiosity and motivates children to learn more about a topic that interests them, whether it is dogs, dancing, or dinosaurs.

GOOD STUFF!

For additional information concerning apps and ebooks, as well as general parenting advice, here are a few resources especially for parents and caregivers.

● AMERICAN ACADEMY OF PEDIATRICS (AAP.ORG). The AAP is the nation's largest group of pediatricians and pediatric specialists dedicated to the health, safety, and well-being of children. Provides revised media-use guidelines, tips, and resources.

● COMMON SENSE MEDIA. Common Sense Media (commonsensemedia .org) is a nonprofit organization dedicated to offering guidance for parents, educators, and advocates to today's complex world of media and technology. It reviews and rates books, movies, TV shows, music, websites, and apps.

● JOAN GANZ COONEY CENTER. The Joan Ganz Cooney Center (joanganzcooneycenter.org) at Sesame Workshop focuses on the role digital media plays in educating children in today's complex media landscape. "Family Time with Apps: A Guide to Using Apps with Your Kids" is a useful short guide, available online in both English and Spanish.

● PBS PARENTS WEBSITE. The PBS Parents Website (pbs.org) offers a treasure trove of guidelines for everything from themed birthday parties and TV programming (for PBS programs) to child development and educational tips, including various media.

● ZERO TO THREE. Zero to Three (zerotothree.org) is an organization dedicated to ensuring that children, from birth to age three, receive the best childhood care, with the help of practical tools, policies, and other resources directed toward parents, professionals, and policy makers. A useful article on screen use for children under age three, titled, "Screen Sense: Setting the Record Straight," can be found on the organization's website.

DEEP DIVE

TIPS FOR READING TOGETHER

The most meaningful connections occur when you and your child enjoy shared attention while reading print or digital stories. Consider these tips for before, during, and after you read together.

Before Reading

Talk about books before you read them.

- Put two books in front of children and say, "Let's choose a book!" Then kids can point to or reach for their choice.

- Look at the front cover together. Ask, "What do you think this book will be about?" For younger children, point and say what you think.

During Reading

Look for ways to make the words and pictures come to life!

- Ask children to help turn the pages. (Babies can't turn pages on their own and young toddlers may want to do nothing but turn pages; however, by 18 months, they may begin to try to follow along with a story.)

- Try using different voices for each character and acting out scenes with gestures or body movements. Read in a sing-along voice.

- Let children chime in with the last word of a familiar line. "The cat in the . . . [hat]!"

- Run your finger under the words as you read to help kids understand that there is a difference between words and pictures. Don't worry about pointing out each individual word—it's important for children to hear the rhythm of language, too.

- Point to and comment on pictures. Ask, "What's happening on this page?"

After Reading

Now it's the perfect time to talk about the story and let your child share what he remembers.

- Ask questions that invite children to think about why certain characters did something or felt a certain way. "Let's go back to this page where Peter looked angry. Why was he mad? What did he decide to do?"

- Encourage children to share their favorite parts of the story (describing them or acting them out).

- Connect the story to kids' lives. ("Have you ever felt the same way as this bunny?")

Knowledge of Print & Its Uses

Children begin to understand the uses and characteristics of written language from an astonishingly early age. They observe the written word all around them—from books, newspapers, and magazines; to words and signage in their environment; to digital texts that appear on television, cell phones, tablets, and other devices. What's more, almost from the moment that they begin to observe written language, they perceive that those words have meaning.

Specifically, a child developing knowledge of print and its uses learns to:

- **SHOW AN INTEREST IN AND APPRECIATION FOR ALL FORMS OF READING.** Young children are naturally curious about written language around them, particularly when a trusted adult models a love of reading and writing. They share comments and questions as they read with you, and they enjoy mimicking Dad reading a novel or Mommy reading the newspaper.

- **EXPLORE THE CONVENTIONS OF PRINT.** Through experience, even very young children become increasingly comfortable with conventions, such as turning the pages of a book from front to back and one page at a time, and reading text from left to right and from top to bottom of a page. They also become aware of basic characteristics of a book, such as the title, an author, and even an illustrator, as well as common features, such as spaces between words and possibly punctuation.

QUICK TIP Bring grandparents, aunts, uncles, or even older siblings into the literary life of your child. Ask Grandpa to read a book to your child that you enjoyed when you were young, and suggest that he tell your child how much you loved the book. Or ask an older sibling to read with your three-year-old. It will forge a lovely bond between them.

- **RECOGNIZE THE PARTS OF A STORY.** Children begin to recognize story patterns, and show an understanding that stories have a beginning, a middle, and an end. They also recognize some details, such as events, characters, and a problem followed by a solution (or cause and effect).

- **UNDERSTAND AND RESPOND TO STORIES AND OTHER SORTS OF TEXTS.** Children may demonstrate their understanding of books by retelling events from a familiar story, acting out the story, drawing parts of it, or choosing to read or learn more on the same topic, such as cars or dinosaurs.

- **RECOGNIZE PRINT IN EVERYDAY LIFE.** Children begin to notice printed text in the world around them, such as on street signs, storefronts, cereal boxes, menus, and other materials that they frequently see in their environment.

- **UNDERSTAND THAT WRITTEN WORDS HAVE MEANING.** Through experience, children come to understand that print is speech that has been written down with a particular sequence of letters, and that print carries meaning, from grocery lists, to signs, to storybooks.

What to Expect from Your Preschooler

AGE 2

At two years old, if not before, your child probably loves being read to, taking pleasure not only in the story itself, but in the interaction between you as the parent (or caregiver) and himself, especially the cuddling that often comes with reading together. From a very early age, he probably enjoys interacting with books, initially as toys, by carrying them around and storing them in bags or baskets. (Board books are perfect for this.) However, very quickly, he will show an understanding of the real purpose of a book. He will see that they contain stories that he finds interesting and pleasurable, and that books are held a certain way, so that words and pictures are readable.

He will often ask a grown-up to read his favorite story, over and over again. When being read to, he might look at pictures, help turn pages, and say repeated phrases out loud at the right time (such as "But the bear snores on" from *Bear Snores On*). He will also begin to interact with books independently by flipping through pages or pretending to read, and using the pictures as clues to describe what's happening in the story.

Two-year-olds also enjoy tactile books, such as *Pat*

QUICK TIP

Eating out in a restaurant can offer a perfect an opportunity to talk about letters and words. Introduce your child to the menu, and ask her if she sees any letters or words that she knows. Some menus include pictures; ask her to identify dishes that she may know and like, like mac-and-cheese, scrambled eggs, or, if your child is used to eating international dishes, she might even find the moo shu pork!

GOOD STUFF!

FAVORITE BOOKS FOR TWO-YEAR-OLDS

- *Goodnight Moon* by Margaret Wise Brown, illustrated by Clement Hurd
- *Good Day, Good Night* by Margaret Wise Brown, illustrated by Loren Long
- *Goodnight Gorilla*, written and illustrated by Peggy Rathmann
- *Bear Snores On* by Karma Wilson, illustrated by Jane Chapman
- *Brown Bear, Brown Bear, What Do You See?* by Bill Martin Jr., illustrated by Eric Carle
- *Jamberry*, written and illustrated by Bruce Degen
- *Pat the Bunny*, written and illustrated by Dorothy Kunhardt
- *That's Not My Kitten* by Fiona Watt, illustrated by Rachel Wells
- *My Very First Mother Goose*, edited by Iona Opie, illustrated by Rosemary Wells

the Bunny by Dorothy Kunhardt and *That's Not My Kitten* by Fiona Watt, that allow children to touch different textures and learn the words for those textures. They also like books that help develop fine-motor skills or contain an element of surprise, such as lift-the-flap books. At age two, they also like books that contain descriptive rhyming words to explain the actions.

At age two, children can begin to retell some familiar story events, usually with the help of a parent or caregiver. They may also start to notice print around them, and understand that words carry meaning, such as the word "Milk" on a milk carton or that a stop sign says "Stop."

AGE 3

At three years old, your child still loves being read to, but will begin to interact with books more deeply. She can recognize and choose her favorite books, and identify and label pictures and characters. She can ask and answer questions about a familiar story, and, with some prompting, retell some of the events. (For example, after having been read a story like *The Three Little Pigs*, she will be able to respond to such questions as "What did the three little pigs use to make their houses?" or "What did the wolf do?" or "What happen to the houses?")

GOOD STUFF!

FAVORITE BOOKS FOR THREE-YEAR-OLDS

- *The Going to Bed Book*, written and illustrated by Sandra Boynton
- *The Very Hungry Caterpillar*, written and illustrated by Eric Carle
- *From Head to Toe*, written and illustrated by Eric Carle
- *The Tale of Peter Rabbit*, written and illustrated by Beatrix Potter
- *Corduroy*, written and illustrated by Don Freeman
- *Make Way for Ducklings*, written and illustrated by Robert McCloskey
- *Here Come the Helpers* by Leslie Kimmelman, illustrated by Barbara Bakos
- *Harold and the Purple Crayon*, written and illustrated by Crockett Johnson
- *Silly Sally* by Audrey Wood
- *The Snowy Day*, written and illustrated by Ezra Jack Keats

At age three, she is beginning to comprehend story structure, and understands the concepts of beginning, middle, and end to a story. She can follow a story from beginning to end, and turn the pages on her own.

She is also noticing and pointing out more words in her world, and she fully understands that they carry meaning. For example, she may know that when the word "Exit" appears, it means she can leave by that particular door. She may also recognize the sign on a favorite restaurant.

AGE 4

At age four, your child still loves being read to, but starts to spend more time interacting with books on his own. He may pretend to read and, using memorized language from a story, to describe what's happening on the pages. (*The*

Monster at the End of This Book is a classic example of a book frequently memorized by four-year-olds!) He can identify story-related events and retell familiar stories in the correct order.

At four years old, he can follow the words from left to right on the page, and may track the text with his finger, especially when you read to him. He may recognize some familiar words in a story, and begin to notice that the words are separated by spaces, and that other markings appear on the page, such as punctuation and page numbers.

Finally, he begins to copy print he sees around him for use in his own play. For example, he might copy the word "Menu" while pretending to be a waiter in a restaurant, or copy words from your grocery list to make a list of his own.

QUICK TIP

It's important to instill a sense of ownership and respect for books in your child. Clear off a low shelf in a family-centered place; create a small set of bookshelves in her room; or just provide a special "Book Basket" in a special place where your child can keep her favorite books.

GOOD STUFF!

FAVORITE BOOKS FOR FOUR-YEAR-OLDS

- **What a Wonderful World** by George Weiss and Bob Thiele, illustrated by Ashley Bryan
- **The Monster at the End of This Book** by Jon Stone, illustrated by Michael Smollin
- **Jake the Philharmonic Dog** by Karen LeFrak, illustrated by Marcin Baranski
- **The Complete Adventures of Curious George** by H. A. and Margret Rey
- **Knuffle Bunny: A Cautionary Tale**, written and illustrated by Mo Willems
- **Horton Hears a Who!**, written and illustrated by Dr. Seuss
- **Too Many Tamales** by Gary Soto, illustrated by Ed Martinez
- **A Bear Called Paddington** by Michael Bond, illustrated by Peggy Fortnum
- **Harry the Dirty Dog** by Gene Zion, illustrated by Margaret Bloy Graham

AGE 5

At age five, your child still enjoys being read to, but is making big steps toward reading on her own. When she pretends to read, she uses the appropriate tone of voice and actual language from a story. When being read to, she can match some spoken words to the words on a page, and follow words from left to right and from top to bottom of a page.

As she gets closer to six years old, she begins to sound out words and notice word patterns in a text. She may now know that a capital letter means the start of a sentence, or that certain letter sequences (e.g., "br" and "sh") have a particular sound.

She also can draw conclusions about a story using details about the characters, events, and story lines. She can reconstruct familiar stories using pictures, text, and props. For example, she might put a sock on her hand and pretend to be the caterpillar from *The Very Hungry Caterpillar*, or she may use her dolls to act out a fairy tale.

She can recognize and respond to print, such as signs in store windows (such as "Pizza") or name cards on gifts, especially her own name, the names of her siblings, or words like "Mommy" or "Daddy."

GOOD STUFF!

FAVORITE BOOKS FOR FIVE-YEAR-OLDS

- *Wild About Books* by Judy Sierra, illustrated by Marc Brown
- *Frog and Toad Are Friends*, written and illustrated by Arnold Lobel
- *Madeline*, written and illustrated by Ludwig Bemelmans
- *The Story of Babar*, written and illustrated by Jean de Brunhoff
- *The Day the Crayons Quit* by Drew Daywalt, illustrated by Oliver Jeffers
- *The Book with No Pictures* by B. J. Novak
- *Pete's a Pizza*, written and illustrated by William Steig
- *Amazing Grace* by Mary Hoffman, illustrated by Caroline Binch

LITERARY "I SPY"

When reading a story that is a special favorite of your child, make a game out of looking for characters or objects that might be hidden on the page. For example, with *Goodnight Moon*, look for the allusive mouse, or with *Good Night, Gorilla*, find the balloon that is somewhat obscured on each page. Or try looking for all the things that are red to teach color identification, or finding objects that begin with the "b" sound to introduce phonetics or the "sounds" of language.

EXPLORING YOUR PUBLIC LIBRARY

Visit your local public library regularly. Allow your child to select a few books in the preschool section that you can read together. Talk about which books you might want to take home because you want to read them again or at a later time. Introduce library procedures, such as using a library card, waiting to borrow a favorite book, and returning books on time. Also talk about library etiquette, such as using an "inside voice" and sitting quietly. Using the library will help instill a deep love and respect for books in your child, as well as a love for the place that houses them.

OOPS & AHA

When my son Lucas was four, we got a pet anole lizard. Lucas was so excited to place the lizard in its new "home"; however, before I realized (too late) just how wiggly and fast it was, the lizard jumped out of his hands and scurried out the window before I could capture it. (Oops!) Lucas was very surprised and upset. I comforted him, and tried to explain that now we knew more about anoles! That night we made up a story, called "The Adventures of Harry the Anole," featuring the lizard who left us too soon! Harry went on several amazing daytime adventures and secretly returned to his tank while Lucas was sleeping, only to leave for another adventure at sunrise. Thus, Harry lived on as part of Lucas's nightly bedtime routine. (Aha!)

—Rosemarie, educator & mom

PLAY & LEARN

LIFE LESSONS

Use reading time to help your child understand the lessons of the stories and then to relate those lessons to his own day-to-day experiences. After you have read a bit of the story, ask him what he thinks will happen next. When the story is finished, ask him what his favorite part was or why he thinks a certain character was feeling a certain way—happy or upset, excited or calm. Then, ask him if he can relate something in the story to something in his own life.

Also talk about the words we use to describe feelings, such as "sad," "frustrated," "surprised," or "joyous." Learning the meaning of these words and recognizing their nonverbal cues helps children to identify and regulate their own emotions, as well as see these emotions in others.

Keep these conversations light and interesting. But don't forget: These sorts of conversations not only will enhance your child's verbal skills, they will provide you with a peek into his inner thoughts and experiences.

GOOD STUFF!

LEVELED READERS

By age five, your child may be almost ready to read, and may even be reading on her own. If so, think about introducing "Beginning Reading" books (also known as "Leveled Readers") to her. Leveled Readers are books organized in "levels" of difficulty from the easy books for early readers, to the longer, more complex books for more advanced readers. Most Leveled Readers are available in a vast variety of subjects, both fiction and nonfiction, including many "licensed" books, such as those featuring *Sesame Street* or Disney characters. Consider your child's interests, favorite television characters, and best-loved authors, and find books that reflect those interests.

Four excellent Leveled Readers series:

- **STEP INTO READING:** stepintoreading.com

- **I CAN READ:** icanread.com

- **READY TO READ:** readytoread.com

- **BOB BOOKS** by Lynn Maslen Kertell and Dana Sullivan, illustrated by John R. Maslen

The Sounds of Language: Phonological Awareness

Phonological awareness is the ability to identify the specific sounds of language. For young children, this involves a child's growing ability to hear, think about, and manipulate units of sound in speech, including words, syllables, onsets and rimes (or the beginnings and the endings of words that rhyme), and phonemes (the 44 units of sound in the English language, such as the sounds represented by individual letters of the English alphabet.)

As children develop their awareness of the sounds of language, they start to:

- **NOTICE AND DISTINGUISH AMONG INDIVIDUAL WORDS IN SPOKEN LANGUAGE.** Young children can hear and understand that there are individual words in spoken language before they learn that written words are separated by spaces on a page.

- **HEAR AND DISTINGUISH INDIVIDUAL SYLLABLES IN SPOKEN WORDS.** Children learn to hear the beats or syllables within words (for "wa-ter," "rain-bow," "play-ground") and can separate them by clapping or stomping.

- **NOTICE THE SOUNDS INDIVIDUAL LETTERS MAKE IN SPOKEN WORDS.** Before they know that individual letters in the alphabet represent sounds, young children begin to hear and play with the 44 individual sounds in the English language. These sounds are called phonemes, like the "m" sound in "map" and the short "a" sound in "sad."

- **IDENTIFY SPOKEN WORDS THAT BEGIN WITH THE SAME STARTING SOUND.** For example, in the story *Lucy the Lazy Lizard*, many of the words start with the "l" sound. Children also become more aware of the different sounds within words, and learn how to separate out a sound. (For example, a child may recognize a hard "g" in "goat")

- **IDENTIFY SPOKEN WORDS THAT RHYME**; that is, end in the same sounds, such as "dog" and "log," both of which end with the "og" sound. Children begin to hear and separate the first and ending sounds in a word. For example, "mop" can be separated into two sounds—"m" and "op." They learn that when the ending sounds of two words are the same, they rhyme. (For example, the words "itsy" and "bitsy" in the "The Itsy-Bitsy Spider" song.)

QUICK TIP Recite or sing a few favorite nursery rhymes to your child as you are preparing dinner, giving her a bath, or getting ready for bed. Not only will your singing serve as a literacy learning moment, but it may serve to calm down an excitable or cranky child.

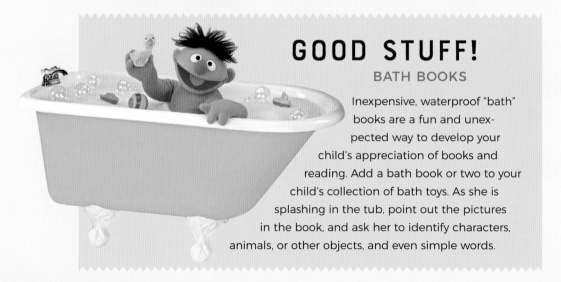

GOOD STUFF!
BATH BOOKS

Inexpensive, waterproof "bath" books are a fun and unexpected way to develop your child's appreciation of books and reading. Add a bath book or two to your child's collection of bath toys. As she is splashing in the tub, point out the pictures in the book, and ask her to identify characters, animals, or other objects, and even simple words.

- **IDENTIFY AND PLAY WITH THE INDIVIDUAL SOUNDS (PHONEMES) THAT LETTERS MAKE.** Older children start to blend sounds to build words ("c," "a," and "t" in the word "cat"). They may also play with sounds to change words by deleting, substituting, blending, or stretching sounds. (Replacing the "c" in "cat" with a "p" makes "pat.")

GOOD STUFF!
FAVORITE "RHYMING" BOOKS

- **Duck in the Truck**, written and illustrated by Jez Alborough
- **Is Your Mama a Llama?** by Deborah Guarino, illustrated by Steven Kellogg
- **Chicka Chicka Boom Boom** by Bill Martin Jr. and John Archambault, illustrated by Lois Ehlert
- **Pretend You're a Cat** by Jean Marzollo, illustrated by Jerry Pinkney
- **Green Eggs and Ham**, written and illustrated by Dr. Seuss
- **Tumble Bumble**, written and illustrated by Felicia Bond
- **Llama Llama Red Pajama**, written and illustrated by Anna Dewdney

What to Expect from Your Preschooler

AGE 2

Two-year-olds enjoy listening to rhymes and may begin to notice rhyming words in familiar songs (such as "Twinkle, Twinkle, Little Star") and books (*Big Red Barn* and *Blue Hat, Green Hat*). They like it when you repeat or sing their favorite nursery rhymes.

AGE 3

Three-year-olds like stories and songs with rhymes, and your child may begin stringing together rhyming words, occasionally saying them out loud (for example,

QUICK TIP Pick out a "rhyming" book that you know is one of your child's favorites, such as *Tumble Bumble* by Felicia Bond or *Green Eggs and Ham* by Dr. Seuss. Find the rhyming words in the story, then, together with your child, make up a new story that includes those particular rhyming words.

"hat," "cat," "rat," and "sat"). He also enjoys tongue twisters with alliteration, such as "She sells seashells by the seashore" or "Peter Piper picked a peck of pickled peppers."

At age three, your child can clap or stomp along with individual single-syllable words in a sentence, another indication that he is tuned into the sounds of language. For example, he may clap for each word while saying, "I want to go to the park!"

QUICK TIP When reading a rhyming story to your child, pause before the "rhyme," and ask him to fill in the missing rhyming word.

AGE 4

At age four, your child delights in listening to and creating rhymes. She may be able to fill in a missing rhyming word. For example, she may be able to call out the rhyme from the well-known book, *Tumble Bumble*: "The baby pig squealed with glee then introduced her friend, the _____ [bee].

She recognizes when words begin with the same sound (alliteration.) For example, she notices that the words "purple" and "pencil" both start with the "p" sound. She can hear separate syllables in words, and can clap out the breaks in words like "pick-le" (two claps) and "co-co-nut" (three claps).

AGE 5

At five years old, your child can figure out whether two spoken words rhyme, such as "bear" and "chair," and can match rhyming picture cards. He can begin to blend beginning and ending sounds to make a word. For example, he says "top" after hearing the "t" sound, followed by an "op" sound.

QUICK TIP Decorate your child's room with the alphabet. Paper a wall with "alphabet" wallpaper, create a design with peel-and-stick alphabet decals, or frame an inexpensive alphabet poster and place it over his bed. As you sing the "Alphabet Song," with your child, point out the letters.

Alphabet Knowledge

In the process of learning to read and write, children learn that the English language is made from the alphabet, which includes letter names, letter shapes, and letter sounds. Young children gradually comprehend that letters and letter patterns represent

52

the sounds of spoken language, and are the basic link between spoken and written language.

Children begin to have an awareness of "letters" very early in their lives. As children develop their knowledge of the alphabet, they start to:

- **IDENTIFY AND NAME UPPERCASE AND LOWERCASE LETTERS.** As young children learn this skill, they may need help telling apart letters that look similar. For example, in lowercase: a/d, b/d, b/p, n/u, i/l, or in uppercase C/G, E/F, I/L, M/N, M/W.

- **IDENTIFY AND MAKE THE RIGHT SOUND FOR EACH LETTER.** Young children may need help telling the difference between the sound a letter makes and its letter name. As they learn the letter sounds, they typically begin with the most useful letters, rather than learning them in alphabetical order. Oftentimes, they first learn consonants ("t," "m," "b," and "s") and short vowel sounds (such as the "u" in "bug" or the "e" in "leg") that can be heard at the beginning of familiar words. Then, in preschool, they may explore familiar three-letter words that begin and end with a consonant (for example, "cat," "hot," "pin"), words that they will begin reading in kindergarten.

GOOD STUFF!
MAGNETIC LETTERS

Magnetic letters—a refrigerator classic—make wonderful teaching tools. For younger children, look for simple, uppercase block letters. As children learn more about letters, add lowercase letters to the mix. Arrange the letters into your child's name, then ask him to name the letters. Write out other words, such as "Mommy," "Daddy," or the names of siblings, and name the letters out loud. Keep an eye out for games and kits containing magnetic letters; your child may enjoy playing games with magnetic letters or an individual magnetic board.

- **RECOGNIZE THAT WRITTEN WORDS ARE MADE UP OF SEPARATE, INDIVIDUAL LETTERS.** Just as children learn to recognize individual sounds in spoken words, they begin to recognize individual letters in written words. As they learn the sounds associated with those written letters, they'll make progress toward becoming readers!

GOOD STUFF!
ALPHABET COOKIE CUTTERS

Alphabet cookie cutters can be used to create letters with other foods—and even other "substances"—besides cookies! Use them to make letters out of morning toast, pancakes, sandwiches, and even gelatin. Think about purchasing an extra set, and use the cutters in a sandbox, to make letters out of modeling clay, or even as designs for your child to trace around.

Sets of cookie cutters containing the 26 letters of the English alphabet, and often numbers from 0 to 9, can be found in kitchen supply stores, bakeries, and the cooking sections of large department stores. Oftentimes, sets can be purchased for under $10.

What to Expect from Your Preschooler

QUICK TIP Show your child, beginning at age two or earlier, the letters that make up her name. Nothing thrills a child more than learning the letters of her name—and then reading and ultimately writing them.

AGE 2

At age two, your child is observing letters and words all around her. As she nears three years old, she may begin to understand and say certain letters, such as the letters in her name, particularly the first letter.

AGE 3

At age three, your child can recognize some or all the letters in his name, and he is starting to recognize a few other letters as well. He can begin to match some familiar letters, possibly both uppercase and lowercase letters. He may be able to produce a few "clear and common" sounds for certain letters, where the letter sounds closely relate to the letter names, such as "b," "t," "m," and "s."

NAMING NAMES

At age four or five, after your child has mastered writing his own name with ease, he may be ready to write the names of other important people in his life. On a sheet of lined paper, list the names of various members of your family, a couple of your child's friends, and perhaps his preschool teacher or his T-ball coach. You might even include the name of your family pet.

Print, using uppercase block letters, or if you think your child is ready, using upper- and lowercase letters. Create a column next to the names, and ask your child to write each name, just as you have done. Ask him to say each letter as he writes it, and then read the full name he has written.

After he has created his list of names, ask him to pick a name from the list and draw a picture or make a card for that person. When the picture is ready, have him write the recipient's name on the card or pictures, and present it as a special gift. He'll feel very proud.

ALL ABOUT ME

To build reading and writing skills, as well as a firm and happy sense of self-esteem, help your child make an "All about Me" book. Plan the project by discussing various subjects your child might want to include, such as "My Family," "My Pet," "My House," "My Favorite Things," or "My Vacation." Using an ordinary spiral-bound notebook or blank book, write the subject headings at the top of the pages, or, if your child wishes, ask her to write the headings, or some of the other names or words. Provide photos, stickers, markers, and crayons, so that your child can illustrate the book herself.

AGE 4

At four years old, your child most likely can name and recognize all the letters of the alphabet, and may be able to produce sounds for several letters. She is beginning to show that she knows that letters grouped together represent certain spoken sounds and tries to sound out simple words she sees, like "bus" or "cat."

AGE 5

At five years old, your child probably recognizes and names most, if not all, the uppercase and lowercase letters of the alphabet. He also tries to sound out letters as he reads and writes simple words. For example, he can read the word "sit" by sounding out the individual letter sounds "s," "i," and "t," and blending the letters together.

Understanding That Words Can Be Written: Early Writing

The moment your child shows that she starts to understand that what we say can be written down to be read by others is an exciting moment for any parent. And it's exciting for the child as well! This realization can come at an astonishingly early age. A child may not yet know letters or possibly very many words, but she comprehends that words being spoken around her are also written. Indeed, early writing skills include drawing, marking, scribbling, and invented spelling.

Specifically, a child developing early writing abilities learns to:

QUICK TIP Whenever your child creates a work of art, always ask her to "sign" her name, even if it comes out wrong. This will get her used to thinking about the letters of her name, and then writing her name—and will also make her feel very important.

- **UNDERSTAND THAT DRAWING AND WRITING ARE WAYS TO COMMUNICATE IDEAS AND FEELINGS.** Young children understand that writing carries meaning and can be understood by those who read it.

- **COPY, TRACE, OR INDEPENDENTLY WRITE MARKINGS, LETTERS, WORDS, NAMES, OR NUMBERS.** Young children may begin writing in many different ways (scribbling, drawing, making wordlike markings), but all of them are steps toward future writing. In early childhood, there is no wrong way to write.

- USE EMERGENT WRITING SKILLS. Young children may use dictation, drawing, early writing, and sometimes invented spelling to share ideas and feelings. Any of these can make a young child feel like an author.
- USE A VARIETY OF WRITING TOOLS. Young children should experiment with different kinds of writing tools, from using their own fingers to write in wet sand, shaving cream, or paint to writing with large and small pencils, crayons, markers, chalk, paintbrushes, and other implements.

What to Expect from Your Preschooler

AGE 2

At two years old, your child probably makes markings on paper, often eagerly scribbling, as her first attempts at early writing. She starts to use drawing and writing to express ideas. For example, she may color a big gold blob, and tell you it's a picture of the family's pet Lab.

AGE 3

At three years old, your child's lines and scribbles are starting to look like letters. As he approaches age four, he can write some letters accurately, particularly those in his own name.

AGE 4

At four years old, your child can write groups of letters (indicating words), but only some are correct and they're probably not in the right order or are written facing the wrong way. She may be able to write all the letters in her own name, but often not in the correct sequence. She is beginning to write simple words, by using their beginning and ending sounds, in a form of invented spelling (for example, "cr" for "car").

WORDS INTO PICTURES

Start a conversation by asking your child to describe an important recent event in his life. For example, "What did you do at preschool today?" Or "What happened at Trevor's birthday party?" Or how he would describe the family cat, his favorite character on television, a beloved toy or "lovey," or anything else that has caught his attention. Then, supply some paper and crayons or markers, and ask him to draw pictures of the event or object. When he is done, write a word or two on the picture, such as "Teacher," "Birthday Cake," or "Lucky, Our Cat"; be sure to add some of the words your child used in your conversation. Then staple his pictures together to create a "book." The result may be a bit of a hodgepodge, but your child will begin to understand that talking (words) can be turned into another form of expression (pictures), then, ultimately, a story (written words on a page or a book). Be sure to praise and congratulate him for all his creativity and hard work!

60

AGE 5

At five years old, your child can write all the letters in his first name, although some of the letters may be out of order, backward, reversed, or not fully formed. As he nears age six, he can write his name with letters in the correct order, using uppercase or lowercase letters (or both). He can now write simple words by their beginning, middle, and ending sounds, but usually with letters still missing. For example, he may write "lit" for "light."

Conclusions

Helping your child develop his early reading and writing skills is one of the most important gifts you can give your child, not only in preparation for preschool and kindergarten, but for his entire learning career. Exposing him to books and other written material, as well helping him to appreciate the sounds of language and the beauty of the written word, is an act that will stay with him his entire life. But, even better—learning about language is fun!

KNOWLEDGE OF PRINT
AND ITS USES

AGE 2	AGE 3	AGE 4	AGE 5
Loves being read to, and interacting with books. • Enjoys carrying books around. • Will often ask a grown-up to read (and reread) a favorite story. • May interact with books independently by flipping through pages or pretending to read. • Enjoys tactile books that teach different textures and the words used to identify those textures. • Enjoys books that teach fine-motor skills.	**Still loves being read to, and begins to interact with books more deeply.** • Can recognize and choose favorite books. • Can identify and label pictures and characters. • Can describe simple actions and the feelings of characters in the books.	**Still loves being read to.** • Starts to spend more time interacting with books independently. • Pretends to read and, using memorized language from a story, to describe what's happening.	**Still enjoys being read to, and is making big steps toward reading on her own.** • When pretending to read, uses appropriate tone of voice and actual language from a story. • Begins to sound out words and notice word patterns in a text, when approaching age 6. • May know that a capital letter means the start of a sentence, or that certain letter sequences (like "br" or "sh") have a particular sound. • Can match some spoken words to the words on a page.
Understands that books are held in a certain way, so that words and pictures are readable. • May look at pictures, help turn pages, and say repeated phrases out loud at the right time. • Uses pictures as clues to describe what's happening in the story.	**Can ask and answer questions about a familiar story**, with some prompting, and retell some of the events in the story.	**Can identify story-related events**, and can retell familiar stories in the correct order.	**Can follow words from left to right** and from top to bottom of a page.

PHONOLOGICAL AWARENESS

AGE 2	AGE 3	AGE 4	AGE 5
Enjoys listening to rhymes. • Begins to notice rhyming words in familiar songs. • Enjoys it when you repeat or sing his favorite nursery rhymes. • Enjoys books that contain descriptive rhyming words to explain actions.	**Enjoys stories and songs with rhymes.** • May string together rhyming words out loud. • Enjoys chants and songs with alliteration.	**Enjoys listening to and creating rhymes.** • May be able to fill in a missing rhyming word in a well-known book.	**Can figure out whether two spoken words rhyme,** such as "bear" and "chair." • Can match rhyming picture cards.
	Can clap or stomp along with individual single-syllable words in a sentence.	**Notices when words begin with the same sound (alliteration).** • For example, notices that the words "purple" and "pencil" both start with the "p" sound.	**Begins to blend beginning and ending sounds to make a word.**
		Can hear separate syllables in words, and can clap out the breaks.	

ALPHABET KNOWLEDGE

AGE 2	AGE 3	AGE 4	AGE 5
Sees letters all around. • May begin to say certain letters, such as letters in his or her name, particularly the first letter.	**Can recognize some or all of the letters in his or her name,** and starts to recognize a few other letters.	**Can name and recognize many letters** • Can identify uppercase and lowercase letters.	**Recognizes and names all the uppercase and lowercase letters** of the alphabet.
	Begins to match some familiar letters, possibly both uppercase and lowercase letters.	**May be able to produce sounds for several letters.**	**Tries to sound out letters when reading, and writes simple words.**
	May be able to produce a few "clear and common" sounds for certain letters particularly where the letter sounds closely relate to letter names.	**Begins to understand that letters grouped together represent certain spoken sounds.**	
		Tries to sound out simple words she sees, like "bus" or "cat."	

EARLY WRITING

AGE 2	AGE 3	AGE 4	AGE 5
Makes markings on paper as first attempts at early writing. • Often eagerly scribbles. • Starts to use drawing and writing to express ideas.	**Makes lines and scribbles that are starting to look like letters.**	**Can write groups of letters,** but only some are correct and are probably not in the right order or are written facing the wrong way. • May be able to write all of the letters in his or her own name, but often not in the correct sequence.	**Can write all of the letters in his or her first name,** although some of the letters may be out of order, backward, reversed, or not fully formed. • Can write his name with letters in the correct order, using uppercase or lowercase letters (or both).
	Can write some letters accurately, particularly those in his or her own name.	**Is beginning to write simple words by using their beginning and ending sounds,** in a form of invented spelling.	**Can now write simple words** by their beginning, middle, and ending sounds, but usually with letters still missing.

3.
HOW MANY BLOCKS ALL TOGETHER?

Early Math

When people think about *Sesame Street*, one of the things they remember is the show's emphasis on numbers, including, in recent years, a musical version of the "Number of the Day." When children watch *Sesame Street*, they learn their 123s, often with the help of that beloved Transylvanian, Count von Count.

But, of course, mathematics is much more than simply identifying numbers and counting. During the preschool years, children grasp the meaning of numbers as they learn how to count objects in a set and label a quantity using a specific number word. They also begin to understand the early math concepts of addition and subtraction, spatial relations, geometric shapes, ordinal numbers, one-to-one correspondence, measuring, sorting, and patterns. Since its inception, *Sesame Street* has offered guidelines for learning these essential math skills, featuring the Muppets of *Sesame Street* and other members of the gang.

The episode featuring Max the Magician is a perfect example. Max magically appears on Sesame Street as Rosita, Big Bird, and Elmo are enjoying snacks with Chris. Everyone is excited to see some real magic. First, Max takes one scarf out of his pocket and puts it with two other scarves to make three scarves—what was two has become three. Everyone is amazed and wants to know the secret to the trick. Max refuses to tell, but Chris, knowing it isn't magic, explains that it's *addition*.

Max's next trick involves making cards disappear one by one. They all agree that this is the best trick they've ever seen and ask Max to tell them how he did it. Max cannot tell because of the Magician's Code of Honor. But, once again, Chris explains that, when Max takes three away, it was just *subtraction*. Max the Magician is stunned that anyone is able to guess the secrets of his tricks and leaves to find tricks that no one will ever figure out. He disappears in a *poof*!

In another episode, a parody of the film *Indiana Jones and the Temple of Doom*, Telly, a lover of triangles, searches for the rarest, most beautiful triangle in the whole world, the Golden Triangle of Destiny. In doing so, young viewers are given a quick course in both geometric shapes and spatial relations.

On their adventure, they come across a shape with five sides, the Golden Pentagon of Destiny, which they discover after finding a clue *under* a giant boulder. Later they find a shape with eight sides, the Golden Octagon of Destiny. At this point, Telly is ready to give up, but while sitting in a chair he feels a sharp, pointed object *under* a cushion. There, at last, he discovers a shape with three sides and three angles: the Golden Triangle of Destiny.

Once you know that math is more than just numbers and counting, you realize that math appears everywhere in our lives! Supporting early math skills can be as easy as involving children in everyday "math moments," such as measuring ingredients for a recipe, setting the table for a family dinner, or choosing the bigger watermelon for a large family gathering.

Children's curiosity and interest in their world naturally lead them to explore a variety of math concepts. For example, they use math when they:

PLAYING WITH MATH AT HOME

Discussing math at home need not be intimidating or anxiety-provoking. You can find plenty of places and situations around the house where math skills can be introduced.

In the kitchen:

- GIVE EVERYONE AT THE TABLE A FEW PIECES OF FOOD, such as crackers or carrots. Ask each child to count the items in his pile. Ask: "Did everyone get an equal, or the same, amount? If not, how many pieces do you need to add to each pile to make them all the same?"

- EXPLORE PARTS OF A WHOLE TOGETHER, a step toward understanding division, as well as the idea of sharing. As you share a sandwich, say, "I'm cutting the sandwich in half so we each get one piece." Or ask, "If there are three pieces of bread and six of us who want some, what can we do?"

In the bathroom:

- USE DIFFERENT SIZES AND SHAPES OF PLASTIC CUPS and measuring cups to play with in the bath and to compare amounts. With younger kids, simply explore the concepts of "full" and "empty" by filling up cups and pouring them out together. Challenge older kids to predict which cup will hold the most water and which will hold the least before pouring water into each cup.

- PLAY "SINK AND FLOAT" IN THE BATHTUB by testing a variety of bath items: a bar of soap, a rubber ducky, a toy car, a dry sponge, empty and full small plastic travel bottles, and bath books. Once you discover which items float and which ones sink, place the items in two separate containers, and then, together, count how many float, and how many sink.

In the bedroom:

- LOOK AT PICTURE BOOKS TOGETHER TO FIND FAMILIAR SHAPES. Rotate the book and point out that the shapes are still the same shapes—no matter which way the book faces. Count the number of sides and angles that make a shape a unique shape.

- AS KIDS LIE IN BED, PLAY "I SPY" TOGETHER, using words like "under," "over," "next to," and "behind." Clue each other in as to what you spy by describing where an object is. You might say, "I spy something *under* the clock" or "I spy something *next* to the bookshelf." Take turns!

DEEP DIVE

THE JOY OF MATH

For many moms and dads, the subject of mathematics arouses a host of negative emotions, ranging from boredom to high anxiety. Just the word "math" evokes stressful memories of tackling eighth-grade algebra or learning high school trigonometry. When it comes to our children, we take pleasure in reading stories together, especially at bedtime, which in many households is a regular part of a child's routine. But somehow the notion of introducing math concepts to our children seems daunting. In fact, some studies have shown that parents harbor a strong belief that while it's important and pleasurable to support their child's reading skills, it is the responsibility of the schools to take care of teaching math. This is unfortunate because the more math activities you engage in at home, the greater children's math achievement will be in school.

What's more, "math anxiety" in parents is quickly passed on to children, causing them to do poorly in math at school and then disliking it. Children don't come with this baggage naturally; Indeed, most young children love counting, sorting, adding, and subtracting in all aspects of their lives.

Here are some suggested activities to overcome any anxiety you may have, and foster your child's love of math: Read books with math themes together; watch television programs that focus on math, such as *Peg + Cat* and *Team Umizoomi*; or, for slightly older preschoolers, work through simple math word problems. Many—perhaps even most—everyday activities involve math: counting flowers in a garden, sorting fruit in a bowl, or finding various shapes at a playground or in your neighborhood.

Remember: Math is so much more than just numbers. For preschool kids, math involves simple addition and subtraction, measuring things, identifying geometric shapes, and completing patterns. Math is everywhere in our everyday lives. And, what's more, math is fun!

- COUNT (say numbers out loud while counting a small pile of books to check out at the library).

- TELL HOW MUCH OR HOW MANY ("There are two birds at the birdfeeder.")

- COMPARE ("I have more apple slices—you have more crackers.")

- PUT THINGS IN ORDER ("I'm first in line for the slide, next is my friend, and Daddy is last!")

- DESCRIBE HOW THEY MOVE in the space around them ("I'll ride my bike around the puddle, over the bump, and between the trees.")

- SORT ITEMS (help sort the laundry by size—large bath towels, medium-size hand towels, and small washcloths).

GOOD STUFF!
MATH APPS & WEBSITES

Here are a few popular apps, web games, and sites that feature math.

Apps

- **ELMO LOVES 123s.** This popular app teaches number identification (and number tracing), one-to-one correspondence (the relationship between two sets of objects; for example, six chairs to six place settings at a dining table; simple addition; and simple subtraction.

- **BEDTIME MATH.** This app addresses how math can be integrated into bedtime reading.

Web Games

Sesame Street web games are available on the *Sesame Street* website, sesamestreet.org/games.

- **BIG BIRD'S BASKETBALL.** This game teaches enumeration and number recognition.

- **ELMO'S WORLD GAMES.** This game focuses on geometric shapes.

- **GROVER'S WINTER SPORTS.** This game addresses number identification (and number tracing) as well as patterns.

- **OSCAR'S ROTTEN RIDE.** This game features relational concepts and spatial relations.

When children are engaged in math activities, encourage them to talk about what they are doing, which will help build their language as well as their math skills. Being able to describe how they approached a problem using their math skills helps build their knowledge and understanding, too. ("My friend needed a baseball glove to play catch, so I shared one of mine—one for him and one for me.") The more "math talk" children use and hear in their preschool years, the more likely they are to understand math language and concepts in the future, and succeed in all subject areas, especially literacy.

The Foundations of Math for Young Children

For two- to five-year-olds, the goals for early math focus on:

- **UNDERSTANDING THAT NUMBERS REPRESENT AMOUNTS** and can be used to compare things. ("I have two toy cars in my basket; my sister has four toy cars in her basket.")

- **UNDERSTANDING THE BASICS OF ADDING AND SUBTRACTING** and using numbers to solve problems. ("I was watching a bird drink from a puddle, then another bird came. There were two birds drinking from the puddle!")

- **THE ABILITY TO MEASURE AND COMPARE OBJECTS.** ("Daddy is taller than me.")

- **RECOGNIZING SHAPES** by their attributes. ("Three sides and three angles make a triangle.")

- **RECOGNIZING THE LOCATION OF OBJECTS IN RELATION TO OTHERS** ("under," "on," "in," "next to," etc.).

- **RECOGNIZING AND USING PATTERNS** (noticing a pattern in a shirt—blue stripe, white stripe, blue stripe, white stripe, etc.; using white and blue crayons to make the same pattern in a drawing).

QUICK TIP Introduce the concept of "ordinal numbers" by asking your child to practice first, second, or third with her stuffed animals, dolls, or other toys. Ask her to line up three stuffed animals in a row. Then ask: "Who is first?" Or give her clues and encourage her to put the animals in the order that you suggest. For example, you might say, "Please place the pink bunny first, the white lamb second, and the brown teddy third."

GOOD STUFF!

MATH STORIES AT BEDTIME

In addition to your child's favorite bedtime story, introduce books about numbers and other math concepts as part of her bedtime routine. Books with math concepts not only provide building blocks for math and language success, but they make math fun! Here are three delightful suggestions:

- *Goodnight, Numbers*, by Danica McKellar, illustrated by Alicia Padron

   In this story, children say good night to the objects all around them and connect them with real numbers in their world. These include not only the ordinary four legs on a cat, but less apparent examples, such as four frogs on a bathmat. You can also turn reading time into a fun and educational game by asking your child lots of questions, such as "What else do you see on that page that comes to four?"

- *Miss Spider's Tea Party: The Counting Book*, written and illustrated by David Kirk

   Part of the popular *Miss Spider's Tea Party* series, this book teaches young children how to count to 12, and one-on-one correspondence.

- *Elmo's Bedtime Countdown* by Lori C. Froeb, illustrated by Tom Brannon

   This novelty book, with fun pull-tabs, features Elmo getting ready for bed as he and young readers learn to count backward from 10 to 1.

- *How Tall, How Short, How Far Away* by David A. Adler, illustrated by Nancy Tobin

   How the ancient Egyptians and Romans used their fingers, hands, arms, and legs as measuring tools.

Numbers and Counting

Number and counting skills are about understanding numbers and how they are used, as well as knowing the order that numbers go in and being able to count the amount in a group of items.

As children build their understanding of numbers and counting, they start to:

- SAY NUMBERS IN THE RIGHT ORDER, without skipping any, just as they learn to say their ABCs.

NUMBERS & COUNTING

Math has its own vocabulary. For example, when counting two dogs and two cats, ask: "How many pets are there all together? If one cat goes away, how many pets are left? Let's count and check how many." Here are several common math words and phrases to use as you talk when counting objects with your child:

- How many?
- How many all together?
- Count to check how many
- Each
- Same amount
- Different amount
- Same number of
- Different number of
- Pair
- Half
- Dozen

COUNTING TO 10 WITH FINGER PLAY

Trace both of your child's hands on a sheet of paper, then help your child decorate the handprints. Make each fingernail a different color, for example, or place a sticker on each finger. When you're done, count the fingers or stickers—from 1 to 10! Then do the same thing with your child's feet, counting his toes, 1 to 10. With slightly older children, do both, then count all the fingers and toes—from 1 to 20!

Use "finger play" to make "lights-out" count! Before you turn off the lights at bedtime, hold up 10 fingers. Then count down together, starting with the number 10: "Ten, nine, eight, seven, six, five, four, three, two, one." [Turn lights off.] "Sweet dreams!"

- **RECOGNIZE WRITTEN NUMBERS** (numerals) and understand that each has its own number word (one, two, three), just as they learn to recognize and name written letters.

- **NOTICE PRINTED NUMBERS AROUND THEM** being used for different purposes (like house numbers, bus numbers, or price signs at the supermarket).

- **UNDERSTAND THAT NUMBERS REPRESENT THE TOTAL AMOUNT OF ITEMS IN A GROUP.** This concept (also called "cardinality") helps children understand that a number, spoken or written, can be used to represent the total number of items. (For example, they ask for three banana slices and know that one is missing when only two are given to them.)

- **UNDERSTAND THAT NUMBERS CAN TELL US THE SIZE OR AMOUNT OF SOMETHING.** Children notice that, in addition to numbers representing a counted collection, numbers, spoken or written, can also tell us the size of something (for example, five blocks tall) or the amount of something (three cups of flour, one gallon of milk).

- **TELL HOW MANY OBJECTS ARE IN A COLLECTION BY POINTING AND COUNTING OUT EACH ITEM.** Placing a finger on each rabbit on a storybook page while counting each one is called "one-to-one counting" or "enumeration." At first, children may skip numbers or count faster than they are pointing. In time, they learn that the number word for the last item they count is the total number in the collection. It takes practice for children to learn how to point to and count out how many items are in a collection.

- **TELL HOW MANY OBJECTS ARE IN A COLLECTION JUST BY LOOKING, WITHOUT COUNTING THEM ONE BY ONE.** This is called "subitizing." For example, immediately recognizing the number of dots on dice without having to count out each dot.

- **COMPARE COLLECTIONS OF OBJECTS.** At first, children compare two collections by lining them up next to each other to see if they have the same amount; for example, lining up two groups of crayons to see which has more. Then, children learn to count up to 10 items and can estimate up to 5 items to see which collection is larger. Finally, children learn how to compare collections and put them in order from smallest to largest. They learn to use language to compare, such as "big," "bigger," "biggest"; or "first," "second," "third," which is known as "ordinality."

73

What to Expect
from Your Preschooler

AGE 2

At two years old, your child probably says a few numbers but not always in the right order. He also may skip a number as he pretends to count, "One, two, five . . ." He understands the meaning of the number words "one" and "two," and can take or give two items when asked. For example, he will give you two crayons or take just one apple slice when requested. He knows when there is more of something, and might complain when a sibling has more of a desired item: "He has more markers!"

AGE 3

At three years old, your child may very well be able to count out loud up to five. She understands that the words ("one," "two," "three") represent an amount. She can count out objects one by one in a group of items up to four, and she knows that three is more than two and two is more than one; for example, she chooses two toy trucks when invited to play with "one or two." At age three, your child also begins to know the order of daily events; starts to identify first and last items in an order; and can recognize a few written numbers (numerals).

AGE 4

At four years old, your child probably counts out loud up to 10. He knows numbers in the right order and can figure out what number comes next when he hears the numbers that come before it; for example, he answers, "Seven!" when asked what comes after "four, five, six . . ." He understands "how many" and can count groups of items up to five. He points to and counts each object and knows that the last number is the total. He is beginning to include counting in his drawings and writing. He counts out five napkins when asked to help set the table for five people, and writes some numbers on a paper he is using as a receipt for a pretend restaurant, although the numbers may be backward or simply number-like

MATH AT THE SUPERMARKET

Adding a little math to a trip to the grocery store doesn't have to take extra time, and it can help engage kids as you are shopping or passing the time in the checkout line!

- **NUMBERS AND COUNTING:** Make a numbered shopping list: "6 apples, 2 containers of yogurt, 4 cans of soup." As you shop for these items, count aloud or, better yet, ask your child to count each item as you add it into the shopping cart.

- **ADDING AND SUBTRACTING:** As you put items into a bag or cart, introduce some simple addition. With your child, say: "I put in three, now you put in two. How many did we gather all together?" Count together to find out. You can also introduce subtraction: "We have five oranges. Maybe we have too many. Let's put one back. How many oranges do we have now all together?"

- **WEIGHING:** Before you weigh your fruits and veggies, ask your child to predict which item will be heavier. "Do you think the cantaloupe will weigh more than the lemon? Why or why not?" Then place your items on the scale. Ask your child: "What number does the arrow point to? How much does it weigh?" Try weighing and measuring items that are close in size, such as an orange and an apple.

- **SHAPES:** Discuss the shapes of various items as you go through the grocery store. Ask your child: "What shape is the cereal box?" or "What shape is the box that the popsicles come in?" At the cheese counter, point out the cheeses that are shaped like triangles, rectangles, squares, or circles.

- **SORTING:** As you pass different displays, talk about how the items are organized or sorted. Point out how all the fruits and veggies are in one place, all the bread is in another; all the meat is in another. When you're in the produce department, point out foods that are sorted by type: All the oranges are in one place, all the apples are in another. Talk about how foods might be grouped or sorted by color (red apples and green apples) or size (large potatoes versus baby potatoes).

- **COUNT PEOPLE IN THE CHECKOUT LINE:** When you get in line, count the number of shoppers ahead of you, then subtract one person each time someone checks out.

READY, SET, COUNT ON

Ask your child to name his favorite number—let's say it's five—then help him to understand that five is always five, no matter how the items are organized. (This is called a "set.") Choose everyday items like toy cars or stuffed animals. First count the items: five all together. Then, ask your child to think of ways to organize his items in a different way. For example, he might arrange his toy cars in two lines, as in a parking lot. Or perhaps he will offer you two animals and keep three for himself. Let your child be creative and see what other ways he comes up with to arrange his chosen items. After he has arranged them, ask him count them again. Emphasize that it's still five! (Or a set.)

Now add some items to this set—let's say, two more animals. Then ask your child, "How many animals are there all together now?" Most kids will start by counting the entire new set from the beginning (from one to seven) before counting the two additions. However, as they start to grasp this concept, children will be able to hold the number of the original set (five animals) without recounting, and then count the additional animals (six and seven) to get the new total (or the number of animals in the new "set"). This math concept is called "counting on."

As your child gets more comfortable with the concept of a "set," challenge him a bit. Cover the original set (the five cars or five animals), add two or three more, then ask him how many there are all together, without him being able to see the original set. You'll know he understands "counting on" if he starts counting by saying "six."

markings. He knows that a higher number represents a larger amount. He can compare two groups of up to five items and knows that the one with the higher number has more.

He uses words like "first," "second," and "last" to describe the order. For example, at the park he might say, "Let's play tag first and play soccer second," or he might notice that two friends also want to use the same shovel in the sandbox and says, "I'll go first, you go second, and Marco can go last." Finally, he can read written numbers (numerals) up to five, and may point to the number five on a house number and says, "There's number five!"

GOOD STUFF!
BOARD GAMES COUNT

Board games are often filled with many opportunities to teach math skills. Classic games, such as "Candy Land," "Chutes & Ladders," "Hi Ho," and "Cherry-O!," teach simple counting skills to young kids. "Money" games like "Monopoly Junior" appeal to slightly older children, and are excellent for strengthening mathematical abilities, especially when a child plays the role of the "banker."

Make playing board games with children a family activity. Ask grandparents, aunts and uncles, caregivers, older siblings, cousins, and friends to join in the fun; however, limit the number of players to four. Even very young children can participate (even if they don't complete the game) with the guidance of an adult or an older sibling.

AGE 5

At five years old, your child will probably be able to count out loud up to 20. She knows the numbers in the right order and can figure out what number comes next without needing to hear the numbers that came before it. She can correctly point to and count out up to 20 objects and can count out loud backward from 5 (and maybe from 10). She correctly answers, "Eleven!" when asked what comes after 10, and can count out 10 playing cards for herself and 10 for a friend when starting a game of "Go Fish."

She has a deeper understanding of numbers' order and value. She knows that, for example, nine is more than eight without having to count it out. She also knows where numbers sit in their order, deciding that five is closer to three than to nine; that any number that follows another is one more; and uses phrases like "greater than," "less than," and "equal to" to compare two numbers.

She understands sequential order (first, second, third) up to 10th. For example, she may line up three or four toy airplanes for "takeoff" and say, "You're first, you're second, you're third . . ." In addition, she represents numbers in her drawings and writing (up to nine), such as creating a drawing of five dogs, after saying, "There were five dogs at the park today."

Adding & Subtracting

Young children build a basic understanding of how to use numbers to solve problems.

As children develop the skills they need to add and subtract, they start to:

- **COMBINE TWO SMALLER GROUPS OF OBJECTS TO MAKE A LARGER GROUP.** Children's early experiences with addition start with counting how many objects are in two groups, putting the two groups together, and then counting the total number of objects. ("I found three acorns. Mommy found two acorns. We have one, two, three, four, five acorns all together!")

- **SEPARATE A GROUP OF OBJECTS INTO SMALLER GROUPS AND THEN COMBINE THEM BACK INTO ONE LARGER GROUP.** Count out a few

CREATE YOUR OWN MATH BOOK

Your child can create her own math book. On each page, suggest that she write a number and then draw items that represent that number. For example, she might write the number 3, then would draw 3 circles, 3 hearts, or 3 people. Start with number 1, and go up to 10 (or more), using a separate sheet for each number. Staple the finished pages together to create a math book.

ADDITION & SUBTRACTION

While exploring the concepts of adding and subtracting, use the following words and phrases to explain new ideas:

- How many all together?
- How many more?
- How many left?
- Take away
- Add
- More than
- Fewer than
- Less than

OOPS & AHA

My daughters, ages three and five, hate being in a car for long drives. I used to just ignore their complaints and let them whine or cry. (Oops!) Recently, I have been more interactive with them, and we have played "number" games, such as "20 Questions" and "Let's Count." Both girls love this and we make it work for both their age levels. Maddy now counts by 5s and 10s; Letty can count to 20 all by herself. (Aha!)

—Jessica, executive assistant & mom

ROLLING THE DICE

Dice present a quick and easy way to help slightly older kids with counting, subitizing, and counting on, as well as adding and subtracting. For example, after your child rolls a pair of dice, count the dots on one die, and then count the dots on the other; ask, "How many dots did you roll all together?" (That's easy addition.)

Consider making a very simple game board by hand. On a sheet of paper, placed horizontally, draw a long row of boxes and number them from 1 to 12 (since the two dice have a total of 12 dots)—or 1 to 20, or even 1 to 100—whatever number you wish. Make the boxes big enough so a child can move freely on the board with her small, chunky fingers and a board piece. You could also simply use the board from any game you may have on hand; you don't need to actually play the game, just practice rolling and moving the dice with your child.

Ask your child to roll her die or dice, and then move her piece across the board. (This will involve simple counting and enumeration.) She might also practice "counting on" (start moving the amount on one die—one to five—then roll the second die, and count on the number of a second die.) Another variation is to count the total of the two dice and then take away one die, and ask, "How many dots are left?" (Subtraction.) As your child grows, she will spend less time counting each dot and will say "five" immediately when she sees five dots. (Subitizing.)

Clearly, playing with dice is an easy way to teach many mathematical skills.

crayons to share with a sibling, then take them back and count to make sure the full set is all there.

- CHANGE A COLLECTION BY TAKING ITEMS AWAY. Children do early subtraction by taking away some of the objects in a group and then counting how many are left. For example, as he is eating a bowl of his favorite berries, he says, "Now there are only three!"

What to Expect from Your Preschooler

AGE 2

At two years old, your child probably understands that adding or taking away items from a group changes the total number. She knows that a collection is made up of parts, and thinks more in a group is better than less. For example, she is enthusiastic about adding "more" of something she likes to her collection of stickers or stuffed animals, and shows frustration when her brother takes some of the cars she is playing with, knowing she has fewer cars: "No! Mine!"

She also knows that parts of a collection can be grouped in different ways, but doesn't yet have the language to express this. For example, she knows that "all" the blocks means not just the blue or red blocks, but the whole group of blocks.

AGE 3

At three years old, your child probably can tell the correct number when one item is added or taken away from a group up to three, although he may not yet have the language to explain what happened. Still, he correctly says, "One!" when asked how many shoes are left, but doesn't explain what happened (you took one away). He also understands that the whole group is a bigger number than its individual items. Most likely, he can't tell you exactly how many there are, especially if it's a group of more than five, but he knows it is more than one and may say a random number he considers to be large.

AGE 4

At four years old, your child can add items in a group up to four. She can also subtract one to three objects and figure out how many are left. For example, she tells you, "Three!" when you say, "I gave you four apple slices. You ate one. How many are left?" She can find different ways to make a group, such as when she is invited to pick out four foam shapes for a collage. She may count out four pink ones, then put back two and replace them with two blue ones, knowing she can take only four.

AGE 5

At five years old, your child may well be able to solve simple word problems with addition and subtraction, up to five. He probably uses a strategy such as counting on his fingers to help. When asked, "What is 2 + 3?," he holds up two fingers on one hand and three fingers on the other, then counts up the fingers to get to five. As he nears six years old, he can make a group of up to five items using different combinations of numbers, and he can also break groups down into smaller groups. For example, when asked to show five fingers, he may show one finger on one hand, then four fingers on the other, then change to two fingers and three fingers. Or he may take apart an orange and count 10 slices, then make two groups—5 for himself, and 5 to share with you.

Measuring & Comparing

As children develop their ability to measure and compare the size, weight, and capacity of different objects, they start to:

- **NOTICE THE DIFFERENCE BETWEEN TWO OBJECTS.** Even very young children can make simple comparisons between two objects. As their vocabulary grows, they can describe the differences they see ("Daddy is tall. Baby brother is short."). In time, they learn that comparisons are relative to each other ("I'm taller than my brother, but shorter than my dad."). Eventually, they learn that comparisons can change over time ("I'm shorter than Mommy now, but when I'm a grown-up, I'll be taller.").

MATH VERSES

Recite or even sing (make up your own tune!) these sweet verses,
both of which are simple and entertaining ways to introduce
addition and subtraction.

Happy Friends

AN ADDITION POEM

One happy friend sings a song. [HOLD UP ONE FINGER.]
Then another comes to sing along. [ADD ANOTHER FINGER.]
La, la, la, ding, ding, dong! How many friends are singing a song? TWO!
Two happy friends sing a song. [HOLD UP TWO FINGERS.]
Then another comes to sing along! [ADD ANOTHER FINGER.]
La, la, la, ding, ding, dong! How many friends are singing the song? THREE!
Continue adding fingers; see how high you can go!

Night-Night

A SUBTRACTION VERSE

Three little babies are dancing in the bed. [HOLD UP THREE FINGERS.]
One lies down to rest his head. [PUT DOWN ONE FINGER.]
Now how many babies are dancing in the bed? TWO!
[REPEAT THE VERSE AND ACTIONS, USING TWO, ONE, AND "NONE." THEN SAY THE FINAL VERSE:]
No little babies are dancing in the bed.
All the little babies went night-night instead!

MEASURING & COMPARING

Here are a few words and phrases to use when talking about measuring things with your child:

- Let's measure!
- How tall are you?
- Which is taller?
- How wide is that wagon?
- How long is that string?

- Longer than
- Shorter than
- Big, bigger, biggest
- Bigger than, smaller than
- Across

- Around
- Height
- Width
- Few, fewer than, fewest
- Less than, more than
- Let's check!

PLAY & LEARN

MEASURE BY THE FOOT

Rulers aren't the only tools that can be used to figure out how long, wide, deep, or high an object is! To help kids build their understanding of measurement, measure using blocks, paper towel tubes—or just about any item—as an informal measurement, rather than a standard unit of measurement. How many blocks tall is your sister? Or trace your child's foot on a sturdy piece of cardboard, cut it out, and use it as a "foot-long measuring tool." Then, measure everyday things around your home: How wide is the doorway? (10 "feet"?)

Make cutout footprints of Mommy's, Daddy's, and a younger sibling's feet. Have fun measuring with each unit and comparing the number of "footprints" and how the number changes in relation to the length of the footprint.

When you measure things with an everyday object that has a standard length (same-size blocks, toilet paper, or paper towel–roll tubes), it is called "informal measurement" because you are not using a formal (or standard measurement) tool, such as a ruler. When doing informal measurement, it is important to line up and connect each item to measure or, if you're using only one item, make marks and count the marks to determine the length, height, width, or depth of the item being measured.

● **COMPARE AND PUT THREE OBJECTS IN ORDER.** Children learn to compare a specific aspect of three objects, such as size, length, speed, and weight, and put them in order ("My hair is long, Aunt Ruthie's hair is longer, Mommy's hair is longest.").

● **MEASURE WITH EVERYDAY ITEMS.** Children start by making comparisons as a way to measure. In time, they learn to make more exact measurements by measuring with familiar objects ("The teddy bear is six blocks tall." "The table is five paper towel tubes long!").

● **MEASURE WITH MEASUREMENT TOOLS.** Eventually, children learn to use the right tool for what is being measured (a ruler for length, measuring spoons for volume, or a scale for weight).

● **USE INFORMATION (DATA) TO ANSWER A QUESTION.** Children may begin to collect data to answer a specific question. (At school, your child may ask classmates what their favorite color is and use tally marks to find out which color got the most votes.)

What to Expect from Your Preschooler

AGE 2

At two years old, your child probably can make simple comparisons between two objects (such as small/big, short/tall, more/less). He notices when one object is bigger than another; for example, he picks the biggest banana from the bunch.

AGE 3

At three years old, your child very likely is beginning to compare two objects in more specific ways (height, length, weight). She can figure out which object is taller or longer by putting them side by side, but probably has difficulty lining them up accurately. For example, she holds two sticks next to each other to see which is longer, but doesn't have the ends lined up, or stands next to a sibling to compare who is taller.

AGE 4

At four years old, your child probably can compare a small group of objects in different ways (length, size, weight) and put them in order. He uses words to compare things, like big/small, long/short, tall/short, heavy/light, and fast/slow. He can compare objects using language like big/bigger/biggest. For example, he may inspect the cake slices at a birthday party and say, "He has a bigger piece than me!"

As he nears five years old, he begins to use everyday objects and measuring tools to measure with. For example, he lines up markers end to end to measure the length of a table or stands on the bathroom scale and is curious about how much he weighs.

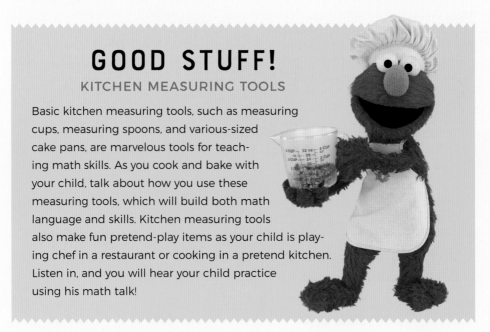

GOOD STUFF!
KITCHEN MEASURING TOOLS

Basic kitchen measuring tools, such as measuring cups, measuring spoons, and various-sized cake pans, are marvelous tools for teaching math skills. As you cook and bake with your child, talk about how you use these measuring tools, which will build both math language and skills. Kitchen measuring tools also make fun pretend-play items as your child is playing chef in a restaurant or cooking in a pretend kitchen. Listen in, and you will hear your child practice using his math talk!

SETTING THE TABLE

The simple act of setting the table offers many ways for children to learn basic math concepts.

- **ONE-TO-ONE CORRESPONDENCE,** an essential math skill, is a perfect example. Ask your child to count how many people will be sitting at the table. Then have her get out the same number of plates, spoons, glasses, and so on—one for each person. You might even hand a child three spoons, and then ask, "Do you need more spoons?"

- **PATTERNING** can also be learned while setting the table for dinner. You can offer a model for a place setting (fork on the left, plate in the middle, spoon on the right, etc.), then let your child repeat the pattern with each place setting. You will need to establish the patterns by laying at least two place settings.

- **WHAT IS DIFFERENT? WHAT IS THE SAME?** Compare spoons (serving spoon to a soup spoon to a teaspoon), plates (serving platters, dinner plates, dessert plates), glasses (sizes, shapes), or any other items.

QUICK TIP

Introducing your child to the concept of "one-to-one correspondence" is an extremely important aspect of the process of learning numbers and counting. For example, you might say: "Grandma and Grandpa are coming over for dinner. We have four chairs; how many more chairs will we need so that *each* person has a chair? Do we have *the same number* of plates? Do we have *more or fewer* napkins as plates?

AGE 5

At five years old, your child probably can make general comparisons and esti-
mates. As she gets older, she can measure with more accuracy, lining up the ends
of two objects to figure out which one is longer. She is also beginning to use measurement words and tools more accurately. She can carefully line up the ends of
two pencils to see which one is shorter and has been used more, or she can use a
measuring cup to help add two cups of milk to a pancake mix.

Shapes & Spatial Awareness

Young children begin to explore geometry through basic shapes, learning how
to identify, describe, and create them. They also build spatial awareness as
they learn to use position words and phrases ("next to," "under," "through") to
describe an object's location.

As children develop their understanding of shapes and awareness of space,
they start to:

- **USE POSITION WORDS.** Children begin to describe the location or position
  of an object with words like "near/far," "above/below," and "in front of/
  behind." In time, children learn that position is relative to other objects
  ("A bridge goes over the water, and a tunnel goes under the river") and can
  change ("Grandpa was living far from me, but now he lives near me").

- **TALK ABOUT DIRECTION.** Children begin to use words like "over," "under,"
  "around," and "through," as they pertain to direction. This language often
  comes up during a game of "Follow the Leader" or "Simon Says," or during
  obstacle course play.

- **IDENTIFY AND DESCRIBE COMMON SHAPES.** Children learn to recognize
  simple shapes (circle, square, rectangle, and triangle), more complex shapes
  (pentagon, hexagon, octagon, rhombus), and learn to name these shapes,
  based on their features. ("This shape has—one, two, three sides, and one,
  two, three angles—it's a triangle!") In time, even if children see a triangle
  turned upside down or elongated, they still recognize that it's a triangle. It's
  important to expose children to different-shaped triangles and label them as
  a "triangle."

DEEP DIVE

COMMON MISTAKES WITH SHAPES

We all can be a little casual when discussing shapes. For example, a ball is technically a "sphere," not a "circle," but a child might label a ball a "circle," especially when looking at it in a picture book or in a photograph.

- SPHERES VERSUS CIRCLES. A ball and the moon are three-dimensional spheres, not two-dimensional round circles; however, one can say a "sphere" is shaped like a circle.

- CUBES. A cube can be a block, but for it to be a cube, each side of the cube must be shaped like a square.

- TRIANGLES. A triangle is a shape with three sides and three angles. The musical instrument, called a triangle, is not a triangle because it doesn't have three angles (there is an opening). A slice of pizza is not a triangle because it doesn't have three angles; instead, two corners are rounded. However, both these items can be referred to as "shaped like a triangle."

- DIAMOND. The correct word for a diamond shape is a "rhombus." A rhombus is a parallelogram; all sides are of equal length, and the opposite angles are also equal.

- HEARTS AND STARS. These are shapes, but they are not geometric shapes.

- **MAKE SHAPES BY COMBINING OR SEPARATING OTHER SHAPES.**
Children begin to play with shapes to make new ones (putting two triangles together to make a square or breaking a rectangular graham cracker in half to make two squares).

GOOD STUFF!
PUZZLES

Puzzles are a great way to introduce children to the concept of shapes. As you "work" the puzzle together, point out the curves, sides, and angles on the pieces, and show how they fit together. Encourage your child to rotate and flip pieces to make them fit together—and use words such as "rotate," "compare," "match," and "substitute" to familiarize your child with the language of math. Ask such questions as, "What might fit instead?" or "This piece has an angle! Where do you think it might go?" Sort pieces by shape. "Let's find all the straight-edge pieces and put them in a pile" or "Let's look at the picture on the box and find where the top and bottom corner pieces go."

What to Expect from Your Preschooler

AGE 2

At two years old, your child can probably match two identical shapes, and can put a circle shape into the circle hole in a shape-sorter toy. She also understands some position words, like "top" and "bottom." For example, she will follow your direction to "Put the book on top of the table."

AGE 3

At three years old, your child can identify a few basic shapes (circle, square, triangle). He also recognizes the placement of objects in relation to others and understands position words and phrases, like "in front of" and "behind." For example, he gets in line behind a friend at the playground when you say, "Wait for your turn behind Stephen," or puts a toy train engine in front when you say, "The engine goes in front of the rest of the cars."

MATH TALK

GEOMETRIC FORMS

Here are words to use when you name and talk about
the attributes of various geometric shapes:

- Shape
- Sides
- Angles
- Length
- Straight
- Round

- Circle
- Square
- Oval
- Sphere
- Cube
- Rectangle

- Triangle
- Pentagon
- Hexagon
- Octagon
- Rhombus

SPATIAL RELATIONS

Here are some words and phrases to use when talking with your child
about the placement of objects, or their location in relation to others:

- Above/below
- Upside down
- Near/far
- In front of/behind
- Over/under

- Top/bottom
- Low/high
- Forward/backward
- Next to
- In between

- Rotate
- Flip around
- Inside/outside

RELATIONAL CONCEPTS

Here are some words and phrases to use when talking about
objects in relation to one another:

- Big/small
- Short/tall

- Short/long
- Fast/slow

- Same/different
- Open/closed

SEARCHING FOR SHAPES IN YOUR ENVIRONMENT

Shapes can be found everywhere! Help your child find and identify shapes in and around your neighborhood. Point out shapes on signs (a STOP sign is an octagon), on buildings (a door is usually a rectangle), in the grocery store (a wedge of cheese is shaped like a triangle), in nature (the face of a full moon is a circle), in your home (a tabletop may be a square, a rectangle, or an oval), at the beach (a beachball is a sphere), at the park (a baseball diamond is a rhombus or a square, even though it's called a diamond; home plate is a pentagon; the other bases are squares.) As you explore shapes, count the sides and angles, and talk with your child about what makes each object a specific shape.

SHAPE DAY

Turn a favorite shape into a daylong game. For example, make today "Circle Day." As you go through your day, ask your child to point out every circle he sees. Keep a list, and then, at the end of the day, count with him to add up how many circles you've seen together. Ask him to draw a picture made with circles. Perhaps even have a pizza for supper, and when he identifies the shape of his pizza slice, suggest that maybe tomorrow can be "Triangle Day."

AGE 4

At four years old, your child will be able to describe basic shapes, even when she sees them in different sizes or positions. She can also name the parts of a shape (sides, angles) and make shapes herself. For example, she can describe a book as "a rectangle—it has two short sides and two long sides."

She understands that a shape can be part of a whole, and, as she nears five years old, she can make a picture or design by combining shapes together. She also uses position words to describe where something is positioned ("over," "under," "behind"); its direction ("up," "down"); or its distance ("near," "far"). For example, she might talk about an outing to a relative's house, "Aunt Donna's house is far away."

AGE 5

At five years old, your child can identify most familiar shapes and some less common ones (like hexagon, trapezoid, rhombus). He is beginning to understand that turning a shape or making it larger doesn't make it a different shape. He can create new shapes by combining others. For example, he knows that a piece of

GOOD STUFF!
TANGRAMS

Tangrams are ancient Chinese puzzles, made up of a square that is divided into seven geometric shapes. Most appropriate for children, age five and older, playing with tangrams heightens children's critical-thinking and problem-solving skills, as they learn how to identify patterns, symmetry, and congruent shapes. Tangrams also encourage fine-motor skills, visual thinking, and logic. Kids enjoy fitting the shaped pieces together to make new shapes and designs. Tangrams come in a variety of sizes and materials, including wood, plastic, and foam.

paper is still a rectangle, even when it's turned on its side, or that he can put two triangular blocks together when he runs out of square blocks for a building.

He understands and uses position words and phrases (like "over," "under," "next to," "between"). He is beginning to create and use simple maps to find objects, and is developing the ability to see positions from more than one point of view, which will help him learn left and right. For example, he can draw a picture of his street and the buildings on it and point out that his house is "next to" the library. He is also learning movement vocabulary used with geometry, such as "slide," "turn," and "flip."

Patterns

Children learn to recognize patterns (items that repeat again and again) and develop thinking skills to copy, continue, or create a pattern. They also build the vocabulary or language to describe patterns.

As children develop their understanding of patterns, they start to:

- **NOTICE AND DESCRIBE SIMPLE PATTERNS.** Simple patterns (also called "AB patterns") have two items that repeat at least two times. Patterns can be seen (cracker, cheese / cracker, cheese / cracker, cheese); heard (clap, stomp / clap, stomp / clap, stomp); and created with motion (jump, hop / jump, hop / jump, hop). As their pattern skills grow, children learn to recognize and describe more complicated patterns, such as:

AABB:
strawberry, strawberry, pretzel, pretzel
strawberry, strawberry, pretzel, pretzel
strawberry, strawberry, pretzel, pretzel

AAB:
flower, flower, bush
flower, flower, bush
flower, flower, bush

ABB:
stomp, clap, clap
stomp, clap, clap
stomp, clap, clap

PATTERNS & SORTING

Here are some words and phrases to use when talking
about patterns and sorting with your child:

- Let's make a pattern!
- What comes next?

- How did you know?
- Let's check!
- Match

- Sort/sorting
- Group

MAKING PATTERNS TOGETHER

Help your child notice patterns all around him—in clothing, in artwork, in books, with food, on fabrics, in music, and in dance. Make patterns together with an assortment of small everyday objects. (Remember: In order to establish a pattern, you need to repeat the pattern at least twice.) For example, if you are coloring together, make a pattern of colors or shapes: three blue circles, one red circle / three blue circles, one red circle. As you are waiting for your food in a restaurant, line up the silverware: fork, spoon / fork, spoon. Then ask your child to add to the pattern. As you are walking down the street, try a little "dance": step, step, stop / step, step, stop.

Any object or collection of objects can be placed into patterns—crayons, pens, colored sticky notes; also, songs and dances are often composed of patterns. Take turns starting and completing each other's patterns. Repeating the pattern out loud will help your child understand the concept of patterning. Whenever he spots a pattern, invite him to guess what will come next.

DEEP DIVE
LEARNING MATHEMATICS THROUGH MUSIC

Music provides a joyful way to introduce basic math concepts and language to young children. In the music vocabulary below, you can see how math is at the core of music. As you make music together with your child—by singing, dancing, playing with musical instruments—you'll be helping your child learn math! When you understand the underlying math concepts, you can, in turn, reinforce your child's grasp of these basic concepts in playful learning moments throughout the day. Here are a few basic musical concepts:

- **RHYTHM** is the **NUMBER** of beats in a musical pattern. Music is developed in groups of two or three. For example, the song "Rubber Ducky" is a 2 beat, and "I Love Trash" is a 3 beat. Children can recognize the difference between a 1-2 beat and a 1-2-3 beat and move their bodies accordingly. You can reinforce these sound and number patterns on simple instruments, such as a drum, a triangle, or maracas.

- **TEMPO** is the pace of music, which can be **FAST OR SLOW** (a relational concept). To demonstrate tempo, play different types of musical tempos and move your bodies to the tempo so your child can see, and then feel, how the tempo changes.

- **DYNAMICS** is the volume of music, which can be **LOUD/SOFT** (a relational concept). To show dynamics, sing a variety of songs, such as a lullaby in a soft voice and belt out a favorite song in a loud "Broadway" voice!

- **PITCH** is the **MELODIC RANGE OF MUSIC**, which goes from **LOW TO HIGH**. To explain pitch, sing a familiar song, such as "Row, Row, Row Your Boat," and play the "Be My Echo" game. Change the range of your voice, alternating between low and high pitches.

- **DURATION** is the **LENGTH** of the musical sound. Sing a song, such as "Twinkle, Twinkle, Little Star," for your children to experience long sounds. For example "Twinkle—Twinkle (long sound) Little—Star (short sound).

- COPY, EXTEND, AND CREATE THEIR OWN PATTERNS. Children learn to play with patterns by creating a new pattern that matches one they see or continuing an existing pattern (cat, dog, cat, dog, cat, dog—what comes next?). They also learn to fill in a missing part (car, truck, truck, car, truck, truck, car, _____, truck—what's missing?). Eventually, they learn to create and describe their own patterns.

What to Expect from Your Preschooler

AGE 2

At two years old, your child probably is interested in patterns and simple sequences, and tries to create patterns with stickers or blocks.

AGE 3

At three years old, your child very likely recognizes simple AB patterns (patterns that repeat two items) and can say the pattern out loud while looking at it. For example, she may point out a pattern in floor tiles—"Look! Gray square, white square, gray square, white square, gray square, white square!"

AGE 4

At four years old, your child probably can extend or fill in the missing part of a simple AB pattern. For example, he can help set the table by continuing your pattern—fork, spoon, fork spoon, fork, spoon—and realizes when a fork is missing. In addition, he can copy a simple AB pattern. As he nears five years old, he can copy more complex patterns, such as following a simple dance step you teach him—step sideways, clap, step sideways, clap, step sideways, clap.

AGE 5

At five years old, your child can extend and fill in missing parts of more complex patterns. She can continue a rhythm you stomp out—short stomp, long stomp, long stomp / short stomp, long stomp, long stomp / short stomp, long stomp, long

NUMBERS AND COUNTING
THROUGH MUSIC

Music and musical instruments offer endless opportunities to experience and play with mathematical concepts. Here are a few suggestions:

- COUNT THE NUMBER OF STRINGS ON A GUITAR (six), a banjo (five), or a ukulele (four). Count the number of black keys on the piano (36) and say the final number of the group of black keys (cardinality), and then count the number of white keys (52).

- SING SONGS THAT INCLUDE A NUMBER, such as "Five Little Monkeys" or "Five Little Ducks That I Once Knew." Use corresponding fingers as you sing the song together.

- SING SONGS THAT INCLUDE HAND OR BODY MOVEMENTS, such as "Itsy Bitsy Spider" and "I'm a Little Teapot." As children do the movements, count each movement and say the final number of movements.

- EXPLORE THE EIGHT-TONE SERIES OF PITCHES (do, re, mi, fa, sol, la, ti, do) that form an "ordinal repertoire" in music. As you or your child plays a xylophone (wooden bars) or glockenspiel (metal bars), count the bars from one to eight in the upward sequence, as the tones gradually ascend from low to high pitches. Then, count down from eight to one, as the downward sequence gradually descends from high to low.

- COUNT THE NUMBER OF INSTRUMENTS YOU ARE ADDING OR SUBTRACTING throughout a particular song as you make music together. For example, start playing a song where you and your child each have 2 maracas, that makes 1, 2, 3, 4—4 maracas all together. Now, take 2 maracas away. How many are left? Let's count! There are 1—2, which equals 2 maracas. Add a tambourine each. Now you have 1—2 maracas and 1—2 tambourines, that's 1, 2, 3, 4 instruments all together.

stomp (ABB). Or she can tell what fruit is missing in a layered dessert—blueberries, melon, pineapple / blueberries, melon, pineapple / blueberries, _____, pineapple. It's missing melon!

GOOD STUFF!
PERCUSSION INSTRUMENT SET

A percussion instrument set, available in a number of different forms, is an excellent toy for beginning a musical education—and closely related mathematical concepts—for young kids. For example, the Frunsi 12-in-1 Musical Instrument Set contains 12 musical toys, including a xylophone, maracas, a wood sounder, a tambourine, a wrist bell, a hand bell, a bell stick, egg shakers, a triangle, finger castanets, mini cymbals, and claves. Such collections are ideal for parents and children to play with together, and for children to learn basic musical concepts.

Conclusions

Throughout their math education, children are learning to think creatively and flexibly, and are experimenting with different approaches to problem solving. These are important tools for children's future success. It helps them move from just thinking about what they can see and touch to thinking about and solving problems about things they can't see; from hands-on activities to word problems, and other less concrete math tasks.

NUMBERS & COUNTING

AGE 2	AGE 3	AGE 4	AGE 5
Says a few numbers, but not always in the right order.	Counts out loud up to five. • Understands that the words "one," "two," and "three" each represent an amount. • Can count out objects one by one in a group, up to four. • Knows that three is more than two, and two is more than one.	Counts out loud up to 10. • Knows numbers in the right order • Can figure out what number comes next when hearing the numbers that come before it.	Counts out loud up to 20. • Knows the numbers in the right order. • Can figure out what number comes next without having to hear the numbers that came before. • Can correctly point to and count up to 10 objects. • Can count out loud backwards from 5 (and maybe from 10).
Understands the meaning of the number words "one" and "two."	Begins to know the order of daily events.	Understands "how many" and can count groups of items up to five. • Points to and counts each object and knows that the last number is the total. • Is beginning to include counting in drawings and writings.	Has a deeper understanding of numbers' order and value. • Knows where numbers belong in their correct order. • Knows that any number that follows another is one more. • Uses phrases such as "greater than," "less than," and "equal to" to compare two numbers.
Understands when there is more of something.	Begins to identify first and last items in an order.	Understands that a higher number represents a larger amount. • Can compare two groups of up to five items and knows that the one with the higher number has more.	Understands sequential order such as 1st, 2nd, 3rd, up to 10th.
	Begins to recognize a few written numbers (numerals).	Uses words like "first," "second," and "last" to describe the order.	Represents numbers in his drawings and writing (up to nine).
		Can read written numbers (numerals) up to five.	

ADDING & SUBTRACTING

AGE 2	AGE 3	AGE 4	AGE 5
Understands that adding or taking away items from a group changes the total number. • Knows that a collection is made up of parts. • Thinks more in a group is better than less.	**Can tell the correct number when one item is added or taken away from a group up to three.** • Probably does not yet have the language to express this concept.	**Can add items in a group up to four.** • Can also subtract one to three objects and figure out how many are left.	**Can solve simple word problems with addition and subtraction, up to five.** • Probably uses a strategy such as counting on his fingers.
Understands that parts of a collection can be grouped in different ways. • Does not yet have the language to express this concept.	**Understands that the whole group is a bigger number than its individual items.** • Probably can't tell you exactly how many there are, especially if it's a group of more than five.	**Can find different ways to make a group.**	**Can make a group of up to five items using different combinations of numbers.** • Can break groups down into smaller groups.

MEASURING & COMPARING

AGE 2	AGE 3	AGE 4	AGE 5
Can make simple comparisons between two objects, such as "big/small," "tall/short," "more/less."	**Is beginning to compare two objects in more specific ways (height, length, weight).** • Can figure out which object is taller or longer by putting them side-by-side.	**Can compare a small group of objects in different ways (length, size, width) and put them in order.** • Uses words to compare, such as "big/small," "long/short," "heavy/light," "fast/slow."	**Can make general comparisons and estimates.** • Can line up the ends of two objects when deciding which is longer. • Begins to use measurement words and tools more accurately.
		Begins to use everyday objects and tools to measure, such as a bathroom scale.	

PATTERNS

AGE 2	AGE 3	AGE 4	AGE 5
Is interested in patterns and simple sequences.	**Recognizes simple AB patterns (patterns that repeat two items).** • Can say the pattern out loud while looking at it.	**Can extend or fill the missing part of a simple AB pattern.**	**Can extend and fill in missing parts of more complex patterns.**
		Can copy both simple and complex patterns.	

SHAPES

AGE 2	AGE 3	AGE 4	AGE 5
Can match two identical shape.	Can identify a few basic shapes such as "circle," "square," "triangle."	Can describe basic shapes. • Can identify basic shapes even in different sizes or positions. • Can name the parts of a shape such as "sides," and "angles." • Can make basic shapes.	Can identify most familiar shapes and some less common ones, including "hexagon," "trapezoid," "rhombus." • Is beginning to understand that turning a shape or making it large doesn't change the shape. • Can make new shapes by combining others.
Understands some position words, such as "top" and "bottom."	Recognizes the placement of objects in relation to others and understands position words, such as "in front of" and "behind."	Understands that a shape can be part of a whole. • Can make a picture or design by combining shapes.	Understand and uses position words such as "over," "under," "next to," "between." • Uses simple maps to find objects. • Is developing the ability to see positions from more than one point of view. • Is learning "left" and "right." • Is learning movement vocabulary, such as "slide," "turn," and "flip."
		Understands and uses position words to describe where something is, including "over," "under," "behind," "up," "down," "near," "far."	

4.
IS YOUR
CHILD A
"STEMIST"?

Early Science

Children are natural scientists or, more specifically, natural STEMists—scientists, technologists, engineers, and mathematicians. When your child is at play, notice how she figures out how things work and investigates the world around her. She is an engineer when building a garage for a toy car; a mathematician when measuring the width and height of the toy garage; a technologist when using a ramp (a tool) to get the cars in and out of the garage; and a scientist when noticing how different cars go down the same ramp at different speeds and travel various distances.

If young children are natural STEMists, what is STEM? STEM education (science, technology, engineering, and math) is a hands-on, experiential approach to learning, which allows children to draw meaning from and reflect on everyday experiences. As preschoolers build their understanding of how the world around them works, they engage in science, technology, engineering, and mathematics as a single

QUICK TIP When you are outside with your child, encourage him to look closely at living things, such as birds, ants, leaves, or flowers. For example, together, check out and count how many different types of birds you see or how many different shapes of leaves you see on the trees. For birds, observe how they fly and where they fly to. Do you see a nest? If you discover leaves on the ground, try to identify which tree they dropped from.

DEEP DIVE

Three Things You Should Know

STEM education is very important, in fact, crucial, in order for our children to perform at top levels. In a world that is becoming increasingly complex, where success is driven not only by *what* you know, but by what you *can do* with what you know, it is imperative for our children, starting during the preschool years, to be equipped with the knowledge and skills to solve problems, gather and evaluate evidence, and make sense of information. These are the types of skills that students learn by engaging in STEM activities.

1. What is STEM?

While it is important to interweave all four disciplines of STEM education (science, technology, engineering, and mathematics) it is also important to understand the skills that each of the four disciplines brings to a STEM curriculum.

SCIENCE

Science is the process of learning about and understanding the natural and physical world. Through scientific inquiry, children build on their existing knowledge of the world around them. The four stages of scientific inquiry are:

- Observing
- Investigating
- Analyzing
- Reporting the Big Idea

Scientific inquiry involves making observations by using your senses; gathering evidence (data) through investigation and experimentation (such as "testing" out ideas); analyzing the evidence and possibly changing or modifying your ideas and concepts, based on the experimentation; and ultimately reporting the big idea of what was learned. This approach to lifelong learning encompasses curiosity and perseverance in the face of mistakes.

TECHNOLOGY

Technology is the process of making a job easier by using physical tools and simple machines, developed by manipulating materials from the physical world. A child, for example, may explore using a stick as a lever to move a large rock that is blocking her path.

ENGINEERING

Engineering is the process of using tools to design a product to solve a problem. Design is not a linear, step-by-step process, and there is never just one correct solution. Instead, designs are often refined and modified to determine the best way to make a device serve a particular purpose. In engineering, a child may build and manipulate a ramp to make objects roll downhill more quickly.

MATHEMATICS

Mathematics is the process of identifying and describing relationships among numbers, patterns, and shapes. It involves drawing attention to the mathematical aspects of a situation, such as asking questions like these: "How many more?" and "How are they alike?" and "How can we tell?" Children engage in mathematics when they sort, classify, analyze, and compare things they encounter through their daily observations. A young child may create a simple chart to record his findings when he explores the bounciness of balls in order to determine which one bounces the highest.

2. What skills underlie STEM education?

- OBSERVING AND QUESTIONING. This stage encourages children to explore their environment in a spontaneous, unguided manner or pose a problem to solve.

- INVESTIGATING. Investigation is about engaging in multiple trials and learning new information along the way. Through this process, children learn skills such as observing, predicting, planning, measuring, and testing out their ideas.

- ANALYZING AND REPORTING FINDINGS. Children analyze problems by looking at the data collected; using their senses; and interpreting the evidence by stating conclusions, making inferences, and drawing comparisons. A young child's conclusions involve restating the question as a statement and providing evidence from observations, findings, and data. The evidence is used to answer and elaborate on the "because" conclusion, rather than proving that an answer is right or wrong.

- REFLECTING ON THE BIG IDEA. Children naturally share what they have done and reflect on their actions and experiences. The "Big Idea" becomes clearer as they reflect on and articulate the "what" and "why" of their actions.

3. Can STEM be taught to preschool children?

Absolutely! Preschoolers are naturally drawn to engaging in STEM activities. It is during these early years that parents can provide the foundational skills in STEM, as well as foster a love of learning. We must remain mindful, however, to approach STEM learning in age-appropriate ways. Young children learn best when engaged in hands-on activities that are of interest to them and are embedded in real-life situations.

integrated discipline and not as four separate domains or subjects. These content domains are connected by the scientific-inquiry skills that are critical to the development of young children's reasoning and problem-solving skills.

To address our nation's weaknesses in the area of STEM education, Sesame Workshop created an integrated preschool STEM curriculum. We focused on specific scientific content areas appropriate for preschool-aged children (specifically natural science and physical science), to be taught through—and together with—scientific-inquiry process skills. These process skills are:

· OBSERVE AND QUESTION

· INVESTIGATE AND EXPERIMENT

· ANALYZE AND REPORT THE FINDINGS

· REFLECT ON THE BIG IDEA (OR, THE LESSON LEARNED)!

These process skills and the content knowledge (the "facts") are the foundation not only for STEM education, but for lifelong learning.

A few years ago on *Sesame Street*, we added the "Arts" to *Sesame Street*'s STEM curriculum, (turning "STEM" into "STEAM") as an engaging tool to help teach preschoolers STEM skills. In one episode, we focused on Zoe, who loves to dance, choreographing a special ballet, "The Dance of the Six Swans," to perform together with her friends. When Snuffy exclaimed, "I always want to leap in the air like a ballet dancer!," his dance partner Alan tried to lift him, but everyone realized that Snuffy was just too heavy.

Gina suggested that they needed to be a little bit creative and think of other ways they could lift Snuffy. As they observed what was around them, Elmo pointed out that Chris was lifting a piece of pie out of a plate with a spatula. Gina explained that a spatula was a kind of lever, and if they designed a bigger lever, they might be able to lift up Snuffy. Using a long board and a crate, Snuffy sat on one end, and Alan tried to lift him by pushing the board down from the other end. But, unfortunately, the board broke.

Undaunted, Gina modeled perseverance ("Don't give up in the face of a challenge or failure!"), and suggested that they try to think of another way they could lift Snuffy. (Trying things out and seeing what works—or doesn't—is a critical

TURNING UP THE STEAM

STEAM (science, technology, engineering, the arts, mathematics) education uses the arts (painting, sculpture, music, dance, and literature) to teach the STEM concept and process skills. For example, a child looking at the sky as the sun is setting can be inspired to create a painting. He asks: "How can I mix paint colors together (science) to make just the right color? He measures (mathematics) the different amounts of paint and compares the colors to the sky. He examines the sky and plans and plots a design that represents his idea (engineering). Through trial and error he remixes the paints using bowls, brushes, and other painter's tools (technology). He learns that he needs more blue than red to make the perfect color purple for the sunset in his painting. The end result—the Big Idea!—is that both the scientific process and the artistic process (the integration of art—"A"—into STEM) are better understood through an engaging, fun activity.

DEEP DIVE
PARENTS AS CO-LEARNERS

As parents, we are often stumped and sometimes even intimidated by our child's "Why" and "How" questions about the natural and physical world because, frankly, we often think we don't have the scientific knowledge to answer the questions accurately. This feeling could lead to avoiding playful learning opportunities that involve exploring, investigating, and learning about nature or how the physical works with your young child. The good news is that you don't need to have all the answers! Join your child as a co-learner and investigate and learn wonderful "Aha!" ideas together. So the next time your child asks a question and you don't have the answer, say, "That's a great question! I don't know the answer. Let's find out together."

Then, as co-learners, guide each other's observations and talk about what you are observing. Remember: Your role is not to give the answers or be a dispenser of facts, which can stifle learning. Instead, empower your child to be an independent thinker and learner. By modeling scientific skills, not only are you enhancing your own knowledge, but you are experiencing the joy and wonder of learning with your child!

This approach to learning helps your child become an active and engaged learner. As a parent, you will be delighted by all you learn from your child's questions and your co-investigations. Remember: It's okay to make mistakes (Oops!), because very often, through your errors, you can discover so much (Aha!)

part of STEM learning.) While looking around again, Zoe noticed a girl jumping rope and suggested using a rope, swung over a beam, and tied around Snuffy's stomach to lift him. They quickly designed a rope solution and tried it out, but no matter how hard Alan pulled, he still couldn't lift Snuffy.

Finally, Gordon came out to help. He looked closely at their design and noticed that they were missing pulleys. Gordon explained that pulleys are great tools to help lift heavy things. He redrew their rope design to include one pulley at the top and one at the bottom. With this new design, Alan was able to easily lift Snuffy high into the air like a swan!

Science Skills & the Scientific Process

Through the lens of science—both natural science and physical science— children build on their understanding of the world. They learn how to adjust their ideas, as new experiences give them new information and more questions to investigate.

This ongoing pathway of discovery is part of the process called "scientific inquiry." Early science skills include exploring, observing, asking questions, predicting, and testing ideas about how things work. Parents can help children develop their science knowledge and vocabulary simply by encouraging them to explore, ask questions, and talk about their discoveries. Most importantly, they learn to persevere and not to give up in the face of failure or setbacks.

Young children start to understand concepts related to the natural and physical world quite early, including living things, weather, force, and engineering. When these science topics are introduced through familiar, everyday experiences and in child-friendly language, young children can learn what might seem like complicated concepts. Children learn how to observe and ask questions. They develop their ability to collect and consider new information and draw conclusions about what they see.

Specifically, as children build their science skills, they start to:

- USE ALL FIVE SENSES TO OBSERVE. They ask questions and gather new information through their eyes, ears, nose, mouth, and skin. Their senses help them identify the problem to solve. ("When my cup is in the sun, I see that the ice goes away and my water tastes warm. What happened to the ice?")

- **USE SIMPLE TOOLS TO OBSERVE.** They use tools (like a magnifying glass, a ruler, a scale, paper, and crayons), when needed, to help them investigate, see up close, measure, and record information.

- **MAKE GUESSES AND TEST PREDICTIONS.** Children participate in simple experiments. They observe and use what they know from previous experiences to make a thoughtful guess about why something is happening (hypothesis). Then they make predictions and test their ideas (putting an ice cube in the sun and one in the shade to see which one melts more quickly).

- **COLLECT AND CONSIDER INFORMATION TO ANSWER A QUESTION.** Children learn to collect information (data) using simple charts, drawings, and photos. They learn how to organize the information so they can read it and draw conclusions. (For example, a child makes a simple chart with a drawing of a sun and a rain cloud and uses a check mark to record the weather each day for a month. From the number of check marks under the cloud, she concludes that it has been a rainy month.) During this process, children may learn that their initial ideas were wrong and will rethink their initial understanding or pose a new question.

- **SHARE AND EXPLAIN CONCLUSIONS.** In time, children learn to report on what they've learned by describing a problem or question they investigated and explain what they discovered. To do this, children need to reflect and think about how and why things happened, based on their observations ("It happened because . . ."). This is an important milestone in cognitive reasoning. (Conclusion: She decides to keep her cup in the shade after discovering that the ice didn't melt as fast there.)

GOOD STUFF!
SCIENTIFIC TOOLS

Here are some tools young, enterprising scientists will find valuable.

Magnifying glasses	Mirror	Drawing pad
Binoculars	Field guide	Paper
Butterfly net	Eyedropper	Index cards
Flashlight	Clipboard	Writing tools

112

SORTING GAMES

Sorting games are an excellent way to help your child learn about observing or, more specifically, how things are different and how they are the same. Be sure to have your child point out these distinct features, and to articulate these observations. Language is key! Younger children enjoy the challenge of organizing all kinds of materials through sorting. Here are a few suggestions:

When you are folding clean laundry, ask your child to help sort by item (towels, underwear, socks) or perhaps pile up all the socks and request that she organize them (by color or by owner—Daddy's socks, Mommy's socks, etc.)

Fill a big box with a random collection of toys, then encourage your child to sort the items in different ways: by color, by size, or by toy category (vehicles, plush toys, action figures, etc.). Within each group, sort by type; for example, for vehicles, by mode of transportation (cars, trains, planes, boats); for plush toys, by type (teddy bears, dinosaurs, etc.). If the items are large or cumbersome, supply two or three boxes, laundry baskets, or shopping bags to hold the sorted items.

SCIENCE TALK

Here is vocabulary that is useful for scientific investigation with young children. Some, if not many, of these words may seem difficult for preschool children, but you will be amazed at how quickly they will understand and use them.

- Observe
- Wonder
- Explore
- Investigate

- Experiment
- Predict
- Estimate
- Hypothesis
- Trial and Error

- Collaborate
- Evidence
- Report
- Document
- Conclude

OOPS & AHA

When James first started asking "Why" questions, when he was about age 2 or 3, my instinct was to simply answer. (Oops!) It took me a little while to control myself to ask him, "Why do you think . . . ?" By doing so, I learned that he was capable of creating a hypothesis. So when he asked, "Why do people have fingers?" I asked him, "Why do you think they do?" He answered, "So they can do the things they need to do." I then asked him to show me what he could do with his fingers, and, during the following days, I pointed out when he and I were using our fingers to do something. Preschoolers are capable of using the scientific method at a basic level if we encourage them to try. (Aha!)

—Sara, educator & mom

What to Expect from Your Preschooler

AGE 2

At two years old, your child probably:

- **LOVES USING HIS SENSES TO EXPLORE.** He likes to explore new objects and test new ideas. You may see this when your child looks at, touches, and smells a pinecone that he found; realizes that shaking different boxes from the cupboard (uncooked macaroni, rice, oatmeal, cake mix) produces different sounds; or sends different objects (acorn, pebble, twig, toy car) down a slide at the playground to see how far and how fast they'll go.

- **IS STARTING TO CONNECT PICTURES TO OBJECTS IN THE REAL WORLD, AND SORT AND ORGANIZE OBJECTS BY SIZE, COLOR, AND SHAPE.** She is also beginning to reflect on experiences and see how they relate to previous ones. You may see this when your child points to her eyes, ears, nose, etc., as you look at a picture book about the body; or sorts a pile of rocks she collected by color and says, "The beach," as she points to one that looks like one she found there.

- **CAN TELL THE DIFFERENCE BETWEEN WHAT BELONGS AND DOESN'T BELONG IN A GROUP.** He may not yet collect information (data) in an organized way, but he can begin to sort and order items by qualities like size, color, and shape. This is the beginning of data collection. You may see this

GOOD STUFF!
BUILDING BLOCKS

Building blocks for kids have been a childhood staple for centuries. Today blocks can be found in every size (tiny to oversized), material (classic wooden blocks, soft "stuffed" blocks, child-safe plastic blocks), shape, and color. Among the best known are Legos, Magna-Tiles, MegaBlocks, K'Nex building sets, and Lincoln Logs. Children gravitate to building blocks almost instinctively and enjoy the creativity of building at all ages.

when your child sorts a collection of balls into big and small bins or notices some misplaced toy food in a bin meant for toy cars and pulls it out (maybe even putting it where it belongs with the other play food!)

AGE 3

At three years old, your child probably:

- **CONTINUES TO BE CURIOUS ABOUT THE WORLD AROUND HER.** She is beginning to ask questions based on what she observes. You may see this when your child asks many "Why" questions: "Why does the sun go away at night?"; "Why do leaves change color?"; "Why can't I fly like a bird?"

- **UNDERSTANDS AND USES LANGUAGE TO TALK ABOUT PREVIOUS EXPERIENCES.** He can connect new information to what he already knows and build an understanding of the world around him. He can also use this information to investigate and explore more. You may see this when your child notices that a puddle has frozen overnight and says, "It's just like the water we put in the ice-cube tray." Or he may observe that "It was cold like a freezer outside last night!" and asks to put an ice-cube tray filled with water outside the next night to see if turns to ice.

AGE 4

At four years old, your child probably:

- **HAS BETTER HAND-EYE COORDINATION AND A GRASP OF MORE WORDS** to help her explore her world more deeply. She asks more questions and can name problems that she can solve. You may see this when your child notices that the leg of a chair is loose, gets her toy screwdriver, and says: "The chair is wobbly; we need to fix it." She may also watch carefully as you use a real screwdriver to tighten the screw, wants to try using it, and asks questions about how screws work to hold the chair together.

- **GETS ACTIVELY INVOLVED IN INVESTIGATING AND EXPERIMENTING.** He may begin to understand that measurement (such as length, weight, and temperature) can be used to compare objects. He is not yet able to use tools (like a ruler or tape measure) accurately, but probably measures using everyday household objects. You may see this when your child uses a crayon to measure how many "crayons high" the table is. He may also line sticks

LET'S GO FIND THE WIND

A wonderful way to introduce even very young children to weather and the environment is to talk about the fascinating aspects of wind, especially with reference to the senses. Here are a few suggestions:

• We can *see* the wind when it creates ripples on a lake as it blows across, or musses our hair, or blows our hat off in an unexpected gust.

• We can *hear* the wind in the rustling of leaves through the trees, or when it unexpectedly blows the back door shut.

• We can *feel* the wind when a soft breeze caresses our cheeks, or as a strong wind makes it harder to ride a bike up a hill!

• We can *smell* the wind when it catches the scent of roses in a garden or hamburgers cooking on an outdoor grill, and blows the wonderful scents our way.

• Can we taste the wind? This is a tough thought! When talking about the wind, ask your child to come up with ways she can see, hear, touch, smell—and even *taste* the wind, and see what she comes up with!

QUICK TIP

Most communities have access, either in their city or at a nearby location, to a natural history museum, a discovery center, an aquarium, a zoo, a botanical garden, or even a child-friendly working farm, where children can learn about nature. Together be captivated by your observations of everything from the gigantic dinosaurs to the trained seals. Pet the baby lambs, feed the ducks, or even milk a cow and collect eggs from a chicken coop on a farm! Spending time in nature offers infinite benefits, including helping in the development of caring, empathetic, confident, inquisitive, and active children.

next to each other to see which is the longest, or suggests making paper airplanes and then testing them to see which will fly the farthest.

- **CAN ORGANIZE INFORMATION SHE COLLECTS INTO SIMPLE CHARTS OR DIAGRAMS.** She is starting to talk about what the information shows and make statements like, "I think this will happen because . . ." For example, she may learn that more people in her family like bananas *because* when she asked everyone what their favorite fruit was (and, with your help, made a simple chart to record their choices), she saw that five people chose bananas and two chose apples.

AGE 5

At five years old, your child probably:

- **IS GETTING MORE CURIOUS AND ACTIVELY ENGAGED AS SHE EXPLORES HER WORLD.** She is curious about things in her world and the larger world she is seeing through television, magazines, and other media. She may experiment in the bath to see how much water she can add to a floating cup before it sinks, or she may suggest checking out more books from the library on a topic she's interested in. "I want to learn more about penguins, like the ones we read about in school."

- **HAS MORE KNOWLEDGE AND EXPERIENCES THAT HELP HIM UNDERSTAND NEW PROBLEMS AND GATHER MORE INFORMATION.** He also is starting to understand that predictions can be wrong, but what is learned through the prediction process can guide us toward an answer. For

GOOD STUFF!
TOOL BELTS AND WORKBENCHES

If your child shows a particular fascination for building, architecture, and engineering, consider getting her a toy tool kit or even a toy workbench for her next birthday. For example, the Black and Decker Junior Tool Belt Kit for ages three and up includes a hammer, wrenches and screwdrivers, and large screws made for little fingers. Many such kits are available for various ages at different prices.

example, he compares current weather conditions to a similar experience he had. "Those look like the dark clouds we saw when we went to the zoo. It rained so hard that day! Let's bring our umbrellas just in case." Later, he may notice that the wind has blown the dark clouds away with no rain. "This weather was different from our zoo day. Sometimes it can be cloudy with no rain. It looks like the rest of today will be sunny!"

- **IS PARTICIPATING IN PROBLEM SOLVING AND EXPERIMENTS.** She is now able to understand and use language to describe the steps in her investigation and explain what she finds. For example, she may carefully explain, "I mixed red and blue paint and made purple. When I added more blue, the purple turned more bluish!"

- **USES SIMPLE TOOLS TO COLLECT INFORMATION AND COMPARE.** He can also make simple charts and diagrams to show what he knows. You may see this when your child uses a ruler to measure different family members' beds and decides which is the longest, or draws a picture of a glass of milk and a glass of water and then adds tally marks next to each as he asks family members what they want to drink with dinner.

Understanding the Natural World

"A child's world is fresh and new and beautiful, full of wonder and excitement . . . Exploring nature with your child is largely a matter of becoming receptive to what lies all around you."

—Rachel Carson, author of *Silent Spring*

Children are innately interested in the natural world. By the "natural world," we mean the study of living things (plants and animals), as well as other natural aspects of our world, including the environment, the weather, changing seasons, and the cultivation of our food.

Introducing young children to the natural world is the first step toward helping them develop a caring attitude toward the environment. Many children today are deprived of frequent positive experiences with the natural world. Richard Louv, author of *Last Child in the Woods: Saving Our Children from Nature-Deficit Disorder*, uses the term "de-naturing of childhood." He and other researchers have found that a lack of positive experiences with nature during the early years can lead to some troubling results, such as attention difficulties; a diminished use of the senses; lack of physical activity, which can produce higher rates of childhood obesity; and the development of unfounded fears of the natural world. Other studies have indicated that children growing up in urban areas may even tend to develop feelings of disgust in relation to natural objects, due to a lack of experience with the natural world.

As young children actively interact with the natural world, they begin to connect related facts to build their overall understanding. Research shows that experiences with nature also contribute to a child's problem-solving ability, creativity, concentration, and observational skills.

As children develop their understanding of the natural world, they start to:

- **OBSERVE AND COMPARE LIVING AND NONLIVING THINGS.** Children learn that living things grow and have needs, such as for water, air, food, and shelter.

- **LEARN ABOUT PLANTS AND THEIR LIFE CYCLE.** They understand that many plants start as a seed, then grow into a plant that eventually makes more seeds (life cycle). They also learn that seeds and plants need sunlight, water, air, and soil to grow.

- **LEARN ABOUT ANIMALS AND THEIR LIFE CYCLES.** They get to know different animals and their names, their life cycles (such as a frog's development from egg, tadpole, and froglet to adult frog), as well as their features (wings, gills, claws, etc.) and their habitats.

- UNDERSTAND ABOUT WEATHER AND THE SEASONS. They observe different kinds of weather (sunny, rainy, windy, hot, cold); how weather changes; the four seasons; and that animals and plants may change the way they look or act as seasons change.

- COMPREHEND WHERE FOOD COMES FROM. Children learn that many foods come from plants and farms; and that food then travels to stores, where we buy it to prepare and eat it at home.

- **LEARN WAYS THAT PEOPLE CAN TAKE CARE OF THE ENVIRONMENT.** Children learn about reducing, reusing, recycling, and respecting the earth.

What to Expect from Your Preschooler

Here are some thoughts about what you can expect your child to comprehend about natural science at various stages.

AGE 2

At two years old, your child probably:

- **UNDERSTANDS SOME OF THE DIFFERENCES BETWEEN LIVING AND NONLIVING THINGS.** She still considers many nonliving objects living, such as stuffed animals and dolls. You may see this when your child tries to feed some of her snack to a doll, or doesn't want to stand near the statue of a person, thinking it is real.

- **RECOGNIZES HIS OWN NEEDS FOR WATER, FOOD, AND SHELTER.** He may begin to help you take care of pets or plants at home. You may see this when your child says, "Kitty's hungry," and wants to help put food in the pet cat's bowl, or helps plant a seed and observes it growing over time, or notices a pet lizard taking shelter under a layer of moss in the tank.

GOOD STUFF!
MAKING HABITATS

Observing insects, worms, birds, fish, and reptiles in their native habitat is endlessly fascinating for kids. In effect, kids can go on a mini-safari, right in their own backyard or in a nearby park, using a few simple products, designed for young children, that are available at pet stores and online. Classic aquariums and terrariums are great to design with your child and teach him responsibility for the care of living things. Another engaging nature activity is to use catching tools and containers to capture and observe all sorts of creatures. Also, numerous kits are available for growing and observing butterflies, ants, ladybugs, praying mantises, and frogs. When purchasing such kits, keep in mind the care and attention each animal will need to develop, grow, and survive until the time of its release, and how best to release the animal to ensure its survival.

- **KNOWS SOME FAMILIAR ANIMALS.** She can name some familiar animals and their features (dog/fur, bird/wings, turtle/shell). She may also know that some animals live outdoors in her neighborhood, some live in the zoo or on a farm, and some live inside as pets.

- **KNOWS THAT WEATHER CAN CHANGE FROM DAY TO DAY.** Depending on her experiences, she may know that there are very cold places with lots of snow and ice, and very hot places, like a desert. However, she may not yet understand that these places exist in the real world (unless she has actually been there herself).

AGE 3

At three years old, your child probably:

- **KNOWS MORE ABOUT LIVING THINGS,** but may still confuse some living and nonliving things. You may see this when she wants to put a blanket on a stuffed animal "because it's cold."

- **KNOWS MORE ABOUT PLANTS.** He probably has had more experiences with plants that help him understand why they need water, sunlight, and air to grow. He may still be unsure as to whether plants are living or nonliving, since they don't move or eat, the way animals do. You may see this when your child says on a rainy day, "I'm sad because I can't play outside, but the trees are happy because they need water." Or possibly, he may see a plant drooping and say, "It's thirsty."

- **KNOWS MORE ABOUT ANIMALS.** She can name more animals and can tell the difference between types of animals, like fish that live in the water and birds that fly in the sky. She is also learning how animals get their food. You may see this when your child points out and names many animals she knows on a farm or at a zoo, or sees a squirrel digging through leaves and says, "He's looking for an acorn to eat."

QUICK TIP It's easy to create a garden, regardless of where you live. You can plant a few rows of herbs, greens, and other vegetables in a small backyard or a whole field of corn if you live on a farm! If you live in an apartment, plant tomatoes, herbs, and even some lettuce or spinach in a few containers by a sunny windowsill. Check to see if your city has a nearby community garden, and then cultivate your own little plot with your child's help.

SCIENCE TALK

Here are some words that will enhance your child's nature vocabulary:

- **ANIMALS:** Insects, reptiles, mammals, amphibians, birds, fish.

- **HABITAT:** A place where animals live and can find food, water, and shelter to sleep.

- **AMPHIBIAN:** An animal, such as a frog, toad, salamander, or newt that:
    - Goes through a big change, called metamorphosis.
    - Lives part of its life on land, breathing through its skin, and part of it in the water, breathing through its gills.
    - Has thin, moist skin, four legs, and a backbone.

- **INSECT:** A small bug that has six legs, two antennae, and usually two pairs of wings, such as flies, crickets, mosquitoes, beetles, butterflies, and bees.

- **REPTILE:** An animal, such as a snake, turtle, lizard, crocodile, or tortoise, that is distinguished by its dry, scaly skin and typically lays soft-shelled eggs on land.

- **CAMOUFLAGE:** To disguise or aid by blending into the background.

- **HIBERNATE:** When animals sleep for a very long time from winter until spring, when it's warm and easy to find food again.

- **METAMORPHOSIS:** When something goes through a really big change (in its life cycle); for example, when a caterpillar changes into a butterfly.

- **NATURE:** Plants, animals, and other things outside that are not made by people.

DEEP DIVE

FOSTERING CHILDREN'S LOVE OF NATURE

By asking simple, open-ended questions, you encourage your child to consider and describe the "answers" that she has observed. The types of questions listed below inspire children to explore nature more deeply and express their observations and thoughts.

EXPERIENCE QUESTIONS:

- What does it look like? Feel like? Sound like? Smell like?

- What kind of living things do you think we'll find outside? At the park? Along the sidewalk? In the garden?

- What do you think the sand will feel like when we get to the beach?

- Let's listen to how different birds make different sounds. Which birds chirp? Coo? Cluck? Quack? Gobble? Go cock-a-doodle-do?

KNOWLEDGE QUESTIONS:

- What do you think? Why do you think that is?

- Let's take a closer look. What can we find out?

- Is it alive? How do you know?

- Do you see its eyes, nose, mouth, ears, etc.? Where?

- What kind of bugs or animals have you seen near our home?

- What other animals have four legs?

- Where do you think this creature lives? Why do you think so?

- What do you think would happen if we planted this here?

- What can we do to keep this plant alive and healthy?

ATTITUDE/FEELING QUESTIONS:

- How do you feel when you're close to this butterfly?

- How do you feel when you're watching a chick hatch from an egg?

- How do you feel when you see a rainbow?

- How do you think the baby duck feels when he's with his mommy?

- **TALKS ABOUT THE WEATHER.** His own experiences help him recognize different types of weather and the seasons where he lives. Travel can help him understand that weather may be different in different places. He often knows what kind of clothes he should wear for the weather. You may see this when your child says, "It looks cold and windy outside. I need my jacket." He may also indicate his knowledge of weather by drawing a picture of a relative at home in a sunny climate, and says, "Grandma can go swimming today because it's hot in Florida, but it's cold here so I have to stay inside."

- **IS BEGINNING TO UNDERSTAND WHERE FOOD COMES FROM.** You may see this when your child says, "Cows made my milk!" or "Chickens lay eggs!" She also enjoys helping with gardening activities. You may see this when your child wants to help you pick lettuce for a salad or eagerly gets a toy shovel to help you plant strawberry plants.

GOOD STUFF!
COOKING WITH KIDS

Cooking with children is an excellent way to introduce scientific processes and additional vocabulary to kids. Indeed, cooking is all about science. Many wonderful cookbooks, focusing on cooking with children, are available. Here are a few of our favorites:

- *Sesame Street: Let's Cook!* by Susan McQuillan

    A collection of 50 healthy, fun recipes for parents and children ages two to five from "celebrity chefs" Elmo, Cookie Monster, Grover, and the rest of the beloved *Sesame Street* gang.

- *Sesame Street: B Is for Baking* by Susan McQuillan

    This book presents 50 nutritious recipes for foods you bake at breakfast, lunch, dinner, snack time, and for special occasions—perfect for getting kids involved in the kitchen with special steps children can do on their own.

- *The Toddler Cookbook* by Annabel Karmel

    This toddler-friendly cookbook features easy recipes for a variety of dishes, from lettuce wraps to crunchy chicken dippers. It offers a fun way to spend quality time together; encourage your toddler to try new foods; and, with step-by-step photos, teach how to measure, sift, mix, and much more!

AGE 4

At four years old, your child probably:

- **UNDERSTANDS THE DIFFERENCE BETWEEN LIVING AND NONLIVING THINGS,** based on his experiences. For example, he knows how people breathe, but may not know how fish breathe. He knows that living things grow and change over time. He also understands more details about the different animals that live on earth and may be able to name some of their habitats. You may see this when your child names and sorts pictures of animals into their species group, such as birds, fish, and insects.

- **NOTICES THE DAILY WEATHER AND KNOWS WHAT KINDS OF CLOTHES TO WEAR.** You may see this when your child observes that it's raining and looks for her umbrella. She probably recognizes that the seasons change, but may not yet know the order of the seasons. She may know that some plants and animals change as the seasons change, but may not be able to tell you what will happen in the next season. She may even see geese in the air and say, "They are flying to a warmer place because it's cold here."

- **KNOWS THAT MANY DIFFERENT KINDS OF FOODS EXIST, AND CAN USUALLY SORT THEM BY TYPE** (fruits, vegetables, meats, etc.). He is beginning to understand that some foods are healthier than others. He is more willing to try new foods if he has helped to prepare them. You may see this when your child picks out a few different pieces of toy fruit and puts them in a bowl when you ask him to make you a fruit salad, or wants to try the new sweet potato dish that he helped you measure ingredients for as you prepared the recipe.

AGE 5

At five years old, your child probably:

- **CAN IDENTIFY LIVING AND NONLIVING THINGS.** When asked why something is nonliving, she may not be able to give clear reasons or may only talk about one reason. For example, she may say a rock is not alive because it doesn't move, but doesn't mention that it doesn't eat, breathe, or grow.

- **WITH HELP FROM A GROWN-UP, CAN CARE FOR A PLANT OR A PET.** He knows that living things reproduce and eventually die, but can't yet explain the details of how that happens. He enjoys learning about many different

MY PET PLANT

Introduce your child to plant care by giving him his very own plant—a houseplant or a particular plant in your yard or garden. Caring for a plant is a good first step for a child, preparing him to own and care for a pet, such as a cat or dog. For slightly older children, you might even begin by planting a seed or seeds. You might suggest that your child give the plant a name, like "Patty the Petunia." Your child will enjoy the silliness, and the naming will give the plant an additional "living quality."

Talk with your child about what the plant needs to live and grow: sunshine, water, and possibly some plant food. Help him to take note that some plants require more sun or water, some less.

CATCH & RELEASE

Kids have been catching fireflies (or lightning bugs, depending on where you live!) on summer evenings for centuries, and they never tire of the pleasure. You don't need any fancy tools or materials to do this. Simply poke a few holes in the lid of a large glass jar, such as a Mason jar or a glass jelly jar. Help your child catch the fireflies, and store them in the glass jar. When you've caught six or eight fireflies, take some time to carefully observe their behavior and use some science vocabulary; for example, you might say, "Let's observe the fireflies for a few minutes, and see what they are doing. How often do they flash their light? Are some fireflies bigger than others, or are they all the same size?" When you and your child are finished observing, gently release the fireflies and allow them to return to their environment. Caution: Release fireflies only at night. If they are released during the day, they are easy prey for predators.

Butterflies are another fascinating insect. Place captured butterflies in a plastic container with a slice of orange, then watch as the butterfly drinks through its proboscis. Like fireflies, butterflies need to be released carefully; however, butterflies can only be released during the day, when it's not cold (below 65°F), raining, or windy. Butterflies sleep at night and their wings are partially solar-powered. Before you release them, make sure no birds are nearby. Birds are their natural predators.

LANGUAGE OF THE GARDEN

Gardens, and working in gardens, offer a delightful way to add to your child's vocabulary. Here are a few examples:

- Water hose
- Water spray bottles
- Bucket
- Hoe
- Rake
- Shovel
- Trowel
- Garden gloves
- Bark
- Branch
- Petals
- Stem
- Pollinate
- Cactus
- Deciduous
- Shrub
- Leaf

STARTING SEEDS

This is an easy science project; even very young children can help with it, and will be fascinated by the results. They will see how a seed serves as the "starting point" for a new plant. When the plant has sprouted, which will happen in about 14 days, transfer the plant to a pot with soil.

SUPPLIES

- 6 or 8 lima beans
- Paper towels
- Water
- Two plastic self-sealing bags
- Masking tape

INSTRUCTIONS

- Select 3–4 lima bean seeds (also known as butter beans) for each plastic bag.
- Wrap the beans in a wet paper towel; insert the wrapped beans in the plastic bag and close the bag firmly. Repeat for the second plastic bag.
- Tape one bag to a window that gets lots of sun. Tape the second bag to a window that is mostly in shade. Avoid excessive heat or cold. No need to water the seeds; condensation from the wet paper towel will keep them moist.
- Observe with your child: Which one sprouts more quickly? Which one is bigger? What color is it? Does it seem to need more water? Does it have a flower? Which one is ready to plant in soil more quickly? Supply your child with a small notebook, and suggest that she record her observations about each plant's growth and development each day.

plants and animals. You may see this when your child remembers in the morning and evening that the dog needs to be fed and helps get the food. He also may have a favorite animal that he likes to talk about, read about, and draw.

- **NOTICES THE CHANGES IN WEATHER AND SEASONS.** She understands that each season brings different weather conditions, but probably still can't list the seasons in their correct order. She can talk about how some plants and animals change as the seasons change, but may not be able to describe what will happen in the next season. You may see this when your child feels the temperatures getting cooler and says, "Winter is coming. I love the snow!" Or she may notice a bird with some twigs in its mouth and says, "Birds build their nests in the springtime."

- **CAN IDENTIFY MOST TYPES OF FOOD (FRUITS, VEGETABLES, MEATS, DAIRY),** and understands that some are healthier than others. You may see this when your child says, "I eat my vegetables because they help me grow strong!" He is also aware people like certain foods and dislike others, including himself. He also knows more about where foods come from and may enjoy growing foods in a garden or in a window box. He may also enjoy helping you look for and count out items on your shopping list as you move through the grocery store.

Understanding the Physical World

So, what's the difference between the "natural world" and the "physical world"? When exploring the "natural world," kids begin to understand the difference between living and nonliving things; that the world is made up of plants, animals, weather, food, and the environment. When learning about the "physical world," children begin to develop their understanding of the physical and human-made world and how things function. Specifically, when learning about the physical world, children begin to comprehend:

- The properties of **MATTER**
- The concepts of **FORCE** and **MOTION**
- The process of **ENGINEERING**

GOOD STUFF!

GREAT BOOKS ABOUT NATURE

Scores of wonderful books are available on the subject of science and nature. Especially valuable are three series that include multiple titles: *Dr. Seuss The Cat in the Hat Learning Library* (*On Beyond Bugs*; *Wish for a Fish*, etc.); *Eyewitness Junior Books* (*Amazing Frogs & Toads*; *Amazing Lizards*, etc.); and *Sesame Street My First Book About:* (*Insects, Reptiles, Fish, Farms*, etc.). And here are some additional books about science and nature topics that will pique your child's interest:

- **The Honeybee Man** by Lela Nargi and Kyrsten Brooker

  The story of Fred, a man who lives in a New York apartment, but raises bees and makes honey, even in the city! Explains to children, especially urban children, where honey comes from.

- **Plants Feed Me** by Lizzie Rockwell

  This beautifully illustrated picture book explains, simply and accurately, how food gets from the garden and farm onto our dining tables.

- **Growing Vegetable Soup**, written and illustrated by Lois Ehlert

  How do vegetables get from seeds and soil to delicious soup? Curious readers will thoroughly enjoy this fresh presentation of the gardening cycle. An easy and tasty soup recipe is included!

- **Because of an Acorn** by Lola M. Schaefer and Adam Schaefer, illustrated by Frann Preston-Gannon

  This book is a celebration of the interconnectedness of ecosystems, inspired by the white oak tree. An acorn leads to a tree, which houses a bird, which scatters seeds, which grow into fruit that nourishes animals who scatter the acorns.

- **Pancake, Pancake, Farm to Table**, written and illustrated by Eric Carle

  A charming story about how Jack orders pancakes for breakfast, but must start literally from scratch. Readers follow the process of making pancakes, starting with the crowing of a rooster! Charming and informative.

"[H]ealing the broken bond between our young and nature is in our self-interest, not only because aesthetics or justice demands it, but also because our mental, physical, and spiritual health depends upon it."

—Richard Louv,
from the Introduction to *Last Child in the Woods*

FROM GARDEN TO TABLE

Introduce your child to the important concepts of where our food comes from and how we get it. In explaining about planting fruits and vegetables, then harvesting, cooking, and eating them, you will be teaching your child about the natural scientific process, including observation, investigation, analysis, and finally, the "big idea," which might be digging into a delicious fresh salad!

If you have a home garden, fabulous! Together with your child, plant seeds for various foods and watch them as they grow: lettuce, spinach, tomatoes, strawberries, even carrots, potatoes, and possibly a few stalks of corn. When the time comes to harvest them, include your child in the process of deciding if a particular plant is ready for picking.

If you don't have a garden at home, take your child to a local farmer's market or farm stand. Talk about how the farmer has grown all these foods, picked them when they were ripe, and brought them to the market. You can even have this conversation in a conventional supermarket. Children are sometimes surprised to learn that those piles of apples or carrots that they see at the local grocery store originally grew on a farm.

Now take your garden greens, vegetables, and fruits, and create dishes that you eat together: a huge fresh salad with lettuce and tomatoes; sautéed spinach (children enjoy seeing how a huge bunch of spinach shrivels to a single serving of cooked spinach); a crudité platter with raw carrots, cauliflower, broccoli, and green beans. If you enjoy baking, consider making a carrot cake or an apple crisp, pointing out how foods begin by appearing one way, but by the time we eat them, they may look very different.

- **EXPLORING THE PROPERTIES OF MATTER.** At an early age, children begin to understand that matter is simply all the "stuff," the objects and materials, around us. They learn that there are three main states of matter—solid, liquid, and gas—and that all matter takes up space and has mass. Children observe the physical properties of objects and materials, and talk about their properties: color, weight, size, smell, relative temperature, and many other aspects. They also learn to connect a material's properties to its possible functions. For example, they might think, "Ice is cold, so if I put it in my cup, it helps make my water colder."

- **EXPLORING THE CONCEPTS OF FORCE AND MOTION.** Through experiences and explanations, young children learn that force is a push or pull that makes something move, stop moving, or change direction. They begin to recognize, explore, and talk about the concept and consequences of force during their play. For example, when playing ball, they learn that if they throw or kick the ball harder, it goes faster and farther.

- **EXPLORING THE ENGINEERING PROCESS.** Through experiences and explanations, children learn that engineering (the "E" in "STEM") is a process of using tools to design and build something for a specific purpose. Engineering can also be used to solve a problem. For example, when two or three children are building a tall block tower, they may come to realize, after seeing it collapse a few times, that the tower needs a sturdy and wide base as a foundation to support the height and weight of the structure. As they figure this out, notice the language they use as they plan, design, and build structures. If you can, provide proper engineering words for tools and construction vehicles (such as "lever," "pulley," "bulldozer," "backhoe," etc.) to build their vocabulary.

What to Expect from Your Preschooler

AGE 2

At two years old, your child probably:

- **OBSERVES PROPERTIES OF MATTER THROUGH HANDS-ON EXPERIENCES.** He is very interested in exploring different materials, such as water, soil, and sand, and enjoys digging in dirt and playing with water in

DEEP DIVE

LOVING THE EARTH

It's never too soon to teach preschool children to "love the earth." The phrase "being green" is commonly used when talking about the environment. For preschoolers, it is important to frame this concept in a way that emphasizes a love for nature, rather than couching it in the notion that "we need to take care of the earth," which implies that it's sick. In other words, "being green" can be defined as "doing things that are friendly to nature and all the living things around us." Here are a few steps to help children love the earth:

• RESPECT. Help children to recognize the beauty of nature and all the living things around us, and to keep the world around us beautiful and protect living things by not littering. Point out a newly emerging spring flower or a beautiful red autumn leaf. Remind your child that plants and trees are alive, so you need to be gentle with flowers and leaves.

• REUSE. Encourage children to reuse materials in their environment. For example, use both sides of a piece of paper; or make a birdfeeder out of a used milk carton. Foster an understanding that, when something is reused, it isn't thrown in the garbage and we reduce waste, which keeps our planet beautiful. Together with your preschooler, come up with examples of how you can reuse materials to show kindness to the natural world.

• REDUCE. Encourage children to reduce their consumption of things, such as paper towels, when they dry their hands with the phrase "using just what we need." Foster an awareness of the consumables that are made from trees (paper, for example), so that a connection is made between reducing consumption and saving trees.

• RECYCLE. Foster an understanding that recycling means to use something you already used once to make something new. For example, a plastic bottle can be recycled to make another bottle, or into a sleeping bag, a park bench, or even clothing. Aluminum cans can be recycled into parts for bikes, cars, and airplanes; paper can be recycled into tissues and cardboard boxes; and glass bottles can be recycled into new bottles and materials to make roads. Model how to place items to be recycled into appropriate bins. Explain how, when we recycle our things instead of throwing them away, we are being kind to our planet by reducing the amount of trash in the world.

CRAYON MELTS

Wax is another substance that can change from a solid to a liquid when heat is applied, and then will become solid again when the wax cools. This is a fun activity, especially since it shows how a common utensil can be reconfigured into an exciting new shape.

Remove the paper from a number of crayons and break them into small pieces. Place the crayon pieces into clean tin cans, according to color. (You might also try creating "new" colors by combining red and blue to make purple, yellow and blue to make green, or red and white to make pink, for example. Point out the color change as you work.) Place the tin cans in a pan of shallow water, place the pan over low heat, and allow the crayons to melt. Pour the heated (now liquid) wax into an ice-cube tray or candy mold. Allow the wax to cool for about 30 minutes, then remove the newly shaped crayons from the molds.

WARNING: Hot wax can burn easily, so preschoolers should only be observers for this activity, and an adult must be present at all times.

the bathtub. He can often sort objects by their features (like hard and soft). You may see this when your child sorts piles of crayons and chalk pieces into their containers.

- **BEGINS TO UNDERSTAND THE CONCEPT OF FORCE AND MOTION.** She understands "pushing" when she pushes her doll's stroller down a sidewalk, as well as "pulling" when she loads her wagon with her favorite animals and dolls. She also begins to comprehend the meaning of added weight. For example, she might load her wagon with lots of toys, realize that it is much heavier, and need to use much more exertion to pull it.

- **CAN USE SIMPLE TOOLS.** He can also solve problems by changing or using materials in a different way. These are the first signs that your child grasps the concept of engineering. You may see this when your child uses a toy hammer to push down a wooden peg, or turns over an empty wastebasket to make a table for his stuffed animals, or finds plastic cups to form "molds" to create a sand structure.

AGE 3

At three years old, your child probably:

- **CAN TALK ABOUT SOME PROPERTIES OF MATTER.** She is beginning to tell the difference between solid and liquid materials. She knows that water can be a solid (ice) as well as a liquid, and demonstrate her knowledge by asking to bring an icicle inside on a cold winter day to watch it "turn to water." When fixing breakfast, you might hear your child say, "The biscuit batter is all gooey." You can then say, "That's right. What do you think will happen when it gets heated in the oven?" You can explain that the gooey *liquid* batter will change to a solid from the heat in the oven. When the biscuits are ready, show your child that the liquid changed to a solid. "Look! The biscuits are hard on the outside and fluffy on the inside, and ready to eat!"

- **LEARNS ABOUT FORCE AND MOTION THROUGH PLAY.** He understands that to move something farther, it needs a bigger push. You may see this when your child knows he needs to kick really hard to make a ball roll a long way, or asks for a "big push" so he can go higher on a swing.

- **EXPLORES HOW TOOLS ARE USED.** She has a better understanding of how people use different materials and ideas to design useful things. You may see this when your child notices a pile of beams at a construction site and says, "The workers are using those to make the building." Or your child wants to stop and watch a bulldozer pushing large loads of dirt or rubble; a construction worker use a jackhammer break up concrete; a crane operator lift a beam up to the higher floors of the building; or the mixing and pouring of cement to make a new sidewalk.

GOOD STUFF!

A FUN LOOK AT
ENGINEERING, ARCHITECTURE, AND SCIENCE:
Books by Andrea Beaty and David Roberts

These three storybooks, each featuring an important "scientific" subject—general science, architecture, and engineering—make introducing scientific topics to kids a joy. The stories are hilarious, and each one includes not only loads of information about the designated topic, but also a social or emotional element (such as fear of making a mistake or intellectual insecurity) that most children will relate to strongly. The rhyming text and the whimsical illustrations are delightful. Each is accompanied by a nonfiction project guide on the same subject.

- *Ada Twist, Scientist*
- *Ada Twist's Big Project Book for Stellar Scientists*
- *Rose Revere, Engineer*
- *Rosie Revere's Big Project Book for Bold Engineers*
- *Iggy Peck, Architect*
- *Iggy Peck's Big Project Book for Amazing Architects*

AGE 4

At four years old, your child probably:

● **KNOWS MORE ABOUT THE PROPERTIES OF MATTER.** You may see this when your child says, "Our house is made of bricks. It's stronger than my cardboard playhouse." He knows that a solid object has a shape, and

LIQUID, SOLID, AND GAS

Showing kids the different properties of water is not only super-easy, it is a topic of infinite fascination for kids. Plan ahead for this activity, since it takes a few hours for the water to freeze, and then melt.

- Fill an ice-cube tray with water. Place the tray in a freezer for a few hours.

- When the ice cubes have frozen, take the tray out and, together, observe what has happened to the water. Ask your child what he sees. How does the ice feel? Is it cold or hot? Is it wet or dry? Is it soft or hard? State clearly that the **LIQUID** (water) has turned to a **SOLID** (ice cubes).

- Next, put the ice-cube tray on a counter and wait for an hour or so. What happened to the ice cubes? Are they still hard? Did the ice cubes melt back into a liquid?

- Now pour the water from the ice-cube tray into a teakettle. (If your child is helping, pour the water first into a paper or plastic cup, and allow him to pour it into the teakettle.) Heat up the teakettle.

- From a distance, watch as it begins to boil. If you have a "whistling" teakettle, it will whistle when the water boils. Explain to your child that the cloudy mist that comes out of the spout is steam, which is a **GAS.** (Also, explain that steam is hot because it is created by boiling water over heat.)

BUILD A BOAT:
WILL IT SINK OR FLOAT?

Children are fascinated by trying out different objects to see if they will sink or float in water. Here's a fun experiment to try as you and your child co-investigate the concepts of "sinking" and "floating." On *Sesame Street*, Murray asked several kids to engineer a boat out of a piece of aluminum foil, and then tested each boat's ability to sink or float, based on the boat's design.

To perform this experiment at home, you'll need four sheets of aluminum foil, 20 large washers (all the same size), and a large pan filled with water.

Together, shape four boats out of the aluminum foil, each in a slightly different shape. For example, make one with a wide bottom; one with a narrow bottom; one with high sides; and one with "wings." Ask your child to form a "hypothesis" about which ones will sink or float the longest. (Remember: A "hypothesis" is an idea about what could happen and why.) Then try to "predict" which boats will float! (To "predict" is to use a little bit of information to guess what will happen.)

Float each boat in the large pan of water. Drop the washers, one by one, into each boat. Count them, and see how many washers it takes to sink each boat. Keep a list of the number of washers it takes for each boat design; note the results on your list; or, better yet, encourage your child to keep a journal and record this experiment and the results in her journal. Was the hypothesis correct? Were you surprised when something you thought would float quickly sank—or vice versa?

QUICK TIP

On Sesame Street, Murray has long been a wonderful leader in helping kids understand science through fun experiments. Check them out at sesamestreet.org/murrayexperiments.

a liquid takes the shape of its container. He has a good understanding of the properties of water. For example, he may help pour water into an ice-cube try, but knows that when it's frozen, it will become ice cubes. He also enjoys seeing how different objects (a washcloth, a bar of soap, a cup, for example) respond in water, depending on the material. He experiments with things that sink and float, and can explain that different materials behave differently; for example, the difference between a dry sponge and a wet sponge, or even that not all stones sink. (A pumice stone usually floats!) He also comprehends the concept of air. For example, if his bicycle tire is flat, he might simply say: "We need to put more air in the tire." With help, he can show how air fills things up and makes things move.

- **IS LEARNING MORE ABOUT FORCE AND MOTION THROUGH HANDS-ON PLAY WITH TOYS.** She is aware of gravity and knows that things fall down. She begins to explore friction, and knows that wheels help things move more easily. For example, she raises the end of a book (a tool) she is looking at to use as a ramp to make toy cars roll faster and farther.

- **IS BECOMING MORE KNOWLEDGEABLE ABOUT TOOLS.** He sees that different tools are used for different functions, and that various tools and materials work together, such as a hammer and nails; a screwdriver and screws; pliers and nuts and bolts.

- **LOVES TO MAKE THINGS OUT OF DIFFERENT MATERIALS.** With help from a grown-up, he is eager to design things for a specific purpose. You may see this when your child asks for help cutting a "door" in a shoebox to make a house for action figures, or pulls an object, like an empty water bottle, from the recycling bin, and says, "I want to make this into a rocket ship."

AGE 5

At five years old, your child probably:

- **KNOWS STILL MORE ABOUT PROPERTIES OF MATTER.** She can identify familiar materials, such as solids or liquids. She can also explain why some materials are better than others for a certain job. (For example, she'll know that a storage bin is made of hard plastic and is stronger than a paper bag.) She can show how air can fill things up and make things move. She can begin to explain how temperatures change things, and comprehends the phenomena of freezing and melting. She also knows that you can mix materials together to make a new substance, and that the change may or

139

may not be reversible. (For example, she will have experienced the act of stirring up cake batter by combining a cake mix, oil, and water, but will understand that the batter cannot be separated back into water, oil, and cake mix.) Or she may announce that she doesn't want to take her popsicle outside to eat because it is hot outside and the popsicle will melt faster. She might also blow a bubble and show how she can keep it up in the air with soft puffs of breath.

- **IS DEEPENING HIS UNDERSTANDING OF FORCE AND MOTION THROUGH HANDS-ON PLAY.** He can explain and show you how using more force makes an object move faster. He can also show how using force can change the direction an object is moving. He is aware of gravity and how it affects different objects. You may see this when your child shows you how he can make bigger and smaller waves in the bathtub by pushing his hands harder or more softly. He also knows that he can kick a ball coming toward him to make it go the other way.

- **IS BEGINNING TO EXPLORE SIMPLE MACHINES,** such as wheels and axles, ramps, and pulleys. You may see this when your child looks for plastic jar lids or large caps from plastic bottles to make wheels for a car she's creating from an empty egg carton. Or she may stop at a flagpole and ask how they pull the flag up, then observe that they use a pulley over which they loop a rope to make it easier to lift heavy things.

Conclusions

Science is how children—as well as (and together with!) parents and caregivers—learn about the many facets of the world around us, from what makes snow fall to how a boat floats. Scientific discovery is based on curiosity, which young children have in abundance! Their desire to explore and their constant questions about the world make them natural STEMists!

THE BOUNCINESS OF BALLS

Even very young children are curious about the properties of different balls. An air-filled beach ball is easy to throw, but perhaps doesn't go very far; a fuzzy tennis ball bounces really high, especially if you bounce it really hard.

Studying the "bounciness" of balls—that is, how high different balls bounce—is a fascinating and fun activity for children of all ages, from younger kids just beginning to observe, to older children ready to take on a more serious science experiment. Here is a scientific approach to this experiment:

OBSERVING

- Collect several balls of different sizes, weights, materials, even color, such as a baseball, a basketball, a beach ball, a soccer ball, a ping-pong ball, and a tennis ball.

- With younger children, simply point out that balls come in a variety of shapes and sizes, and that they bounce differently. With older children, ask them to predict which ball will bounce the highest. Ask your child to formulate some questions: "What makes certain balls bounce the highest?" or "Which ball will bounce from the floor to the ceiling?"

INVESTIGATING

- Together, plan a little test, keeping variables constant (for example, how much pressure is being exerted).

- On a piece of paper or in a journal, record the "bounciness" of the balls—which one bounces the highest, the fastest, etc. Rate the balls in a list or, perhaps, on a graph.

- Ask your child to think about his findings, and to try some additional experiments: What will happen if we bounce the ball on a different surface? What will happen if we bounce the ball from a higher point? What will happen if we fill the balls with more air?

ANALYZING AND REPORTING

- Talk with your child about his findings. With a very young child, you might ask the simplest question: Which ball bounced the highest?

- With an older child, ask him to look at his journal or graph, and draw a scientific conclusion. For example, he might have thought that a tennis ball would bounce the highest, but he learned that the ping-pong ball bounced even higher. Ask him to say why he thinks that is so.

REFLECTING ON THE BIG IDEA

- Your child has learned that some balls bounce higher than others, and how to look at multiple factors when conducting an experiment.

SCIENTIFIC BUBBLES

What kid doesn't enjoy a playful bubblefest! And to make it much more interesting, this one involves a number of fascinating scientific criteria. First, the bubbles are created with a special "bubble formula"; but, even better, the bubbles are made especially inventive when you "engineer" your own bubble wands. You can make both the bubble formula and the bubble wands with your child.

To make the bubble wands, you'll be using "engineering" skills. Take a few pipe cleaners, tie them together at the ends, and shape them into a variety of different forms: circles, squares, rectangles, or stars. Try making a very large circular wand! (*Fun Fact*: The shape of the bubble is always round, no matter what the shape of the wand—but it's still fun to experiment!)

To make the "bubble formula" you'll need:

- ½ cup dishwashing liquid
- 2 cups water
- 2 teaspoons sugar
- A dab of food coloring (optional)

Measure the bubble ingredients into a shallow pan and mix well. Together with your child, dip your engineered wands into the mixture, then blow gently through the wands. What happens with your engineered wands? Are bubbles bigger? Smaller? Does a square wand produce a square bubble? Does a giant wand produce a giant bubble?

If your child is old enough, ask her to record what she's learned, or record it in a journal for her. Also, pose other "problems" involving the bubbles. See how large you can make your bubbles! Experiment with your "bubble formula" (such as by adding more dishwashing liquid) and the shape of the wand to see if bubbles can be bigger. If you are outside, observe if the bubbles are blowing in a certain direction. Ask your child what she thinks that says about what the wind might be doing. Is the wind making the bubbles move in a certain way?

SCIENCE SKILLS & PROCESS

AGE 2	AGE 3	AGE 4	AGE 5
Loves using his senses to explore.	**Continues to be curious about the world.** • Is beginning to ask questions based on observations.	**Has better hand-eye coordination and more words to help explore the world.** • Asks more questions. • Can name problems and solve them.	**Is getting more curious and actively engaged in exploring the world.** • Is beginning to interpret the world through various forms of media: television, books, etc.
Is starting to connect pictures to objects in the real world. • Sorts and organizes objects by size, color, and shape. • Is beginning to reflect on new experiences and see how they relate to previous ones.	**Understands and uses language to talk about previous experiences.** • Can connect new information to old, and build an understanding of the world. • Can use information to investigate and explore the world.	**Gets actively involved in investigating and experimenting.** • May understand that measurement can be used to compare objects. • Although he cannot use tools, such as a ruler, he may actively "measure" things.	**Has more knowledge and experiences that help explain new problems and information.**
Can tell the difference between what belongs and doesn't belong in a group. • Can sort and order items by qualities such as size, color, and shape.		**Can organize information into simple charts or diagrams.**	**Is participating in problem solving and experiments.** • Is able to understand and use language to describe an investigation.
			Uses simple tools, such as a ruler, to collect information and compare. • Can create simple charts and diagrams.

UNDERSTANDING THE NATURAL WORLD

AGE 2	AGE 3	AGE 4	AGE 5
Understands some of the differences between living and nonliving things.	**Knows more about living things, but may still confuse some living and nonliving things.**	**Understands the difference between living and nonliving things.** • Knows that living things grow and change.	**Can identify living and nonliving things.** • With parental help, can care for a pet. • Knows that living things reproduce and die. • Enjoys learning about plants and animals.
Recognizes the need for water, food and shelter. • May help feed pets.	**Knows more about plants.** • Understands that they need water, sunlight, and air to grow. • May be uncertain if plants are living or nonliving, since they don't move or eat the way animals do.	**Notices the daily weather.** • Knows the correct clothes to wear. • Notices seasonal change, but probably cannot put seasons in order.	**Notices the changes in weather and seasons.** • Understands that different seasons bring different weather conditions. • Can discuss how some plants and animals change with seasons.
Knows some familiar animals. • Can name some animal features.	**Knows more about animals.** • Can tell the difference between types of animals. • Understands how animals get their food.	**Knows that many different kinds of foods exist, and can sort them by type.** • Knows that people like different foods. • Knows that some foods are healthier than others.	**Knows that there are many different kinds of foods and can sort them by type.** • Enjoys food shopping. • Enjoys helping to prepare foods. • Enjoys growing foods.
Knows that weather can change from day to day. • May know that some places are cold, while others are hot.	**Talks about the weather.** • Knows what kind of clothes he should wear for the weather conditions. • Understands seasons.		
	Is beginning to understand where food comes from. • Enjoys helping with gardening.		

UNDERSTANDING THE PHYSICAL WORLD

AGE 2	AGE 3	AGE 4	AGE 5
Can use simple tools, such as a toy hammer.	**Explores force and motion through play.** • Understands that to move something farther, it needs a bigger push.	**Is learning more about force and motion through hands-on play with toys.**	**Is deepening his understanding of force and motion through hands-on play.**
Observes properties of matter through hands-on experiences. • Explores materials such as water, soil, and sand. • Enjoys playing with water in a bath.	**Explores how tools are used.**	**Loves to make things out of different materials.**	**Is beginning to explore simple machines, such as wheels, ramps, and pulleys.**
	Can talk about some properties of matter.	**Knows more about properties of matter.**	**Knows more about properties of matter.**

5.
THINKING IT THROUGH!

Problem Solving & Other Skills for Learning

A few years ago, in a show segment on *Sesame Street*, titled "All Good Things Come to Those Who Wait," Cookie Monster participated in a game show and demonstrated a range of strategies preschoolers can use when controlling their behavior and delaying gratification for a reward. Guy Smiley, the game-show host, explained the rules of the "Waiting Game" to Cookie Monster. He tells Cookie, "If you wait to eat this cookie till I get back, you get two cookies!" (This segment was a "play" on the famous Marshmallow Test, designed by Dr. Walter Mischel, to assess children's ability to control behavior and resist impulse in the face of a desired reward.) For a second, Cookie Monster sees that it is a good idea to wait and eat TWO cookies, but—no surprise—he has a very difficult time resisting the cookie on the plate right in front of him. Fortunately, he is stopped by a group of singers who remind him of a simple phrase, "All Good Things Come to Those Who Wait," and give him a strategy to control his desire to eat the cookie: to sing a song to distract himself. When that strategy doesn't work, the singers provide a few other strategies, including using his fingers to make a "frame" around the cookie to pretend it's only a picture of a cookie; playing with a toy to shift his attention away from eating the cookie; and telling himself that the desired cookie is really a smelly, stinky fish! By the end of the song, enough time has passed and Cookie is rewarded with TWO cookies, as promised!

148

Cookie Monster proved to be such an excellent role model to teach self-regulation strategies that *Sesame Street* developed *Cookie's Crumby Pictures*, a series of parodies on classic movies that teach self-regulation and executive function skills.

The first four chapters of this book are devoted to teaching your child important foundational academic skills (language, literacy, mathematics, and science). However, it may come as a surprise to learn that self-regulation skills—including problem solving, initiative, curiosity, independence, and executive function—are every bit as important as basic academic subjects to success in school.

Self-regulation is the ability to recognize and manage one's emotions and control behaviors. For example, talking quietly when in a library; resisting the impulse to hit someone when we're angry; and overcoming frustration and per-severing to complete a difficult task. The cognitive skills needed to regulate our emotions and control our behavior are called executive function skills. To put it another way, executive function skills are required in order to exercise self-regulation. The technical term "executive function" refers to a child's ability to:

- Focus her attention on a task;

- Shift attention in order to see other possible solutions or transition to a new activity;

- Use information stored in her memory and apply it to a task;

- Remember the rules when controlling her behavior; and

- Plan and persist at a task.

Kindergarten teachers value these skills because they help children learn academics, form and navigate friendships and other relationships, and develop healthy habits. Moreover, during the preschool years a child's ability to learn these skills increases significantly. Children are not born with self-regulation and executive function skills; instead, they need to be modeled by parents, caregivers, and other adults; practiced; and nurtured.

Because self-regulation is so critical for learning, we put these cognitive learning skills at the core of *Sesame Street*'s whole-child curriculum. In 2013, the *Sesame Street* writers chose Cookie Monster as the ideal character to teach these skills and strategies because of his impulsive nature, his obsession with eating cookies, and his willingness to keep trying in the face of failure. We believed it was important for children to see how Cookie persevered at a task, and learned how to use different strategies. Children require a "toolbox" of strategies that need to be modeled and nurtured repeatedly in order for this information to become part of their working memory and recalled when needed.

Thinking & Problem Solving

In order to be successful at school, not only do preschool children need a firm grounding in the academic subjects (literacy, math, and science), but they also require skills for learning *how* to learn—that is, how to use their fast-accumulating knowledge and understanding. The ultimate goal is to enhance children's ability to maneuver through their everyday lives and experiences effectively and appropriately, at home and in school. This starts with developing strong thinking (logic and reasoning) skills, which in turn help children take in information and understand how things in their world are related. This helps them make decisions more independently and rely less on an adult to solve their problems.

Young children use their thinking and problem-solving skills in everyday experiences when they persist at building a stable block structure, complete a puzzle, peel the paper from a crayon to have more crayon to draw with, or take the perspective of another to resolve a conflict.

It's tempting to step in and take over, but children build their problem-solving skills through self-discovery. When they try out their own solutions and fail, it is through these mistakes that they learn. With your encouragement, they can find an answer and understand their choices. You can help by talking through their thought process out loud ("The tower fell down! Why do you think it fell? What could we do to the bottom so that the tower doesn't fall down again?").

Critical-Thinking Skills or "Thinking It Through"

Watch your child as she navigates through her day. Notice her emerging critical-thinking skills as she curiously asks lots of questions; figures things out using prior understanding or newly gathered information; experiments with different solutions; shows resilience; and perseveres at a task. For example, observe as she tries to figure out where to hide when playing hide-and-seek ("I can't hide in the same place because Mommy will find me"); how to divide a sandwich to share with her four friends; and how to make green paint to finish her picture of the backyard.

As children build their ability to think critically and problem-solve, they start to:

QUICK TIP The next time you snuggle with your child and share a storybook, use it as an opportunity to practice reasoning and thinking skills. If the story is new to your child, ask him to predict what will happen on the next page or at the end of the story. As you read the story together, ask him questions like these: "How is the character feeling?"; "Why is the character feeling that way?"; "Why did the character act that way?"; "Could the character have made a different choice?" As you talk about outcomes of the character's actions, ask "What if . . . ?" questions and perhaps even ask your child to make up a new ending or add another character.

150

QUICK TIP

To develop a confident problem solver, remember to communicate the idea that "It's okay to make mistakes; everybody makes them." Children who aren't afraid to make errors and learn from their mistakes are more likely to try new things, take safe risks, and persist at a task. Talking about mistakes *you* make encourages your child not only to identify his own errors, but also to consider other solutions and think about information in a new way. So the next time you burn the roast chicken, or forget to pick up the dry cleaning, let your child hear you say, "Oops, I made a mistake, it's okay! Next time, I'll set the oven timer so I don't burn the chicken." Or "I'll write a sticky note so I'll remember to pick up the dry cleaning."

● **MAKE CONNECTIONS** between similar situations and previous experiences to complete a task or solve a problem. ("I lost some of my crayons when I tried carrying them all in my hands to the doctor. When I go to Grandma's, I'll bring them in my backpack.")

● **NOTICE CAUSE AND EFFECT.** Learn to recognize when one thing makes another thing happen. ("When I poke a bubble, it pops!")

● **COMPARE, CONTRAST, AND SORT.** Observe how things are different and the same by exploring qualities like color, shape, and size. Noticing and matching things by specific qualities help deepen their learning (like sorting laundry by color).

● **CONSIDER DIFFERENT OPTIONS.** Learn to weigh possible solutions to solve a problem. Pause and think carefully about each choice before making a final choice. ("I could go around the puddle or go through it. If I go through it, I'll get wet.")

● **EVALUATE THEIR CHOICE.** Learn to reflect on the solution or decision they make and decide whether it works. If it is not the best choice, they may try another option. ("My feet are wet from walking in the puddle. I'll put my boots on so I can keep splashing.")

151

GOOD STUFF!

PUZZLES AND MORE PUZZLES!

If there's a single plaything that helps to promote a wide array of problem-solving skills, it's a puzzle, from a simple wooden peg puzzle, shape sorter, or nesting boxes to a complicated multipiece jigsaw puzzle. Children exercise sorting and organizational skills, plan their approach (Tackle straight edges first? Start with the corners? Begin by connecting like colors?), then make comparisons and persist with a thought-provoking task.

AGE 2

At two years old, your child probably:

- **IS DISCOVERING WAYS TO SOLVE PROBLEMS MORE ON HIS OWN.** He is understanding cause and effect, and using previous experiences to find solutions. You may see this when your child steps on a box to reach a toy he's not tall enough to reach unassisted; is able to find a simple hidden object; completes a simple shape puzzle; or realizes that he can get a reaction from you when he makes very loud noises with a toy or a musical instrument.

- **SORTS OBJECTS BY A FAMILIAR QUALITY**, such as size, color, weight (as he nears three years old). You may see this when your child groups together large and small toy cars; stacks a tower of blocks from largest to smallest; creates a string of beads in a favorite color; selects the lighter bags of groceries to help carry and leaves the heavier ones for a grown-up.

AGE 3

At three years old, your child probably:

- **IS MORE THOUGHTFUL WITH HER PROBLEM SOLVING.** She watches to see what other people do and asks more questions. You may see this when your child asks for help with her solution (has you hold up her completed drawing while she adds tape to hang it on the refrigerator); or watches how siblings shoot baskets, which she tries to copy.

- **UNDERSTANDS CAUSE AND EFFECT.** He recognizes when one thing makes another happen. You may see this when your child plays with toys or games that have buttons, levers, and moving parts, such as a wind-up toy or a jack-in-the-box; gives his baby brother a favorite toy when he's upset to encourage him to stop crying; interacts with simple computer or digital touch games (layering colors with a drawing program or trying to keep a car on course in a racing game).

- **SOLVES PUZZLES** with large pieces of 10 or fewer.

PET ADVENTURES

Select a pet (your family's dog, your neighbor's cat, your cousin's pet lizard, one of Grandpa's tropical fish) and, together with your child, make up an adventure story about the animal. Think about a place the pet might travel to, and then figure out how she will get there, what she will see, and how she will get back home again. Perhaps she got lost when she went out for a walk. Or perhaps she was trying to visit an old friend and had to travel miles to do so. Don't be afraid to be silly!

As you develop the story, use some of the following questions and phrases to build your child's critical-thinking skills and perseverance as a storyteller:

- What do you think will happen?

- What should we do next?

- How do you know?

- What makes you think so?

- Show me how you figured that out.

- What if . . . ?

- I predict that . . . !

- Let's analyze this / think about this.

- Let's try something else. Let's come up with another plan.

- I'm thinking!

- How would you feel if that happened to you?

- What would you do?

- **SORTS OBJECTS** based on one quality, such as color, size, or shape. You may see this when your child helps put away clean spoons and forks in their place in a drawer or separates out favorite items in a snack mix.

AGE 4

At four years old, your child probably:

- **USES MORE COMPLEX STRATEGIES TO SOLVE EVERYDAY PROBLEMS.** She considers different options more carefully before deciding on the best one. You may see this when your child figures out which crayon is missing from a small box of crayons by looking at which ones are still there (also called "deductive reasoning"); tries to connect two puzzle pieces that look like they go together, rather than trying to make any two pieces fit together.

- **ORDERS OBJECTS FROM SMALLEST TO LARGEST** and describes the difference ("Mommy's shoes are big, Daddy's are bigger, Grandpa's are biggest").

- **SORTS OBJECTS INTO MORE THAN TWO GROUPS.** For example, he helps to separate clean laundry into piles for himself, his mom, and his brother.

- **IS BEGINNING TO GROUP OBJECTS BY ONE QUALITY AND THEN REGROUP BY ANOTHER QUALITY,** and explain why (as she nears five years old). You may see this when your child groups a collection of leaves or rocks by color and then by shape, or separates toys by type (cars, dolls, balls) and then re-sorts by which ones she'll use inside and outside.

AGE 5

At five years old, your child probably:

- **IS SOLVING PROBLEMS WITH MORE CARE.** She considers different solutions and the possible results of each one. You may see this when your child thinks through a few ways to fix a "broken" fort made of sofa pillows and blankets, and tries one solution and then another.

- **SORTS OBJECTS BY A FAMILIAR QUALITY AND THEN RE-SORTS THEM.** You may see this when your child separates hair ties or barrettes by color and then by size; or identifies items to be recycled, then groups them into paper and plastic.

- **SORTS OBJECTS BY MORE THAN ONE QUALITY AT THE SAME TIME,** switching the sorting rules when asked (as he nears six years old). This ability to focus on a new rule shows flexible thinking. You may see this when your child creates four piles of building bricks—big red rectangles, small red rectangles, big blue squares, and small blue squares—then combines them into two groups when asked to separate by big or small size; chooses beads for a necklace, separating them by color and shape (green flower beads, green circle beads, purple butterfly beads, purple square beads).

Initiative & Curiosity

Children are active and engaged learners when they explore topics that they are interested in learning more about. They express their curiosity through questions and take initiative in discovery through their play, experimentation, and storytelling. Curiosity is a commodity that most preschoolers possess in abundance, along with the drive that pushes them to know more. A confident, curious child is sure she can master a task or become an expert at something . . . at *every*thing! She needs only a little encouragement from a parent, caregiver, or teacher to grow those positive attitudes into full-fledged skills for learning.

Curiosity leads children to:

- **SHOW AN INTEREST.** This tends to express itself in a lot of "Why" questions—and in questioning the initial answers you supply with even *more* demanding "Whys," as well as "Who," "What," "Where," and "When" questions. Your child is seeking new information and building on his existing knowledge. Foster your child's curiosity and initiative by engaging in activities within the topic he's interested in. For example, if he loves insects, explore different habitats to find them, purchase insect kits to grow and care for bugs, read stories about bugs, and visit science and nature centers.

QUICK TIP It's okay *not* to know something. Instead of blundering your way through a response when you don't have an answer to a question, try modeling curiosity and initiative by saying, "That's a great question. Let's find out together. How do you think we can find out?"

- **CONFIDENTLY TRY SOMETHING NEW.** You may notice your child saying, "I can do it myself!" "I can climb up there—let me try!" "I know how—I'll show you." Your curious child will display an eager willingness to tackle new challenges and proudly share any new learning.

- **IMAGINE AND PRETEND.** You will see your child observe reality and then think beyond what she sees—"I can fix Teddy's arm. I know how to give a shot. I'm a doctor now!" "These are my superhero wings. Watch me! I'm flying!" Her curiosity has encouraged her to imagine new possibilities and strategize her place in those pretend worlds.

- **THINK CREATIVELY.** Not only can your child create elaborate pretend worlds, but he is able to see existing real-world objects and make them symbols for something else entirely. For example, a box becomes a fort, a row of chairs a ship on a daring shark safari.

GOOD STUFF!
BOOKS FOSTERING CURIOSITY & INITIATIVE

Stories and experiences that foster curiosity or encourage a child's initiative tend to share a common trait: They revel in the question of "What *next*?" and the wonderful possibilities that question opens up.

- ***Another Monster at the End of This Book*** by Jon Stone, illustrated by Michael Smollin

  This best-selling sequel (and its earlier classic, *The Monster at the End of This Book*) captures *Sesame Street's* playful approach to learning. A child's curiosity grows as he follows Elmo and Grover, and their foiled plans to find what's at the end of the book.

- ***Don't Let the Pigeon Drive the Bus***, written and illustrated by Mo Willems

  When a bus driver takes a break from his route, an unlikely volunteer driver—Willems's famous pigeon—insists on taking his place. Silliness prevails, but most kids will know how to respond. A playful approach to foiled plans by a master humorist.

- ***Press Here*** by Hervé Tullet

  What will happen when you press the yellow dot, shake the pages of this book, or clap once, twice, three times? Although the pages may be plain paper and the illustrations the simplest shapes and colors, they become interactive in a child's vivid imagination.

- ***The Book with No Pictures*** by B. J. Novak

  Every child will try to guess during the first read precisely *what* the magnificent thing is going to be. Repeated readings will drive home the value of hard work and lots of creative thinking.

- **IS INTERESTED IN FEELINGS—HER OWN AND OTHERS'.** Curiosity helps to channel attention, allowing a preschooler the time and focus to assess her emotions and actions, and consider how they might affect her family, friends, and classmates.

The expression of a child's natural curiosity—the characteristic that makes each of them tiny scientists and scholars—allows children to acquire new knowledge, learn new skills, set goals, and engage in task persistence in order to achieve those goals.

"I think, at a child's birth, if a mother could ask a fairy godmother to endow it with the most useful gift, that gift should be curiosity."

—*Eleanor Roosevelt*

QUICK TIP

Practice "active listening" whenever you are talking to your child. Show that you're actively listening by repeating back what your child says. For example, after telling you a story about his day at the park, say, "You said you went to park and then a little boy had a ball and you got mad. Why did you get mad? What happened next?" When you rewind your child's speech this way and ask questions designed to elicit helpful information, you are showing interest in and attention to what he's saying, as well as demonstrating a process for how to gather information, which fosters critical thinking.

157

What to Expect from Your Preschooler

AGE 2

At two years old, your child probably:

- **LIKES TO EXPLORE HOW THINGS WORK** and how one thing can make another thing happen (cause and effect). You may see this when your child takes apart and puts together a simple puzzle or toy, or drops a bath toy into the water and reacts when it makes a big splash.

- **OBSERVES AND IMITATES OTHERS** when trying to solve a problem and during pretend play. Most of her thinking comes from her direct experiences. You may see this when your child watches as her siblings dip a bubble wand and blow bubbles, and then tries it herself; or pretends to talk on a real or toy phone, holding it to her ear, and carrying on a conversation.

AGE 3

At three years old, your child probably:

- **IS VERY CURIOUS ABOUT THE WORLD AROUND HIM.** He asks lots of questions about a variety of topics. "How did the spider make the web?"; "What are crayons made of?"; "Where does snow come from?"

- **IS STARTING TO SOLVE PROBLEMS MORE THOUGHTFULLY.** You may see this when your child waits for another child to leave the bottom of the slide before sliding, saying, "We'll bump into each other if I slide down now."

- **USES OBJECTS TO REPRESENT THINGS** in her drawings and in play. This helps her consider ideas and possibilities beyond what is right in front of her. For example, she draws shapes to make a face and says, "That's Daddy!"

- Begins to pretend-play with one or two other children.

AGE 4

At four years old, your child probably:

- **IS EAGER TO LEARN ABOUT A VARIETY OF TOPICS.** He uses his growing vocabulary to ask more focused questions and find answers. For example, he may ask deeper questions about things that spark his interest, like "How does the batter turn into pancakes?"; "What makes them puff up?"; "What makes pancakes smell so good?"

- **CONTINUES TO SOLVE PROBLEMS THOUGHTFULLY,** without having to try every possible solution. She may choose sturdy materials (blocks, books) to build a ramp for her cars, knowing a piece of paper would be too flimsy and bend, or she turns a box into a playhouse, choosing to turn it upside down so the sturdy bottom creates a roof.

- **IS BEGINNING TO PLAN AND REPRESENT IDEAS** in drawings, creations, and play. You may see this when your child talks through how he will draw a truck he saw outside before he draws it, or considers the things he'll need to bring to school in the fall and packs a backpack, pretending it's the first day of school.

- **ENGAGES IN PRETEND-PLAY** with two or more children. She gives and takes on different roles and talks about her actions during pretend play. You may see this when your child pretends to be a bus driver, takes tickets, and tells other family members to be the passengers.

158

EASY GAMES, STRONG SKILLS

Many simple games already in every parent's arsenal can help support executive function skills. Here are some suggestions, as well as how to vary the play to enhance learning!

- **I SPY.** Start this game by looking for objects that have a specific color ("I spy something green!") or shape ("I spy something that is shaped round like a circle!"). When your child is ready for more of a challenge, you can combine attributes, such as "I spy something that is round like a circle and you can eat it." This game fosters focused attention, flexible thinking by shifting your attention, and working memory (holding on the rules of the games).

- **SONGS TO SING IN THE ROUND.** Start by singing "Row, Row, Row Your Boat" together, then have your child wait to sing again until you motion to start the song from the beginning while you continue to sing to create the round. For older preschoolers, add more singers, which makes it more challenging, as your child needs to focus on his own singing while others are singing the same song out of step.

- **"SIMON SAYS."** This fun and simple game helps your child build working memory of the game rules (do only what Simon says to do and ignore the other directive), focus her attention to hear the phrase "Simon says," practice self-control (resist the temptation to do the directive when hearing the action), and follow directions. For older preschoolers, you might make this game a bit more challenging by stacking actions: "Simon says, bark like a dog and wiggle your puppy tail."

AGE 5

At five years old, your child probably:

- **IS BEGINNING TO LOOK FOR INFORMATION AND ANSWERS FROM DIFFERENT RESOURCES** (such as books, TV, and grown-ups). You may see this when your child wants to make a paper airplane and remembers that his brother has a book that shows how, or asks to go to the zoo to find out more about monkeys.

- **IS BEGINNING TO THINK THROUGH PROBLEMS** and conceive of different possible solutions. She is starting to predict what will happen with each solution before choosing one. You may see this when your child wants to add glitter to her picture, decides that glue will work better than tape to make it stick to the page, and says, "Glue will be stickier than tape."

- **IS REPRESENTING IDEAS, PLACES, AND OBJECTS IN HIS DRAWINGS AND PLAY.** This shows abstract thinking, the ability to imagine things beyond what is right in front of us. You'll see this when your child cuts out rectangles of paper and draws on them to make dollar bills for playing store, or sets up a coffee table as a pretend cashier station, using a dish towel as a conveyor belt.

160

GOOD STUFF!
WHAT HAPPENS NEXT?
Picture-Sequencing Cards and Puzzles

Available in packs of simple rectangular cards or in jigsaw puzzle–shaped pieces, these sets of images tell a wordless story in a sequence of three to six pictures. Inquisitive children try to guess what comes next, predicting the outcome from visual clues, looking for images that match and reveal a beginning, middle, and end. If your child has an especially active storytelling bent, you can prompt him to make up his own stories, from the plain cards, by mixing and matching images from various sequencing, anticipating what would happen in these more mixed-up scenarios. These are produced by several different manufacturers, and are available through teachers' stores and sites.

- **ENGAGES IN PRETEND PLAY WITH OTHER CHILDREN.** She is planning and negotiating with others about roles, actions, and stories. You may see this when your child talks through the pretend menu and then opens a play restaurant with cousins or friends, deciding together to take turns being the chef when everyone wants that role.

Executive Function Skills

Executive function skills give your child the ability to control his thoughts, actions, and emotions, allowing him to engage in goal-directed behaviors. Specifically, executive function skills are:

- **WORKING MEMORY:** The ability to hold relevant and past information in one's mind and use that information to recall prior knowledge when solving a problem; remember and follow directions or rules; match cards in a memory game; plan an activity; and be a critical thinker.

- **FOCUSED ATTENTION:** The ability to focus your attention on a task or a goal and not be distracted by competing thoughts or other behavior. This type of attention helps your child to process information and directions and stay focused on the task until completion.

- **FLEXIBLE THINKING:** The ability to shift your attention to focus on another solution and assess a range of possibilities; or transition from one activity to another, and approach a situation in different ways (take on a different role in pretend play, or sort the same item based on different attributes, such as color versus size or shape).

- **SELF-CONTROL:** The ability to resist a strong inclination to do one thing and instead choose to do what is appropriate; delay the reward of gratification (such as waiting to the end of the birthday song before blowing out the candles); and minimize frustration and persevere to complete a difficult task.

These skills take time and practice to develop and are learned through modeling. Moreover, the preschool years are a critical time for their development, as children are experiencing rapid growth of the brain's prefrontal cortex at this age. It is these skills—as much if not more than knowing the ABCs and 123s—that teachers value as the most important school-readiness skills because these are the skills they need *in order to* learn.

161

PLAY & LEARN

WHAT'S THE SAME? WHAT'S DIFFERENT?

As children approach a problem, they can be encouraged to think about using several different ways to tackle it. One way to get children to view things in a variety of ways is to play "What's the Same? What's Different?"

Ask your child any question that pops into your mind or that relates to something you are doing: "How are dogs and cats the same? How are they different?"; "What's the difference between a car and a bus? How are they the same?" "You had a slice of pizza and an orange for lunch. How are they the same? How are they different?"

Give your child a few minutes to think about the question and figure out the common characteristics. Make an effort to elaborate on her answers, and possibly urge her to see other similarities and differences. This game can be played anytime—while riding on a bus or in the car, while reading a story together, when you are shopping at the grocery store, or when she is drawing a picture.

Observing Executive Function Skills in Your Child

QUICK TIP

Check out these *Sesame Street* videos that illustrate the concept "one of these things is not like the other." In one, Cookie and Ernie discuss what is the same and different about various "round" foods. In the other, Monsters discuss the characteristics of things that fly. Both serve as great examples of executive function, of how a child needs to shift attention around the same set of items in order to sort them for a different solution. Find these videos at sesamestreet.org/sorting.

As children build their executive function skills, they start to:

- **USE THEIR WORKING MEMORY** to remember relevant information (such as remembering different items the family needs at the grocery store while you shop together). They are learning to remember and follow the order of the steps in a routine, the rules of a game, family or classroom rules, and directions.

- **STICK WITH A TASK, EVEN WHEN IT GETS CHALLENGING**, and show self-control by not getting frustrated and giving up when the task gets difficult. They also maintain focused attention when there are distractions (such as getting fully dressed in the morning, rather than stopping midway to play with their toys).

- **ENGAGE IN THE "POWER OF YET"** when they are learning new skills, such as writing their name, swimming, or learning a new dance. They begin to remember that it takes time and lots of practice to learn something new. They need to be reassured that they can do it, but not just "yet." If needed, they may break the task into smaller, more manageable steps to gain mastery bit by bit.

- **THINK FLEXIBLY** about different solutions to a problem or situation by switching rules (for example, remembering to use an "inside voice" when inside and an "outside voice" when outside). They are able to change roles when playing pretend play; consider someone else's point of view ("If I share my crayons, my friend can draw, too"); and smoothly move from one activity to the next (willingly putting toys away when it's time to go outside).

- **PLAN AHEAD**, by learning to anticipate needs while preparing for an activity ("I'll need my pail and shovel to play in the sandbox at the park"). They can set goals and develop steps to complete them ("I want to learn how to kick a soccer ball into the net, so I'm going to practice with my mom"), and make a plan when deciding what to play with friends.

163

- **CONTROL IMPULSES THROUGH SELF-REGULATION.** He is able to wait his turn at the slide or wait to be called on for an answer at story time. He can wait patiently, and possibly uses a strategy to help himself wait.

What to Expect from Your Preschooler

AGE 2

At two years old, your child probably:

- **CAN REPEAT A SEQUENCE OF TWO OR THREE ITEMS.** You may see this when your child recites a set of three numbers you tell him ("1, 2, 3," "5, 6, 7," etc.) or a short list of fruits you want to get at the store.

- **REMEMBERS ONE RULE AT A TIME.** She can switch to another rule when it isn't the opposite of the first rule. You may see this when your child puts books away on one shelf and toys on another, or waits in line for her turn on a slide and knows she needs to move away from the bottom of the slide when she's done.

- **REMEMBERS ONE- OR TWO-STEP DIRECTIONS.** You may see this when your child follows directions to put his coat and hat on a hook, or remembers that hand washing includes soaping first, then rinsing.

- **RESISTS A STRONG TEMPTATION TO DO SOMETHING OR DELAYS A TREAT BRIEFLY** (under a minute). She still needs support from a grown-up to follow "don't" requests. You may see this when she finishes her carrots before she eats her cookie, when asked.

- **BEGINS TO UNDERSTAND WHAT OTHERS ARE TRYING TO DO.** You may see this when your child wants to help someone who is trying to open a door while carrying a heavy bag, notices a grandparent struggling with a suitcase and runs to lend a hand, or helps another child find the right items to stock a game of pretend astronaut.

QUICK TIP Praise your child for the process of her work—focusing on a task, using productive strategies, or persisting after a setback—rather than on the quality of the finished product. This type of praise instills a positive attitude toward learning, as well as building resiliency and confidence, especially in the face of failure, to explore tasks of varying degrees of complexity.

164

AGE 3

At three years old, your child probably:

- **CAN REPEAT SEQUENCES OF THREE OR FOUR ITEMS.** You may see this when your child recites a set of four numbers you tell him ("1, 2, 3, 4," "5, 6, 7, 8," etc.) or a short list of animals you've chosen to look for at the zoo.

- **CAN REMEMBER TWO RULES AT THE SAME TIME.** She can also switch to an opposite rule when asked. You may see this when your child follows directions in a game to jump five times and then run to the finish line, then follows reverse directions to run to the finish line and then jump five times.

- **REMEMBERS DIRECTIONS WITH TWO OR MORE STEPS.** You may see this when your child follows when asked to brush his teeth and then put on his shoes and a coat.

- **RESISTS A STRONG TEMPTATION TO DO SOMETHING OR DELAYS A TREAT** for a longer time (about three minutes). She can sometimes follow "don't" requests on her own. You may see this when your child remembers not to run indoors, or will busy herself with coloring while she waits for a baked treat to finish cooking.

- **IS BEGINNING TO UNDERSTAND THAT PEOPLE HAVE DIFFERENT PERSPECTIVES.** You may see this when your child makes comments like, "Grandma says it's too hot outside, but it feels just right to me."

DEEP DIVE

HELPING YOUR CHILD DEVELOP EXECUTIVE FUNCTION SKILLS

Developing your child's executive function skills takes time and practice. You can help by modeling the following strategies and, as you do, talk about what you are doing. You are your child's most important teacher and she observes your behaviors and follows your lead. Remember, your actions often "speak" louder than your words.

Working memory

- Create a mental picture of the items or rules to be remembered. ("In my mind, I'm picturing the stick of butter and the carton of milk that we need from the store.")

- Use memory tricks, like noting how many things there are to remember ("We need to bring three things to Grandma's house—fruit salad, napkins, and spoons") or repeating a rhyme to help remember the rules ("Now and then, it's okay, but don't eat candy every day!").

- Say the rules or steps out loud. This is also called "self-talk." (When preparing to brush his teeth, say, "Squeeze toothpaste, brush, rinse!")

Self-Control

- Use physical "tricks," like covering up a tempting object or having your child sit on his hands until he is permitted to touch the object.

- Sing a song, play with another toy, or think about something else to pass the time and focus your attention on something else. Describe what you are thinking about to your child.

- Use your fingers to make a "picture frame" around a desired object so you think of it as a *picture* of it and not the real thing at all.

- Think about a temptation as less tempting, such as imagining that a present is an alligator, something you wouldn't want to touch. Share what you are imagining with your child.

- Use self-talk to keep the goal in mind. ("I need to wait, but then it will be my turn on the ride.")

Focused Attention

- Make a plan for an activity or establish the steps of a morning or evening routine to help your child keep a focused attention throughout the activity.

- Once a plan is established, use a self-talk strategy, such as a chant, to keep a focused attention until the task is completed. For example, a morning routine chant might be: Wake-up, potty time, eat and brush my teeth; or a bedtime routine chant might say: Soapy water, warm pajamas, brush our teeth, storytime, then we say night-night!

Flexible Thinking

- Use self-talk to think about the big picture. ("Oh, I see, there are two ways to play this game. I can match by color or shape.")

- Create reminders of appropriate behaviors. (Hang and refer to a sign on the bedroom door that says "Quiet Time" with a related drawing of a bed, book, or blanket.)

AGE 4

At four years old, your child probably:

- **CAN REPEAT SEQUENCES OF FOUR TO FIVE ITEMS.** She can repeat two to three of those items in reverse order. You may see this when your child remembers all the stops you need to make as you run errands together. "We need to go to the post office, get books at the library, pick up baby sister, and go home." Or she talks with a friend about a few places you went, starting with the last stop on the trip. "We picked up baby sister and before that we got books at the library."

- **CAN REMEMBER TWO PAIRS OF RULES AT THE SAME TIME.** You may see this when your child follows directions when asked to put crayons and markers on the top shelf, and scissors and paper on the bottom shelf.

- **REMEMBERS DIRECTIONS WITH MULTIPLE STEPS.** She may begin to follow instructions on her own. You may see this when your child remembers to hang up her coat, wash her hands, and put away her school bag when she gets home.

- **RESISTS A STRONG TEMPTATION OR DELAYS A TREAT** for a longer time (5 to 10 minutes). He can control inappropriate reactions when they are brought to his attention. You may see this when your child picks up the pieces and puts away one game before taking out another when asked, or waits patiently for a turn on a swing.

- **SORTS THINGS BY ONE QUALITY AND THEN BY ANOTHER.** You may see this when your child helps separate fruits and vegetables while unpacking groceries, then decides which go in the refrigerator and which go on the counter.

- **UNDERSTANDS WHEN SOMEONE HAS DIFFERENT PREFERENCES OR KNOWLEDGE ABOUT A TOPIC.** You may see this when your child mentions that her brother loves apples but she loves oranges, or says, at the zoo, "I want to know more about zebras. Let's go read the sign."

AGE 5

At five years old, your child probably:

- **CAN REPEAT SEQUENCES OF FIVE TO SIX ITEMS.** She can repeat three to four of those items in reverse order. You may see this when your child names

QUICK TIP

Throughout the *Cookie's Crumby Pictures* series, Cookie Monster models executive function skills (by saying while gesturing) how to "Stop" (holds hand up), "Think" (points finger to his temple), "Control Yourself" (take a deep breath), and "Remember" (using self-talk to remind oneself to focus attention on the task). Visit sesamestreet.org/cookiecrumbyplaylist to see the shows.

PLAY & LEARN

PROMPTING WORKING MEMORY

When modeling and practicing strategies to help build your child's executive function skills, it's important to use gestures to help increase their understanding of the behaviors. This playful approach will also help your child remember to use these strategies.

- **STOP AND THINK:** Put your hand out like a STOP sign, take your index finger, and tap the temple of your forehead.

- **FOCUS:** Make "binoculars" around your eyes to remind your child to focus her attention on a task or activity.

- **REMEMBER:** Take your index finger and tap the temple of your forehead. A similar approach is used in an active-listening ritual. Begin with a call to action—"Let's listen with our whole body." Then lead your child through the steps:

- **EYES WATCH.** Point to your eyes.

- **EARS LISTEN.** Point to ears.

- **VOICE QUIET.** Put finger to lips in *shhhh* gesture.

- **BODY CALM.** Take a deep, calming breath.

five or six ingredients for a favorite recipe in order as he helps get them out, then says (three or four of) them in reverse order as he puts them away. Or, he talks about the activities of the day from morning to evening or the last few from evening backward.

- **CAN REMEMBER A DEPENDENT RULE** (when one situation is directly tied to or causes another). You may see this when your child knows that if the weather is rainy you'll take the bus, but if it's sunny you'll walk.

- **REMEMBERS DIRECTIONS WITH MULTIPLE STEPS** and follows instructions without repeat reminders. You may see this when your child puts away toys when you say, "It's dinnertime," then washes her hands and helps set the table.

- **RESISTS A STRONG TEMPTATION OR DELAYS A TREAT** for a longer time (15 to 20 minutes) if there is an incentive. He can control inappropriate reactions on his own. You may see this when your child, while grocery shopping, waits until after checkout to get a more appealing snack from your grocery cart, rather than eat the one brought from home.

- **SORTS THINGS BY ONE QUALITY AND THEN BY ANOTHER EASILY AND QUICKLY.** You may see this when your child groups small and large toy vehicles, then shifts to put cars together, trucks together, etc.

- **ADJUSTS HIS BEHAVIOR TO SUIT THE SETTING.** You may see this when your child uses a loud voice when playing outside at the park and a quieter voice at the library.

Conclusions

While it is important for children to prepare for kindergarten by learning academic skills, it is even more important for them to develop their self-regulation and executive function skills. As kindergarten teachers will attest, teaching children content knowledge is joyful when children come to school with a love of learning, initiative, perseverance when faced with frustration and failure, and they're not afraid to take safe risks and learn from their mistakes. Self-regulation and executive function skills are critical for learning, and the preschool years are a critical time for developing these skills through playful learning activities.

REASONING & PROBLEM SOLVING

AGE 2	AGE 3	AGE 4	AGE 5
Is discovering ways to solve problems more independently. • Understands cause and effect (how one thing can make another thing happen). • Is able to find a simply hidden object. • Matches objects that go together.	**Engages in more thoughtful problem solving. Observes what other people do and asks questions.** • Watches how siblings play a game and imitates them.	**Uses more complex strategies to solve everyday problems.** • Considers different options more carefully before deciding on the best one. • Figures out which crayon is missing from a small box of crayons by looking at which ones are still there. • Tries to connect two puzzle pieces that look like they go together.	**Is solving problems with more care. Considers different solutions and the possible results of each one.** • Thinks through a few ways to fix a "broken" fort made of sofa pillows, then tries one solution.
Sorts objects by a familiar quality. • Groups together large and small toy cars.	**Understands cause and effect.** • Gives a baby brother a favorite toy when upset to help calm the baby down.	**Orders objects from smallest to largest and describes the difference.** • "Mommy's shoes are big, Daddy's are bigger; Grandpa's are biggest."	**Sorts objects by a familiar quality and then re-sorts them.** • Separates hair ties or barrettes by color and then by size. • Identifies items to be recycled, then groups them into paper and plastic.
	Completes simple puzzles.	**Sorts objects into more than two groups.** • Helps separate clean laundry into piles, such as shirts and pants.	**Sorts objects by more than one quality at the same time, switching the rules when asked.** • Creates four piles of building blocks by size and color. • Chooses beads for a necklace by color and shape.
	Sorts objects. • Helps put away clean spoons in their correct place. • Separates out favorite items in a snack mix.	**Is beginning to group objects by one quality and then regroup by another quality.** • Groups a collection of leaves by color and then by shape. • Separates toys by type, such as cars, dolls, balls and then by where they will be used.	

EXECUTIVE FUNCTION SKILLS

AGE 2	AGE 3	AGE 4	AGE 5
Can repeat a sequence of two or three items. • Recites a set of three numbers you say ("1, 2, 3" "5, 6, 7" etc.) or a short list of fruits you want to get at the store.	**Can repeat a sequence of three or four items.** • Recites a set of four numbers you say ("5, 6, 7, 8") or a short list of animals you've chosen to look for at the zoo.	**Can repeat sequences of four to five items.** • Can repeat two to three of those items in reverse order. • Remembers all the stops you need to make as you run errands together. • Talks with a friend about a few places you went starting with the last stop on the trip.	**Can repeat sequences of five to six items.** • Can repeat three to four of those items in reverse order. • Names five or six ingredients for a favorite recipe in order when getting them out, then says them in reverse order when putting them away. • Talks about the activities of the day from morning to evening or the last few from evening backwards.
Remembers one rule at a time. • Can switch to another rule when it isn't the opposite of the first rule. • Puts books away on one shelf and toys on another. • Waits in line for turn on a slide and knows to move away from the bottom of the slide when done.	**Can remember two rules at the same time.** • Can switch to an opposite rule when asked. • Follows directions in a game to jump five times and then run to the finish line, then follows reverse directions to run to the finish line and then jump five times.	**Can remember two pairs of rules at the same time.** • Follows directions when asked to put crayons and markers on the top shelf and paper on the bottom shelf.	**Can remember a dependent rule (when one situation is directly tied to or causes another).** • Knows that if the weather is rainy you'll take the bus, but if it's sunny you'll walk.
Remembers one- or two-step directions. • Follows directions to put coat and hat on a hook. • Remembers that hand washing includes soaping first, then rinsing.	**Remembers directions with two or more steps.** • Follows when asked to brush teeth and then put on shoes and a coat.	**Remembers directions with multiple steps.** • May begin to follow instructions on own. • Remembers to hang up coat, wash hands, and put away backpack after arriving home.	**Remembers directions with multiple steps, and follows instructions without repeat reminders.** • Puts away toys when you say, "It's dinnertime," then washes hands and helps to set the table.

EXECUTIVE FUNCTION SKILLS (cont'd)

AGE 2	AGE 3	AGE 4	AGE 5
Resists a strong temptation to do something or delays a treat briefly (under a minute). • Still needs support from a grown-up to follow "don't" requests. • Shifts to another activity when asked to put a toy away. • Finishes eating carrots before eating a cookie, when asked.	**Resists a strong temptation to do something or delays a treat for a longer time (about three minutes).** • Can sometimes follow "don't" requests on own. • Remembers not to run indoors. • Stays busy coloring while waiting for a baked treat to finish cooking.	**Resists a strong temptation or delays a treat for a longer time (five to ten minutes).** • Can control inappropriate reactions when directed. • Picks up pieces and puts away one game before taking out another when asked. • Waits patiently for a turn on a swing.	**Resists a strong temptation or delays a treat for a longer time (15 to 20 minutes) if there is an incentive.** • Can control inappropriate reactions on his own. • When grocery shopping, waits until after checkout to get a snack.
Is beginning to understand what others are trying to do. • Wants to help someone who is trying to open a door while carrying a heavy bag.	**Understands when someone has different preferences or knowledge about a topic.** • Mentions one friend loves apples but another loves oranges. • Says at the zoo, "I don't know much about zebras, but the zookeeper does, so I'll ask her."	**Sorts things by one quality and then by another.** • Helps separate fruits and vegetables while unpacking groceries, and then decides which go in the refrigerator and which go on the counter.	**Sorts things by one quality and then by another easily and quickly.** • Groups small and large toys vehicles, then shifts to put cars together, trucks together, etc.
		Is beginning to understand that people have different perspectives or opinions. • Makes comments like "Grandma says it's too hot outside, but it feels just right to me."	**Adjusts his behavior to suit the setting.** • Uses a loud voice when playing outside at the park, and a quieter voice at the library.

INITIATIVE & CURIOSITY

AGE 2	AGE 3	AGE 4	AGE 5
Likes to explore how things work. • Cause and effect—how one thing can make another happen. • Takes apart and puts together a simple puzzle. • Drops a bath toy into the water and reacts when it makes a big splash.	**Is very curious about the world.** • Inquires about everything: "How did the spider make the web?" "What are crayons made of?" "Where does snow come from?"	**Is eager to learn about a variety of topics.** • Uses growing vocabulary to ask more focused questions and find answers. • Asks deeper questions about things that spark interest. "How does the batter turn into pancakes?"	**Is beginning to look for information and answers from different resources, such as books, TV, and grown-ups.** • Wants to make a paper airplane, and remembers that Mommy has a book that shows how. • Asks to go to the zoo to find out more about monkeys.

INITIATIVE & CURIOSITY (cont'd)

AGE 2	AGE 3	AGE 4	AGE 5
Observes and imitates others when trying to solve a problem or with pretend play. • Watches as siblings dip a bubble wand and blow bubbles, then tries it herself. • Pretends to talk on a toy phone. • Is confused when you say. "Let's take this bike for a spin," thinking you literally mean spinning around on the bicycle.	**Is starting to solve problems more thoughtfully without having to try every possible solution.** • Waits for another child to leave the bottom of a slide before sliding down. • Chooses white paint to lighten a color, instead of black.	**Continues to solve problems thoughtfully without having to try every possible solution.** • Chooses sturdy material to build a ramp for cars, knowing a piece of paper would be too flimsy. • Wants to turn a box into a playhouse, choosing to turn it upside down so the sturdy bottom creates a room.	**Is beginning to think through problems and different possible solutions.** • Is starting to predict what will happen with each possible solution before choosing one. • Wants to add glitter to his picture and decides that glue will work better than tape to make it stick.
Begins to use an object to represent another thing as they engage in pretend play. • A broomstick becomes a horse or a block is a phone.	**Uses objects to represent things in drawings and in play.** • Draws shapes to make a face and says, "That's Daddy!" • Uses props to pretend play, such as drinking from empty cups during a tea party or using rubber bands for spaghetti when making dinner.	**Is beginning to plan and present ideas in drawings, creations, and play.** • Talks through how to draw a truck after seeing it but before drawing it. • Talks about things to bring to school and packs a backpack, pretending it's the first day of school.	**Is representing ideas, places, and objects in drawings and play.** • Shows abstract thinking, the ability to imagine things beyond what is visible. • Cuts out rectangles of paper and draws on them to make dollar bills for playing store. • Sets up a coffee table as a pretend cashier station.
	Begins to engage in pretend play with one or two other children. • The role play is simple and models what they see, such as playing "Mommy" and "Daddy" with a baby doll.	**Engages with two or more children in pretend play.** • Takes on different roles and talks about these roles during pretend play. • Pretends to be a bus driver, taking tickets, and tells other family members to be the passengers.	**Engages in pretend play with other children.** • Plans and negotiates with others about roles, actions, and stories. • Talks through a pretend menu and then "opens" a play restaurant with friends, deciding together to take turns being the chef.

6.
CELEBRATE YOU, CELEBRATE ME

Feelings & Friendship

I n children's early years, the areas of the brain that support social and emotional functions are developing very quickly. Children learn to understand and manage their feelings by practicing behaviors like taking deep breaths to calm down, not hitting others when they're angry, and resisting impulsive behavior, such as taking a friend's toy without asking. They learn to recognize others' feelings (empathy), show compassion, take turns, and cooperate. These are foundational skills for lifelong social and emotional success.

Throughout the years, *Sesame Street* has featured a range of story lines—such as the death of Mr. Hooper, Big Bird losing his nest (his home) when a hurricane hit Sesame Street, and Baby Bear becoming a big brother—to help young children develop the skills to manage big emotions. In the aftermath of September 11, 2001, we created four stories (coping with loss, bullying, appreciation of firefighters and fire safety tips, and cultural awareness) to help children build resiliency during challenging times.

We also developed a story to help children navigate friendships and model how to be an "upstander" to a friend in a difficult situation. When Big Bird's pen pal, Gulliver, comes to visit Sesame Street for the first time, Big Bird is so excited to meet his new friend face-to-face, to show him around, and to introduce him to all his friends. Gulliver, also a bird, is equally excited to meet and play with Big Bird. Gulliver keeps asking to meet Big Bird's best friend, who he assumes is another bird. So he's very surprised to meet Snuffleupagus, who is clearly a different creature altogether!

In an exasperated voice, he says, "Big Bird, I don't want to play with him, I only want to play with birds just like us!" Big Bird expresses surprise, puzzlement, anger, and finally sadness, but most importantly models how to be an upstander. He responds to Gulliver by saying, "Snuffy is my best friend. If you won't play with him, then I won't play with you." After Big Bird talks about how they can all play together, Gulliver realizes how hurtful his behavior has been and together they sing the alphabet and continue to have fun on their playdate.

Understanding, Expressing, and Managing Emotions

Even as adults, we are sometimes tempted to lose control when we feel frustrated, angry, or disappointed. So imagine how difficult it is for a young child who does not yet have the vocabulary to express or control her emotions. The fact is, children need a toolbox of self-regulation strategies to help understand, express, and manage their emotions and behave in more reflective and purposeful ways during emotional moments. These skills are critical for building and maintaining friendships, and are also necessary skills for school readiness.

The ABCs of Self-Regulation

Self-regulation skills (which include executive function skills) form the basis for the conscious control of thoughts, actions, and emotions. These skills enable children to respond to situations in a more purposeful, thoughtful, and controlled manner, so that their reactions are less impulsive and more reflective.

While the process of learning these skills can be difficult for young children, it is during the preschool years that rapid growth of these skills occurs.

A child's ability to control her behavior and to regulate her emotions is a combination of three self-regulation skills: affective, behavioral, and cognitive.

(A)FFECTIVE

Affective skills represent the ability to recognize, understand, and manage feelings. The first step to regulating feelings is to have the language and vocabulary to name and accurately label one's emotions (and the emotions of others). Children often have mixed emotions and need to understand how to differentiate between them. For example, your child may not understand that it's okay to feel both happy and sad when her mother leaves and her grandmother babysits. It is also important to provide clarification when a child labels a feeling wrong. For example, your child may express anger when her friend has a toy that she wants, but the true emotion is jealousy, not anger. Providing the correct name to the emotion helps your child understand what she's feeling and then determine how to regulate her emotional reaction.

(B)EHAVIORAL

Behavioral refers to how a child learns to act with regard to his feelings, resulting from a particular situation or experience. For example, instead of crying because he is told he can't have a toy, he learns to express his emotions in a socially appropriate way, such as by using a calm-down strategy. When a child has the ability to self-regulate, he is able to avoid impulsive behavior, delay immediate gratification, and develop "friendship skills," such as the ability to view a situation from another person's

QUICK TIP

BELLY-BREATHING WITH TEDDY

Taking belly breaths calms strong emotions. To encourage your child to practice belly-breathing the correct way, play "Belly-breathing with plush friends." Have your child lie down on her back and place a teddy bear or another stuffed animal on her belly. Lie down next to her, and put another stuffed toy on your belly. Model taking slow deep breaths, watching the animals move slowly up and down as you both breathe in and out.

perspective. Perspective taking is an important foundational skill, necessary for developing empathy, compassion, manners, and resolving conflicts.

In order to perform these skills and behave appropriately, a child must be able to manage and control his own emotions. For example, when a child grabs a toy from another child, the child whose toy was taken away must first recognize what he is feeling (angry), and think ahead about how to respond. For example, he might think, "What if I push?" "What if I grab the toy back?" "What if I use my words?" He needs to learn to take a moment, recognize and understand what he is feeling, then think of the best strategy to manage his emotions and behavior.

As you are helping your child learn good behavior skills, acknowledge that this process is difficult, and learning these skills takes time and practice. It's important to validate your child's feelings, and to provide support and encouragement.

(C)OGNITIVE

Cognitive skills refer to the executive function skills that enable a child to have conscious control of thoughts, actions, and emotions. These skills include: "focused attention," or being able to shift attention ("flexible thinking") in order to figure out other ways to solve a problem; "inhibitory control," or stopping automatic, inappropriate responses and using more appropriate, thoughtful behaviors; "working memory," or connecting past experiences with future experiences or remembering a calm-down strategy; "making a plan," coming up with an idea to create something or to solve a problem; "perseverance," or sustained motivation and resisting the urge to give up; and "monitoring performance," or making a new plan if the current one isn't working.

QUICK TIP

One of the most effective ways to help your child manage frustration, persevere in the face of a challenge, and boost self-respect is to teach him the concept of the "power of *yet*." Explain to your child that you can't do something *yet*, but by practicing and not giving up, he will overcome obstacles, learn new skills, and reach his desired goals.

CALM-DOWN STRATEGIES

Here are 10 simple calm-down strategies kids can learn to use when they start to feel overwhelmed by their feelings:

1. Belly-breathe.

2. Take a walk, run around, or dance to your favorite tune—move!

3. Draw a picture.

4. Count to 10.

5. Snuggle with a favorite stuffed toy, blanket, or other lovey.

6. Read a book in a quiet space.

7. Shake a glitter jar and watch the glitter float down while taking deep breaths.

8. Sing a song.

9. Hug yourself.

10. Self-talk. Use a simple phrase ("I can do this if I rest for a minute") to overcome a strong emotion.

OOPS & AHA

Because of his shy, slow-to-warm-up temperament, my son Lucas found new transitions emotionally challenging. So on his first day of a new summer out-of-town day camp, Lucas, age five, was scared and nervous. When the bus arrived, he got hysterical and wrapped himself in my sundress. I tried my best to stay calm and supportive, but, inside, I was an emotional wreck. Perhaps he wasn't ready for day camp, I thought.

When I got to my office, I called the camp to check in on him. The counselor said, "He's fine and seems happy!" While relieved to hear this report, I wasn't totally convinced and continued to worry. (Oops!) So, I was surprised and delighted when Lucas got home that afternoon, and exclaimed, "Mommy, that was the *Best Day Ever!*" My lesson (Aha!) was not to get caught up in his big emotions and trust that he could use the strategies we had practiced to manage his emotions and adapt to new experiences.

—Rosemarie, educator & mom

STOPLIGHT GAME

This game is one application of "Breathe, Think, Do" and offers a fun way to help your child learn how to pause for a moment between an impulse and an action, and to think about the options he has to regulate his feelings.

- **RED LIGHT: STOP.** First, encourage your child to belly-breathe. Remind him that belly-breathing will allow him to calm his strong feelings.

- **YELLOW LIGHT: PAUSE, MAKE A PLAN.** Once he has calmed down, help him to understand what the problem is and what he is feeling. It's important for you to recognize and validate his feelings. Together think about things he can do to feel better, as well as strategies (or plans) to solve the problem.

- **GREEN LIGHT: GO.** After helping him choose a plan, let him try it out. If the plan doesn't work, go back to the "Yellow Light," think about why that didn't work, and try a different plan.

Breathe, Think, Do!

When your child is overwhelmed by big feelings, the best remedy for regaining control is the concepts of "Breathe, Think, Do":

- BREATHE: Encourage your child to "belly-breathe." Put her hands on her belly and show her how to take three slow, deep breaths in through the nose and out through the mouth.

- THINK: Help your child think of different things she can do to feel better, such as counting to 10, taking a walk, or drawing a picture.

- DO: Together, choose a plan and try it out! If the plan doesn't work, try something different. For example, if he becomes impatient while waiting for his turn on the swing, say, "I know it's really hard to wait for a swing. Let's think of something else you can do until it's your turn." While he waits, he can ride his a tricycle, go down a slide, or perhaps even push his friend on the swing. These strategies will help your child understand that shifting his attention and focusing on something else can help him stay calm and be patient.

GOOD STUFF!
BREATHE, THINK, DO APP

Check out the "*Sesame Street* Breathe, Think, Do" app. This bilingual (English and Spanish), research-based app helps your child learn this important self-calming strategy as well as important "feeling" vocabulary. Your child will also enjoy silly animations and playful interactions.

OTHER STRATEGIES FOR SELF-REGULATION

Whether your child is angry because he doesn't want go home after a happy afternoon at the park, agitated because he is overtired, or super-excited because he is about to celebrate her birthday, you can help him learn specific strategies to calm his body and regulate his emotions.

- USE "FEELING WORDS." Not having the vocabulary to express how they feel can cause your child to act out. To help your child talk about his feelings, you might say, "I notice you're rubbing your eyes and getting easily upset.

Are you feeling frustrated because you're tired?" As you use these emotional vocabulary words, he'll begin to pick up on feeling words and use them on his own.

- **ENCOURAGE SELF-TALK.** Oftentimes, it helps to simply say what you are feeling out loud to yourself. Show your child how to use her "feeling words" to identify his feelings, and then to start to think of ways to calm down or feel better.

- **READ A BOOK TOGETHER, AND TALK ABOUT THE CHARACTERS' FEELINGS.** You might say, "Lucy is covering her eyes and clinging to her dad. How do you think she feels?" Or you could say, "It looks like Lucy feels afraid. Do you remember when you felt afraid of the dark? What else might make someone feel afraid?" As your child learns to label and understand his own feelings and those of others, he'll realize that what makes him feel a certain way may be different from what makes someone else have that same emotion—and that is okay!

- **PLAY "FEELING CHARADES."** Act out a feeling and ask your child to guess which one it is. For instance, if you're frustrated, you might cross your arms and furrow your brow. Then let him have a turn!

- **RECOGNIZE BODY CLUES.** Talk with your child about clues inside her body that help her tell the difference between comfortable and uncomfortable feelings. For instance, if she is angry, she may feel hot; or if she feels happy, she may feel relaxed. When you help your child describe how an emotion is making her feel physically, you create an opportunity to teach your child about more complex emotions. For example, if she sees someone with a toy that she wants, she may label her feeling as anger. By discussing the situation and guiding her through expressing her feelings, you can show her that she is actually feeling jealous (a more complex emotion), not angry.

- **CREATE A "CALM-DOWN BOX."** Empower your child to calm down on his own by creating a "calm-down box," which he can easily access when he needs some emotional release and to calm down. Fill a box with games, art supplies (including crayons and paper so that he can draw a picture of something that makes him feel happy and modeling clay to mold to relieve frustration), a teddy bear or another favorite stuffed toy for him to hug, and even add a glitter jar!

- **USE HER IMAGINATION.** When a child feels anxious, using her imagination can help her find creative ways to "escape" big feelings and calm down.

Encourage your child to think of a place or situation that makes her feel happy: It may be going to her grandparents' house, cuddling with Mom, or playing with her sibling. Have her close her eyes and imagine that place or situation. Ask her open-ended questions to help her get a clear picture, like these: "What are you thinking about?" "What does the room smell like?" "What kind of game are you playing?" Let her know that whenever she feels that she needs to calm down, she can close her eyes and go to her special place.

GOOD STUFF!
MAKING A GLITTER JAR

When a child is feeling upset, a glitter jar can be used as a calming strategy to help regulate her feelings. The glitter inside the jar symbolizes how the child's feelings are swirling around inside her. As your child watches the glitter settling down, it has a peaceful, calming effect on her, and helps her calm down.

Supplies

- Water

- Glitter glue

- Glitter

- A 16-ounce to 30-ounce clear jar, such as a Mason jar (plastic, not glass)

Instructions

Fill the jar about ¾ of the way full with warm water. Be sure to measure how much water you're using.

For every cup of water you use, add 2 to 3 drops of glitter glue to the jar.

Add the glitter to the jar until it is ½ inch to ¾ inch deep from the bottom of the jar.

Secure the lid tightly. For extra protection, add glue to the inside of the lid's lip before closing, and allow the glue to dry before shaking the jar.

Shake the jar, then sit and watch the glitter as it settles back down onto the bottom of the jar—and your child settles down as well! You just may find this calming as well.

DEEP DIVE
MODEL CALMNESS

You are your child's biggest role model and supporter. It is as important for you to practice the strategies you are teaching your child. She'll be watching and will mimic everything you do. Here are a few ideas for modeling self-regulation:

• **MANAGE YOUR BEHAVIOR.** If you feel frustrated or angry, allow your child see the strategies you use to calm yourself down. You might take three deep breaths; use self-talk ("Oh, no, I've burned the pizza! What will we have for dinner?"); or model and label your feelings with your own "feeling words" ("I'm feeling frustrated today. I need a hug!"). By seeing and hearing you calm down from a frustrated state, your child will feel empowered to use similar strategies to calm himself down as well.

• **RECOGNIZE AND VALIDATE YOUR CHILD'S FEELINGS.** Take time to consider how your child may be feeling, relate it to his physical cues, and talk about those observations, using "feelings talk." For example, you might say, "I notice your head is down and your lip is pouting. Are you feeling disappointed?" Also, let him know that it's okay to have more than one feeling at the same time. For instance, he may feel excited about school, but also anxious about separating from you.

• **MANAGE YOUR CHILD'S BEHAVIOR.** When your child has these stressful or emotional moments, brainstorm together ways that will help him feel less anxious. For example, suggest that he carry a comfort object like a family photo or a favorite toy car, in his pocket or backpack when he goes to school. Or practice self talk, like saying to himself, "OK, just take a deep breath" when he's feeling angry, or "I am brave" when he's feeling scared." If he's feeling anxious, while waiting for his turn on a swing; suggest that he count to five; or when he's feeling anxious on the way to a doctor's visit, think about singing a favorite song to keep calm. Finally, sometimes all children need to calm down is a big hug.

What to Expect
from Your Preschooler

AGE 2

At two years old, your child understands what she is and is not allowed to do but can't yet stop herself from doing something she isn't supposed to. You may see this when your child pokes at the pet cat or pulls its tail, throws toys, or unravels the entire roll of toilet paper.

Two-year-olds also get overwhelmed by strong feelings. Your child experiences basic emotions (happy, sad, scared, etc.), but can get overwhelmed by stronger or more complex ones. He needs a trusted grown-up to help him name them and model how to manage them. He can comfort himself when upset with a lovey (a special toy or blanket). You may see this when your child eagerly snuggles his favorite blanket after a bump or a fall, or cries and protests when he has to give back a borrowed toy and needs your help to return it.

She can express her wants and needs through actions and some words. She is becoming more independent and wants to do more things "on her own." She is more defiant now, but as she nears three years old becomes more willing to cooperate and can be redirected toward positive behavior. You may see this when your child responds to your requests with lots of "no's"; tells you when she's wet, hungry, or thirsty; draws on a piece of paper and not on the table itself when asked (as she nears three years old).

AGE 3

At three years old, your child shows a range of feelings and uses words to describe simpler ones. ("I'm mad. He took my toy.") He can get upset when his routine changes unexpectedly. Moving smoothly from one activity to the next and following rules and routines (like hand washing and tooth brushing) get easier as he gets older (closer to four years old).

She is starting to use self-control and wait for what she wants, and she is learning how to see a situation from different points of view. For example, when your child waits her turn at a water fountain, she might say, "We're thirsty. When she is finished drinking, it will be my turn."

She is also showing more independence and doing more things by herself. She is beginning to understand the idea of belongings (mine, yours, ours, his, hers), and is more willing to listen and respond to others when there is a challenge. Examples of your child's independence show up when she puts her toys away by herself, puts her clothes on herself, and is more willing to give back a toy a sibling was playing with and play with something else.

AGE 4

At four years old, your child will show greater independence by doing things herself, such as when she puts on a coat without help, asking only when needed, or wants to make her own sandwich. She is learning how to read a situation and use self-control. Also, she is starting to wait more patiently, using skills taught by the grown-ups around her. For example, she might sing a song to distract

GOOD STUFF!
CONTROLLING BIG EMOTIONS

Here are a few books that speak effectively to preschoolers about how to get control of big emotions.

– **Belly Breathe** by Leslie Kimmelman, illustrated by Lindsay Dale Scott
    This charmingly illustrated rhyme describes the concept of "belly-breathing" for the youngest readers.

– **The Feelings Book**, written and illustrated by Todd Parr
    This book vibrantly illustrates the wide range of ever-changing moods we all experience.

– **Lots of Feelings**, text and photographs by Shelley Rotner
    In this expressive photo essay, simple text and photographs introduce emotions, such as happy, grumpy, and thoughtful, and how people show these feelings.

SEE IT, SHOW IT, SHARE IT

Building a strong "feelings vocabulary" is like building a muscle—it takes exercise, practice, and hard work! Try these exercises to help your child practice expressing himself:

SEE IT. When children can visualize emotions or actions, they'll learn the words that describe those emotions more easily. Take out a family photo album, a child-friendly magazine, or a picture book. Point to a person or character and say, "How do you think he/she is feeling?" If your child says, "happy," build on that. You might say, "She looks really, really, happy. Another word for really, really, happy is 'joyful.'"

SHOW IT. Children will be more likely to remember a new word if they experience its meaning, either emotionally or as a physical action. One way to help your child experience emotions is to come up with a movement or facial expression for each word that you learn together. For example, if the word is "exhausted," suggest that she flop over and give a really big yawn.

SHARE IT. Encourage your child to describe his feelings as he tells you about things he did that day. Ask him questions like, "How did you feel when you petted that big dog?" Or "How did you feel when Jack wouldn't share the swing at the park?" Remind him of words he has already learned to describe emotions, such as "happy," "scared," "mad," and "tired."

OOPS & AHA

When my son was young, his favorite show was *Sesame Street* and his favorite part was Big Bird's friendship with Mr. Hooper. When Will Lee (Mr. Hooper) passed away, I thought it might be best to shield my youngster from the truth about his death. (Oops!) *Sesame Street* announced that they would address Mr. Hooper's death on-screen and I trusted that the show we loved would address the subject the best way possible. We watched as a family that day to help our son through the sad situation, and we all learned a lot about how both children and adults can handle grief and come through hardships together. (Aha!)

—Jane, mom

FEELINGS TALK

Children learn to recognize and talk about their feelings, using words like "happy," "sad," "surprised," "frustrated," "angry," and "scared." They start to understand that their feelings can change over time or in different situations. In time, they realize that they can have more than one feeling at once; for example, being both excited about going to a birthday party, but anxious about seeing people they don't know.

Here are a few common "feelings words" to use when talking about feelings with your child:

- Happy
- Sad
- Angry
- Scared
- Sorry

- Proud
- Excited
- Frustrated
- Disappointed
- Worried

- Jealous
- Disgusted
- Tired
- Love

OOPS & AHA

As a teacher of young children with special needs, I like to reward children when they display positive learning behaviors. Most kids enjoy selecting a toy or extra screen time, but one of my students didn't seem motivated by any of my choices. (Oops!) I began to notice that he was most engaged when I spent one-on-one time with him. (Aha!) Sometimes the most powerful motivator to offer kids is not a material item, but more time, attention, and encouragement from those who believe in them.

—Kerri, teacher

herself from frustration while waiting her turn; or count to 10 or breathe deeply (belly-breathing) to help her calm down.

As she nears five years old, she is starting to manage strong feelings with words. For example, she might say, "I feel a little scared when we get on the bus. Will you hold my hand?" or uses self-talk by saying, "It's okay, we can fix it!" to herself when trying to manage her disappointment when a favorite toy breaks.

AGE 5

At five years old, your child probably can identify and respond to his own needs. He finds a place to sit so he can see during a story at the library or puts on a sweater when he is cold.

He manages his feelings successfully most of the time, with help from grown-ups. He can follow a familiar strategy to help him focus his attention, such as "eyes watching (cup hands around eyes), ears listening (cup hands around ears), voice quiet (hold a finger to the lips), body calm (deep breaths and hands in lap)." You may see this when your child shares that he's worried about an upcoming dental checkup or doctor's visit, or takes a deep breath and hugs himself when he gets too excited or feels aggressive.

He is starting to apply rules and behaviors to new situations. You may see this when your child puts toys away at a friend's house, just as he does at home. He also gets in line at the water fountain at the playground, just as he does at school.

QUICK TIP While it is important for children to share a lot of things, it is also okay for children to have preferences. For example, it's natural for a child to have certain toys or games that have special meaning for them. It may make playdates go more smoothly if you put away certain special toys that don't need to be shared. Letting your child set aside one or two prized items can give him reassurance and encouragement to share other things. At the same time, make sure your child is respectful of other people's possessions, and remind him not to touch others' things without permission. Finally, when you see your child sharing well with others, congratulate him on his kind and generous behavior. It helps to reinforce the behaviors you want to see, and lets your child know you appreciate his efforts.

Developing Relationships

Once children begin to understand and control their own emotions, they quickly realize that others—parents, siblings, friends, neighbors—have feelings as well, and they begin to learn how to understand those feelings. As children build their relationship skills, they start to:

- RECOGNIZE AND NAME THE FEELINGS OF OTHERS. Children learn that others may have feelings that are different from theirs. They learn to recognize the feelings of others through facial expressions and body language. ("Baby sister is so happy—she's smiling and clapping her hands.")

- CARE ABOUT THE NEEDS AND FEELINGS OF OTHERS. Children begin to notice that others have feelings, and express that they care by showing support or by helping (giving a hug or drawing a picture to cheer up a friend; or helping to look for a sibling's lost toy).

- COOPERATE WITH OTHERS. Children learn to work together, solve problems, and resolve conflicts cooperatively, such as by taking turns with pails and shovels while building a sand castle in the sandbox with a friend.

Seeing your child's first friendships emerge can be a very special milestone. Younger children may be interested and want to play near other children, but as they get older, they begin to engage more with preferred playmates, and, with help, learn how to join a group of children playing.

Self-regulation skills, such as resisting impulsive behaviors (the urge to grab an interesting toy when another child is playing with it or hitting someone when angry); sharing, taking turns, and cooperating with others; and being able to empathize and consider the perspective of someone else, are essential behaviors for developing and maintaining friendships. As with other skills, your child's ability to develop and build friendships takes time and practice.

Some key messages children need to learn about what it means to make and be a friend, include:

- UNDERSTANDING WHAT A FRIEND IS. Children learn that a friend is someone who they care about, enjoy spending time with, and have fun with together and who feels the same way about them.

192

Model being a good friend, and lead by example. In your day-to-day interactions with family members, friends, colleagues, and anyone else you meet, think about your tone of voice and the words you use to show appreciation and compromise. By modeling good friendship skills and caring behavior in your own relationships, you show your child exactly what those skills look like up close. Include your child when you are doing something that helps others and explain why. For example, let her help you bring soup to a sick friend or relative to demonstrate empathy.

- **FRIENDS HAVE SIMILARITIES AND DIFFERENCES.** They learn that a friend can look different and have different likes, wants, and needs than their own, but what's most important are the things they have in common with each other. Friends appreciate these differences because they make each friend special in his or her own way.

- **FRIENDS SUPPORT AND CARE ABOUT EACH OTHER.** They help each other, work together, play fairly, and do other kind acts, such as cheer each other up, share, and take turns.

- **FRIENDSHIPS ARE DEVELOPED.** Children make and keep friends by inviting others to play, and learning how to join a group. For example, your child might bring chalk to join a group of children drawing on the sidewalk together, or ask to join a game of tag.

- **FRIENDS CAN ARGUE.** Children learn that friends don't always agree or like the same things, but they can still remain friends. When conflicts arise, friends need to try to understand each other's feelings, needs, and wants, and respond in a kind and respectful way.

What to Expect from Your Preschooler

AGE 2

At two years old, your child probably recognizes and responds to the feelings of others. She understands the emotions of familiar grown-ups (facial expressions, body language, encouragements), and looks for similar expressions when engaging with new people and places. For example, she may frown when she sees someone cry or smile when she sees someone laugh. She may want to help or give comfort in the same ways that she likes to be helped or comforted. For example, she may give some of her crayons to a friend who wants to color, too, or brings a diaper when baby brother needs to be changed. She may offer her favorite toy to another child who's upset.

He also shows strong emotions with body language more than words, because he may not yet have the words to verbally express how he feels. For example, he crosses his arms when told it's time to go and doesn't want to.

She is interested in other children and wants to make friends. She may be able to take turns, but still needs your help with sharing and resolving conflicts. She is more likely to play alongside another child, rather than with another child, often copying the same activity but doing it separately. You will notice that your child gets excited when she sees a familiar friend at the park and wants to dig in the sandbox together or starts to build a train track when she sees her brother doing it.

194

QUICK TIP

Making an effort to learn someone else's language is a way to express kindness and respect for another's sense of pride in his family's culture and traditions. Look up suggestions for how to say a few simple words and expressions in his language, such as "Hello," "Thank you," "Let's play," and other friendly words. Talk to your child about why you are using another language, and encourage him to learn and use a few simple words with his friends and neighbors, such as saying "*Hola!*" or "*Bon soir!*"

GOOD STUFF!

WE'RE THE SAME, WE'RE DIFFERENT

Here are a few videos about embracing differences and similarities that can be found on *Sesame Street*'s YouTube channel. Enjoy them with your child, and be sure to ask lots of questions:

- **THE COLOR OF ME**
- **BEAUTIFUL SKIN SONG**
- **THE AMAZING SONG**
- **COUNT ME IN**
- **I LOVE MY HAIR (AVAILABLE IN ENGLISH OR SPANISH)**
- **SPANISH ME, ENGLISH ME**

DEEP DIVE

PRESCHOOLERS NOTICE DIFFERENCES

For preschoolers, noticing differences among people is a natural way of trying to make sense of the world. But sometimes, our children make observations that trigger us to say "Shhhh," especially when they talk about physical characteristics, such as skin color, hair texture, physical limitations, or behaviors associated with autism. For young children, noticing differences does not necessarily mean they are placing negative value on these differences. However, when you shush your child or say, "We don't say that!" or "We are all the same on the inside," you send the message that they did something wrong and they shouldn't talk about differences.

Preschoolers are not color-blind and they notice differences from a very young age. Noticing racial and ethnic characteristics does not mean that your child is racist, prejudiced, or discriminatory. It just means that he is an observer of his world, and his natural curiosity leads him to ask questions.

So what do you do if your child says something? Instead of reacting because you feel embarrassed or uncomfortable, acknowledge your child's observation. Say something like this: "Yes, that child is in a wheelchair" or "Yes, that woman's skin is dark brown" or "Yes, that child is upset right now and is flapping her arms." Acknowledge how differences make each of us unique and special, and point out and talk about how your child shares many similarities with other children, such as what they like to do, their feelings, and their needs.

So if your child asks to play with the brown boy who lives upstairs, and your instinct is to reply "Don't say that!," take a deep breath, and calmly talk about skin color. Describe your own skin color, and the color of your child's skin, and how all skin colors are beautiful. And then continue on to talk about all the fun things that will happen when that little boy comes over to play.

LET'S MAKE FRIENDS

Here are some playful strategies to help your child
develop strong friendships:

- **TALK ABOUT FRIENDSHIP.** Read books focused on friendship and talk with your child about what it means to be a good friend. Ask: "Do you think the boy in the story was a good friend?" "What would you do if your friend . . . ?" Ask him who are his friends. Ask, "Why is Jack your best friend?"

- **SHARE, TAKE TURNS, AND TRADE.** The ability to share is one of the essential elements of friendship. Sharing, however, is difficult for young children. In fact, it is not expected for two-year-olds to share, which is why in toddler centers there are multiple amounts of the same item. To help your child learn this important school-readiness skill, provide everyday moments to practice these prosocial skills.

  Sharing means that the desired item can be broken down into smaller parts. For example, you can share a cookie, a stack of stickers, or a pile of crayons. If there is only one red crayon, then your child needs to take turns with another child in using that crayon.

  Taking turns involves patience (your child must wait to use the swing) and perspective (your child must understand that another child wants a turn on that swing as much as he does). Try playing "My Turn, Your Turn" with your child. For example, the next time you are mixing batter, say, "We're going to play 'My Turn, Your Turn.' I will stir the batter five times. Then it will be your turn to stir."

  Trading is similar to taking turns, except that neither child has to wait. Practice trading with your child by handing her a toy to play with while you play with another toy. You might even set a timer and say: "You will play with your toy while I play with my toy for 10 minutes." When the 10 minutes is up, trade the toys back—and reset the timer, if you wish.

- **ROLE-PLAY.** Act out different situations and use specific language as you play together to help your child learn what it means to be a good friend. For example, "Let's share these blocks and build a garage together and take turns 'driving and fixing' the cars. During your role-play, practice strategies she can use when she has a conflict with a friend, including calming down, labeling and expressing her feelings, and thinking of a solution to a problem.

• **JOIN SOCIAL GROUPS.** Help your child make new friends by giving her strategies and language to use when joining others at play. One strategy is to have your child contribute to the play by offering an idea to expand the play. So, rather than asking "Can I play with you?," first notice how the children are playing and think about how your child can join in. For example, you can say: "Those children are drawing with crayons, and you have these markers. Maybe you'd like to share so you can use both in your drawings." Also, encourage your child to invite others to play by modeling questions he can ask, such as, "Do you want to play blocks?"

• **RESOLVE CONFLICTS.** Conflicts are a natural part of preschool life, and children need tools to resolve these conflicts and renegotiate the friendship. Knowing how to use "feeling words" to describe a problem, instead of grabbing or hitting, is an important skill that will help your child react in calmer and more thoughtful ways. The next time a conflict arises, encourage your child to label how she is feeling, such as, "That made me angry because . . ." By labeling her feelings, your child becomes better at understanding problems when she has a social conflict with her peers. It is also important to help your child notice how others may be feeling during a conflict. Encourage her to ask questions, such as, "Are you okay?" or "How are you feeling?" to help her understand the perspective of others.

• **PRACTICE FORGIVENESS.** When there is conflict, help your child understand that the friendship is not over and model ways he can rebuild it. One strategy is to help your child become aware of how his behavior upset his friend. Young children are not always aware of how their actions affect others. There's a difference between "intentional" and "accidental" and "oblivious." Have your child take the time to think about his behavior and, when he's ready, apologize to his friend.

AGE 3

At three years old, your child probably separates more easily from you when left with a familiar grown-up (a babysitter at home or a teacher at school drop-off). He shows concern for others' feelings and can show he cares (empathy). You may see this when your child hugs a friend who fell down or brings a favorite toy when baby sister is crying.

He's more interested in making friendships and may show interest in certain friends and seek them out to play, such as bringing a truck to join children creating a pretend construction site. With your help, he is learning how to take turns, share, resolve conflicts, and join a group of children. He might go to an adult for help when a friend takes a toy he wants to play with.

AGE 4

At four years old, your child probably interacts more with familiar grown-ups and shares her interests with them. You may see this when your child talks to a neighbor about her garden, or she shares details of a recent trip to the zoo with relatives.

She shows concern for other people's needs and feelings, and she is starting to express why someone might feel a certain way. You may see this when your child asks a friend if he is okay after she witnesses that child's feelings being hurt. She might then explain what's happened, using words like, "He's mad because someone took his teddy bear."

She is more interested in playing with other children than playing alone. She may have a special friendship with a particular child, calling her "my friend," and can start or join in play with small groups of children. She is building her cooperation skills as she practices taking turns. As she gets older, she can share more easily and is able to offer simple solutions to conflicts. You may see this when your child suggests taking turns when she and a friend want to use the same toy. If she sees children pretending that the slide at the playground is a boat, for instance, she may say, "Let's pretend it's a pirate ship."

AGE 5

At five years old, your child probably interacts with trusted adults easily and shares interests with them. You may see this when your child engages in more detailed conversations with relatives at a family gathering. He invites a visiting family member or friend to play a game or look at a favorite book together.

She begins to understand that people can have different feelings about the same thing (especially as she nears six years old). You may see this when your child says, "I like to knock down blocks, but Joanna doesn't."

He also starts to identify "best" friends. He wants to please his friends and may have a closer friendship with one child in particular. He can also play with a larger group of children, working collaboratively and sharing his own ideas. These friendships begin to last longer, because he is starting to negotiate and compromise to solve conflicts as he nears six years old. For example, when he wants to ride the same bike as a friend, he might suggest, "You can ride it first, then I'll ride it."

GOOD STUFF!
BIG BIRD—AND OTHERS—ON BULLYING

A few years ago, Big Bird was bullied by a group of birds that excluded him from their club because of his physical features (too yellow, feet too big, and way too tall). The story provided an opportunity to model what bullying behaviors are and how friends can be upstanders and help a victim of bullying by going to a trusted adult.

- Watch "The Good Birds Club" (sesamestreet.org/goodbirdsclub) with your child to see how Abby and Elmo are upstanders and report when Big Bird is being bullied.

- Watch a panel of experts discuss the topic of bullying at sesamestreet.org/anti-bullying.

DEEP DIVE

BULLYING IN PRESCHOOL

Yes, your child can engage in bullying behaviors or be a victim of bullying, even in preschool. However, not all aggressive behaviors are acts of bullying. In fact, the term is often misunderstood and misused. Here are some useful thoughts on the subject of bullying:

- **WHAT IS BULLYING?** Bullying is a specific type of aggressive behavior in which a child or group of children with more power (for example, if they are bigger, older, or have more friends) acts with the intent to harm another child and the mean behavior is usually repeated. Bullying may take many forms and includes physical (hitting and kicking) and emotional (mean name-calling as well as social exclusion).

- **IS TEASING BULLYING?** Teasing is actually very common in children's play relationships, similar to how adults would use sarcasm to bond or connect with someone. Among friends, one might tease someone, but it occurs in a friendly, back-and-forth banter, rather than being rooted in a power dynamic where one person takes control and wants to humiliate someone or put someone down.

- **IS NAME-CALLING A FORM OF BULLYING?** If name-calling is a recurring pattern, characterized by a power differential with the *intent* to use the name to put the child down and make her feel bad, then this is an act of bullying.

- **HOW TO KNOW IF MY CHILD IS BEING BULLIED?** Signs to look for in your child: doesn't want to go to school; shows concern about what he wears or brings to school; has unexplained changes in his sleep or appetite; and has unexplained crying episodes.

- **WHAT SHOULD I DO IF MY CHILD IS BEING BULLIED?** Remember that being victimized is very scary for a child, so it's important that you make her feel safe. Stay calm and listen to your child and don't be so quick to react in an emotional way.

- Remember: Bullying is a planned act by someone who has power over the victimized child. Refrain from telling your child to confront a bully, as this may put the child at greater risk for being hurt. Praise your child for coming to tell you and to gather the facts so you are in a better position to help him with the situation.

- **HOW DO I KNOW IF MY CHILD IS BULLYING OTHER CHILDREN?** One indicator is if you receive reports from teachers that your child is engaged in repeated aggressive behaviors with peers. Or, you may observe her bullying her siblings. What's important is to understand the underlying reasons for these intentional acts of aggression, and take steps to deal with them.

- **IS BULLYING A RITE OF PASSAGE?** No! Adults must neither accept nor ignore this hurtful and harmful behavior.

- **DO I CALL THE PARENT OR THE SCHOOL?** It's almost always best to contact the director of the center or school to discuss your concerns and have the director bring the parents in to discuss the situation. It is useful to have a third party involved in that conversation. Calling the other parent and saying, "I think your kid is bullying my kid," even if you are calm on the phone, may elicit denial or a negative reaction. Putting someone on the defensive, even if you have a friendly relationship with her, can create a back-and-forth and a he-said/she-said situation.

- **HOW CAN FRIENDS HELP?** If your child sees another child being bullied, tell him to go to a trusted adult who will listen and intervene.

- **IS REPORTING DIFFERENT FROM TATTLING?** Tattling is when you are trying to get someone in trouble, even though no one is getting hurt physically or emotionally. Reporting is when you are trying to help someone out of trouble because someone is getting hurt physically or emotionally. This distinction is important to understand because it takes courage for a child to come to an adult for help for fear of being bullied himself.

GOOD STUFF!

BOOKS ABOUT FRIENDSHIP

Here's a wonderful collection of books about the many facets of friendship:

- *Sesame Street Circle of Friends* by Naomi Kleinberg, illustrated by Tom Brannon *Sesame Street* friends show what it takes to be a good friend.

- *We Are All Alike . . . We Are All Different*, written and illustrated by the Kindergarteners of Cheltenham Elementary School. Photographs by Laura Dwight.
    This charming book, written by children for children, reinforces multicultural and antibias learning.

- *The Family Book*, written and illustrated by Todd Parr
    Whether you have two moms or two dads, a big family or a small family, a clean family or a messy one, Todd Parr assures readers that no matter what kind of family you have, every family is special in its own unique way.

- *Shades of People* by Shelley Rotner and Sheila M. Kelly
    A photographic book showing people of different nationalities—and different colors.

- *Sesame Street Celebrate You! Celebrate Me!* by Leslie Kimmelman, illustrated by Tom Brannon
    Sesame Street friends celebrate everyone's similarities and differences. This interactive book features Julia, who has autism.

- *We're All Wonders*, written and illustrated by R. J. Palacio
    This picture book, based on Palacio's bestseller *Wonder*, introduces young children to the importance of "choosing kind" when confronted with people who are different.

- *One*, written and illustrated by Kathryn Otoshi
    A beautiful book that teaches young readers about accepting each other's differences, but also imparts much about numbers, counting, and primary and secondary colors. A visual treat!

- *I Walk with Vanessa* by Kerascoët
    A beautiful, compassionate story in which a young bystander who witnesses hurtful behavior becomes an upstander and recruits more upstanders.

Building Friendships

When children can successfully navigate playing together, they feel better about themselves, display greater self-confidence, and are more sensitive to other children's feelings. Give your child plenty of opportunities to explore friendships with other children through playdates, visits to the park, and time with other young family members or neighbors. Informal sports activities or organized classes, such as music, dance, science, and nature are also great ways give your child a chance to get to meet and play with other children.

The Importance of Kindness

Kindness is the glue that holds relationships together. It is imperative that children understand and practice being kind. But kindness needs to be modeled by adults—both what it looks like and what it feels like. Praise your child for being kind and talk about how she feels (the intrinsic reward) when doing kind acts. Being kind benefits others and makes your heart feel good.

In 2017, Sesame Workshop strengthened its commitment to encouraging kind behaviors (the "kinder" aspect of our mission to help kids grow Smarter, Stronger, and Kinder) by developing a curriculum that defined the building blocks of kindness, which are:

EMPATHY. Empathy is the ability to recognize the feelings of others and care about their needs. Young children haven't yet developed the cognitive ability to do this yet, but they respond positively

QUICK TIP

Be kind to animals. Remind children in any hands-on encounter with a pet to be gentle and watch an animal's body language to gauge how it might be feeling. Changes in the movements of a pet's ears and tail are clues, as are expressions like narrowed eyes and bared teeth. Stop the interaction if a pet seems uncomfortable. Messages of respect apply to tiny animals, too.

QUICK TIP

To help your child understand the meaning of "kindness," use the word "kind" instead of "nice" to encourage or praise acts of kindness. So if you want your child to help another child, instead of saying, "Be nice!" say, "Be kind, and help that little girl up steps." If you observe your child sharing or helping, avoid saying, "That was nice of you!"; instead, say, "That was kind of you!"

203

SPREADING KINDNESS

Here are 20 suggestions to help you model kindness and engage your child in acts of kindness with you.

1. Play fair: Take turns, share, trade, cooperate.

2. Have your child invite a few friends over and include someone new in the group.

3. Display good manners, such as saying "Please" and "Thank you." Encourage your child to do the same.

4. Hold open a door and let someone exit before you enter.

5. Model being kind to people you meet by saying, "Have a nice day!" "How are you?"

6. Give someone a compliment.

7. Offer a tissue or a hug when someone is sad.

8. Return something you find that's been lost by someone.

9. Lend a helping hand to someone who seems lost or confused: "Can I help you?"

10. Encourage your child to help clean up after playing and eating.

11. Send a "Thinking of You" card to a friend or relative. Encourage your child to send a "Thinking of You " drawing to Grandma.

12. Check on an elderly or homebound neighbor; bring, soup, cookies, or flowers.

13. Express how much you care by holding hands, blowing a kiss, giving a hug.

14. Make treats for community helpers, such as police officers or firefighters.

15. When dining in a restaurant, thank your server for good service. Leave change in tip jars, on the table, and explain to your child why you are doing it.

16. Send a gift package of cookies to someone serving in the military. Involve your child in baking the cookies.

17. Let someone skip ahead of you in line (especially a younger child on a bathroom line!).

18. Donate gently used toys, books, clothing, or shoes to those in need. Involve your child in picking out the items, and boxing them.

19. Together with your child, help make and deliver food to local homeless shelters.

20. Make a donation to a nature conservancy, shelter, zoo, or animal sanctuary, if possible.

GOOD STUFF!
GOOD BOOKS ON KINDNESS

Here are some useful books for helping preschoolers understand the concept of kindness:

– ***Sesame Street: K is for Kindness*** by Jodie Shepherd, illustrated by Tom Brannon

    Elmo learns about being kind to others as he works to earn his Monster Scout Kindness Badge by helping his friends and neighbors.

– ***Sesame Street: Kindness Makes the World Go Round*** by Craig Manning, illustrated by Joe Mathieu

    Elmo's mom surprises him with a camera for World Kindness Day and asks him to find kindness on Sesame Street.

– ***Have You Filled a Bucket Today?*** by Carol McCloud, illustrated by David Messing

    This guide to daily happiness shows kids that kindness and appreciation of others go a long way toward making this world a happier place for everyone.

– ***Here Come the Helpers*** by Leslie Kimmelman, illustrated by Barbara Bakos

    This charming view of police officers, firefighters, emergency medical technicians, and other community friends gives younger readers a look at important helpers in their neighborhood.

– ***You, Me and Empathy*** by Jayneen Sanders, illustrated by Sofia Cardoso

    The rhyming text and comfortingly familiar settings in this story take the big idea of "empathy" and make it both playful and understandable enough for older preschoolers.

QUICK TIP

Be kind to the earth. Reduce, reuse, recycle, and respect! By reducing waste and using just want you need, you are being kind to our planet. As parents, model good use of water and electricity; reuse paper before recycling it; use water "bottles/flasks" to reduce plastic; recycle glass, plastic, and metal items to reduce waste; plant trees or gardens; pick up trash on the sidewalk, in the park, on the beach; bring eco-friendly/reusable bags to the grocery store. As you engage in these activities, talk to your child about how these acts of kindness are helping the earth.

if you take everyday opportunities to model and encourage kindness skills in an age-appropriate way. For example, ask questions like these: "Look at his face. What do you think he is feeling?" to help your child develop empathy.

COMPASSION. Once children are able to turn the focus away from themselves, the next step is to cultivate in them compassion, or the awareness that someone might need help and the desire to provide it. Raising empathetic children is important, but we also need to encourage children to act on their feelings for others through words and behaviors.

RESPECT. When children learn to be respectful, they place a high value on themselves, others, and their environment, which leads to kind behavior. One component of being respectful is having good manners, a learned behavior that can best be developed and reinforced through modeling.

Conclusions

Understanding and controlling one's emotions, using self-regulation strategies, and being kind to others by being empathic, compassionate, and respectful are among the most important attributes a child needs to develop, not only for school readiness, but to establish and maintain good personal relationships throughout their lives. As parents, you are the most important teachers of effective self-regulation skills through modeling, practice, and patience.

UNDERSTANDING, EXPRESSING, AND MANAGING EMOTIONS

AGE 2	AGE 3	AGE 4	AGE 5
Understands what is and is not allowed. • Can't yet stop from doing something that is not permitted. • Pokes at the pet cat or pulls its tail. • Throws toys. • Unravels a whole roll of toilet paper.	**Shows a range of feelings, and uses words to describe simpler ones.** • Gets upset when the routine changes unexpectedly. • Moves smoothly from one activity to the next. • Rules and routines, such as tooth brushing, get easier.	**Shows independence by doing things on own.** • Puts on a coat without help, asking only when needed. • Wants to make own sandwich.	**Can identify and respond to own needs.** • Finds a place to sit in order to see during storytime. • Puts on a sweater when cold.
Gets overwhelmed by strong feelings. • Experiences basic emotions (happy, sad, frightened, etc.), but can get overwhelmed by them. • Needs a trusted grown-up to help name feelings and model how to manage them. • Can comfort self when upset with a lovey, such as a special toy or blanket. • Eagerly snuggles favorite blanket after a bump or fall. • Cries and protests when needs to give back a borrowed toy, and needs an adult help return it.	**Is starting to use self-control and wait for a desired item.** • Is learning how to see situations from different points of view. • Waits for a turn at a water fountain, saying, "When she is finished drinking, it will be my turn."	**Is learning how to read a situation and use self-control.** • Is starting to wait more patiently, using skills taught by the grown-ups. • Sings a song to manage frustration while waiting to have a turn. • Counts to 10 or breathes deeply (belly-breathes) to help calm down.	**Manages feelings successfully most of the time, with help from grown-ups.** • Can follow a familiar strategy to help focus attention: eye watching (cup hands around eyes); ears listening (cup hands around ears); voice quiet (hold finger to the lips); body calm (hands in lap). • Shares worries about an upcoming dental checkup or doctor's visit. • Takes a deep breath and hugs self when too excited or feels aggressive.

BUILDING RELATIONSHIPS

AGE 2	AGE 3	AGE 4	AGE 5
Recognizes and responds to the feelings of others. • Looks for reassurance from a familiar grown-up (facial expressions, body language, encouragements) when exploring and engaging with new people and places. • Responds to the expressions of others (frowning when seeing someone cry or smiling when seeing someone laugh). • May want to help or give comfort in ways that he or she likes to be helped or comforted. • Gives crayons to a friend who also wants to color. • Brings a diaper when baby brother needs to be changed.	• **Separates more easily from you** when left with a familiar grown up (a babysitter at home or a teacher at preschool).	**Interacts more with familiar grown-ups and shares interests with them.** • Talks to a neighbor about the garden. • Shares details of a recent trip to the zoo with relatives.	**Interacts with trusted adults easily and shares interests with them.** • Engages in more detailed conversations with relatives at a family gathering. • Invites a visiting family friend to play a board game or look at a favorite book together.
Shows strong emotions with body language more than words. • Crosses arms when told it's time to go and doesn't want to. • May not yet have the words to verbally express feelings.	**Shows concern for others' feelings.** • Can express caring behavior. • Hugs a friend who fell down. • Brings a favorite toy when baby sister is crying.	**Shows concern for other people's needs and feelings.** • Is starting to express why someone might feel a certain way. • Asks a friend if she is OK, if that child's feelings are hurt. • Explains, "He's mad because someone took his teddy bear."	**Begins to understand that people have different feelings about the same thing.** • Says "The fire truck siren hurts Jordan's ears but not mine."

BUILDING RELATIONSHIPS (cont'd)

AGE 2	AGE 3	AGE 4	AGE 5
Is interested in other children and wants to make friends. • May be able to take turns but still needs a parent's help with sharing and resolving conflicts. • Is more likely to play alongside another child, often copying the same activity, but doing it separately. • Gets excited when meeting a familiar friend at the park. • Wants to dig in the sandbox or build a train track when seeing others doing it.	**Is more interested in making friendships.** • May begin to play more with a preferred friend. • With a parent's help, learns how to take turns, share, resolve conflicts, and join a group of children. • Is also noticing how people are the same and different, such as comparing skin and hair color and identifying boys and girls.	**Is more interested in playing with other children than playing alone.** • May have a special friendship with a particular child, calling her "my friend." • Can start to or join in play with small groups of children. • Is building when cooperating skills when practicing taking turns. • Can share more easily and is able to offer simple solutions to conflicts. • Suggests taking turns when a friend wants to use the same toy. • Sees children pretending the slide is a boat, and says "Let's pretend it's a pirate ship."	**Starts to identify "best friends."** • Wants to please friends and may have a closer friendship with one child in particular. • Can also play with a larger group of children, working collaboratively and sharing own ideas. • Friendships begin to last longer. • Is starting negotiate and compromise to solve conflicts. • Works together with other children to build a garage out of blocks for a toy truck. • Wants to ride the same bike with a friend, and suggests, "You can ride it first, then I'll ride it."

7.
HAPPY HEALTHY MONSTERS!

Strong Bodies, Smart Choices

When childhood obesity became more and more prevalent in our society, the *Sesame Street* team decided to address this health issue (and other health problems) as a critical educational and societal concern. Toward this end, we established a company-wide initiative, called "Healthy Habits for Life," which included a comprehensive health curriculum that guided content for *Sesame Street* the show, as well as many popular *Sesame Street* books, apps, games, and activities. Resources were also created for parents, educators, and caregivers and can be found at sesamestreetincommunities.org.

Not surprisingly, parents are central in establishing their children's health habits, both as role models and as facilitators. When adults model healthy habits and routines in all aspects of life (eating, sleeping, exercising, hygiene, etc.), children naturally start practicing healthy habits themselves. It is during the preschool years that healthy (or unhealthy) habits for life are established. As children start to understand and appreciate how their bodies work and what their bodies can do, they also begin to learn what they need to do to stay healthy and strong.

While health has always been a part of *Sesame Street*'s whole-child curriculum, for the "Healthy Habits for Life" initiative, we redefined the building blocks for developing healthy habits. Specifically we focused on:

- Practicing good hygiene;

- Eating nutritious foods;

- Being physically active; and

- Getting enough rest.

As we developed the "Healthy Habits for Life" initiative, we also evaluated the habits of our beloved Cookie Monster—most particularly, his eating habits, of course. In a segment titled "A Cookie Is a Sometime Food," Hoots the Owl helped Cookie Monster learn through song that fruits are an "anytime food," but cookies are a "sometime food." Cookie can't have a *cookie* anytime he wants one, but *other* foods are appropriate and available, and among them are foods that Cookie Monster will love!

These simple, down-to-earth terms, "sometime" and "anytime," were chosen in order to provide a simple, accessible vocabulary for parents and caregivers to use with children when talking about making healthy food choices. No, we didn't turn Cookie Monster into a "Veggie Monster," as some critics speculated; nor did we turn cookies into a forbidden food. Instead, we modeled how to make smart choices while also teaching what the body needs and the types of foods that give sustained energy in order for us to play and learn. Watching Cookie Monster enthusiastically embrace healthier food choices empowered children watching to make smarter choices, too: If Cookie Monster can do it, so can they!

When Kids Build Healthy Habits

As children build their knowledge of healthy habits, they acquire a range of new skills and start to:

- **NAME BODY PARTS AND SENSES.** Children learn to identify the different parts of the body and what they do. They connect the five senses—sight (eyes are for seeing), sound (ears are for hearing), taste (a mouth or tongue are

212

for tasting), smell (a nose is for smelling), and touch (skin is for touching)—with their related body parts.

- **PRACTICE GOOD PERSONAL CARE AND HYGIENE.** As children grow and learn, they begin to name and participate in their own basic health care. These include such activities as washing hands, brushing teeth, taking a bath, covering her mouth and nose when coughing or sneezing, and using the potty.

- **IDENTIFY HEALTHY FOODS.** Children learn that foods can range from more healthy to less healthy; that certain are "sometimes" foods (those higher in sugar and fat—such as cookies!) and others are "anytime" foods (including fruits and vegetables). They understand that eating healthy foods, including a nutritious breakfast each morning, gives their bodies energy. They learn that eating a variety of colorful foods ("eating a rainbow") is good for their bodies. They may need to try new foods several times before they develop a taste for them. A parent's encouragement that healthy foods help us grow strong can be very motivating as a child explores new tastes.

- **PARTICIPATE IN REGULAR PHYSICAL ACTIVITY.** Children learn that being active and exercising help keep their bodies and minds healthy and strong. They also learn that they can be physically active in a variety of ways, from very energetic exercise, like running, jumping, and biking, to less intense exercise, like walking and stretching. They start to understand the importance of drinking water, especially during and after exercise.

- **UNDERSTAND THAT SLEEP AND REST ARE IMPORTANT.** Children learn that rest and sleep help recharge their bodies and give them energy to play and be active.

Body Parts & How to Care for Them

When a child knows how the body works, its parts, and how they function, he is better able to understand why and how to care for it. Through playful interactions, including games and songs, such as "Heads, Shoulders, Knees and Toes," "Hokey Pokey," and "Simon Says," with commands such as "Simon says . . . touch your nose!" or ". . . hop on one foot!" your child is building his knowledge about body parts.

As children learn their various body parts, they'll begin to connect them with their functions. For example, even a very young child learns quickly that eyes are for seeing; a nose is for smelling; skin is for touching; ears are for hearing; and a tongue is for tasting. She also begins to reason and make choices based on her knowledge of how certain body parts work. For example, she might realize that bending her knees helps her to hop higher or that eating too much makes her tummy hurt. Your child also learns about how visits to the doctor and dentist are necessary and important in keeping the body healthy and strong.

214

QUICK TIP

In a classic *Sesame Street* storybook, *Grover's Own Alphabet*, Grover twists and bends his body parts into the letters A through Z. Let your very young child direct you to do the same, by choosing a letter. As you move to make its shape, label each part of the body you're using: "To make an A, I'll stretch my arms *waaaay* over my head and use my hands to make the point. Then I'll move my feet far away from each other. My tummy is the middle of the A." For some letters, work together to make the shape.

GOOD STUFF!
GETTING TO KNOW YOUR BODY

Lots of entertaining books, apps, and toys are available to help even very young children learn about their bodies.

Here are a few books to help preschoolers celebrate the wonders of their bodies:

- *Inside Your Outside: All About the Human Body* by Tish Rabe, illustrated by Aristides Ruiz

  Part of the Cat in the Hat's Learning Library, this book offers an accessible and amusing tour through all the biological facets of the human body.

- *My Amazing Body* by Ruth Martin, illustrated by Allan Sanders

  An excellent resource with bold cartoon-colorful art, this title utilizes dozens of flaps to reveal what's underneath the skin.

- *Sesame Street We're Different, We're the Same* by Bobbi Kates, illustrated by Joe Mathieu

  Sesame Street's friendly Monsters, birds, Grouches, and humans are only a fraction of the manifold faces and bodies that kids will encounter in this book, which blends body-part vocabulary with lessons about diversity and kinship.

TALKING SENSE

It's important for children to be able to identify, label, and recognize the body parts associated with the five senses and how the two are related. For example, when eating an apple, talk about how all your senses are engaged: "This apple makes all my senses happy: My eyes help me see colors to pick the green apples. My ears hear the crunch when I bite it. My nose sniffs its wonderful fresh smell. My tongue tells me how good it tastes, sour or sweet!"

Below is language you can use to help define and explore the senses with your preschooler:

- **SIGHT.** Use "eye" words, like "see," "watch," "observe," and "look." "Focus your eyes and see all the shapes around us right now. How many do you see?"

- **HEARING.** Use "ear" words, such as "listen," "echo," "quiet," and "loud." "My ears can hear the sound of a bird. What do your ears hear?"

- **SMELL.** Use "nose"-related words, such as "sniff," "scent," "odor," "fragrance," "smelly," and "stinky." "Let's use our noses to smell these socks to see if they're dirty."

- **TASTE.** Explain how we use our "tongue" to lick and taste. "This ice cream tastes so good in my mouth as a special treat when it's hot outside."

- **TOUCH.** When you talk about how things feel, you might use words like "dry," "moist," "sticky," "gooey," "slimy," "fluffy," "spongy," "hard," "soft," "smooth," and "rough."

DEEP DIVE

TIPS FOR A WELL VISIT

Your child's health care team helps keep him healthy so he can play, learn, and grow! Consider these tips to help any visit to the doctor go smoothly:

Preparing Yourself for the Checkup

- **WRITE DOWN QUESTIONS ABOUT YOUR CHILD'S HEALTH BEFOREHAND.** This is a great way to start a conversation that will keep you involved in your child's care. You might ask about:
  - Your child's height, weight, vision, movement, and overall health.
  - Milestones your child should be meeting.
  - Things you can do to help your child stay healthy.
  - When the next visit will be.

Preparing Your Child

- **KIDS MAY BE SCARED.** Explain that doctors and nurses keep us healthy and make us better when we're sick.

- **LET YOUR CHILD KNOW WHAT WILL HAPPEN.** ("The doctor will check different parts of your body to make sure they're healthy. I will stay with you the whole time.")

- **HONESTY IS KEY AS WELL.** Don't make promises you aren't sure can be kept. If you don't know whether a child's due for a shot, reduce stress about it by being frank: "We can't be sure yet whether you need a shot. But if you do get one, I'll hold your hand the whole time and it won't be so bad. It might feel like a pinch, but it will be over so fast." What you *can* promise: a hug and perhaps a special activity together afterward.

- Before the visit, invite your child to pretend that he is the doctor! Let him feel and listen to your heartbeat, or ask him to look into your mouth while you say, "Ahhhhh!"

What to Expect
from Your Preschooler

AGE 2

At two years old, your child probably knows some body parts, inside and out, particularly the ones representing the senses: eyes, ears, nose, and mouth. She is also becoming aware of how her body behaves and can express certain feelings in simple terms. You may see this when your child pats her tummy and says, "Tummy hurt!"

She is also beginning to understand that she'll go to the doctor when she is sick. She may understand that some visits are just checkups and that others help her when she's not feeling well: "Tummy feels better now." She also is beginning to understand that she occasionally visits the dentist to keep her teeth healthy and strong.

QUICK TIP

Scores of books are available at libraries, at bookstores, and online that feature stories of well-known characters—from Elmo and Daniel Tiger to Corduroy, Caillou, and the Berenstain Bears—and their adventures visiting a doctor or dentist. Although the stories vary, seeing familiar characters in these potentially stressful situations can ease children's fears.

GOOD STUFF!
FROM THE INSIDE OUT

Skeletons don't have to be scary—or relegated to Halloween. These fascinating kits help kids understand how their bodies are constructed.

With *Human Skeleton Magnetic Accents* by Teacher Created Resources, kids develop a greater understanding of how their bodies are built by assembling a skeleton with these oversized magnets, on the fridge or any other metal surface. With *Melissa & Doug's Magnetic Anatomy Set*, a paper doll–like activity with wooden boy and girl figures, allows kids to "build a body" with pieces that layer over a basic skeleton.

HAPPY HEALTHY MONSTERS!

GOOD STUFF!
DOCTORS' KITS FOR KIDS

Many professional physicians have fond memories of their first toy doctor's kit, used for setting a "broken" arm on a doll or prescribing a shot for a teddy bear with an upset tummy. Doctors' kits remain popular with children to this day, and they are perfect toys for preschoolers because they allow kids to become familiar with a variety of medical items (syringes, bandages, medicine bottles) and behaviors, and such familiarity helps to alleviate fears of visiting the doctor. Many types of doctors' kits, at a wide range of prices, are available at toy stores and online.

AGE 3

At three years old, your child may well know some internal parts of the body (tummy, bones, heart, teeth, tongue), and may talk about what they do. He also might talk about some ways to stay healthy. For example, he might say, "My bones help me stand up." Or, after a bedtime glass of milk, he may tell you, "I need to brush my teeth now."

218

QUICK TIP

Watching someone else have a positive experience during a doctor's visit can help kids when it's time to do so themselves. The *Sesame Street in Communities* website offers videos, such as "A Great Doctor Visit" and "Visit the Dentist." You can also find videos, including "Bebe Goes to the Doctor When Sick" on *Sesame Street*'s YouTube channel. Watch these videos together with your child and then talk about what happened during the visit. Try role-playing after you watch, taking turns playing doctor/nurse/dentist and patient, using a toy doctor's kit or household objects as props. Visit sesamestreet incommunities.org./ topics/health

AGE 4

At four years old, your child knows more about internal body parts. She may point to her chest and say, "My doctor helped me listen to my heart. It's pumping blood in my body." Or, at a birthday party, she may point out that "My lungs helped me blow out the candle."

AGE 5

At five years old, your child understands how certain behaviors keep us healthy. He might say something like this: "I can see a plane way up in the sky. That's

TEDDY'S EXAM

Role-playing with baby dolls and stuffed toys like teddy bears allows children to prepare for a doctor's visit and to work through any big feelings after a visit during which they might have needed a shot or had a minor procedure. For example, you might suggest that your child give Teddy doses of medicine, listen to his heartbeat, or apply an adhesive bandage to his paw. Children will often pretend-play that a doll has a broken bone, enjoying the drama and action of putting on a "cast." Or you may see your child assign a stuffed friend an allergy, if she, a family member, or a playmate has been diagnosed with one.

During such doctor play you may introduce and use language such as:

- INJURIES AND OTHER "OUCHIES." Together, you might describe these as a "hurt," "pain," "bump," "bruise," "cut," "scratch," "infection," and the too-common bloody nose and "boo-boo."

- TOOLS OF THE TRADE, such as bandages, ointment, medicines like an antibiotic, and terms used in exams, such as "heartbeat," "stethoscope," "thermometer," "plessor" (the rubber reflex hammer), "otoscope" (for checking ears), "ophthalmoscope" (for checking eyes), "blood pressure cuff," or "shot."

- COMMON, MINOR CONDITIONS AND ILLNESSES might include a "cold," "influenza (flu)," "headache," "toothache," "stomachache," "sunburn," or "infection"—and related symptoms like a "runny nose," "sneeze," "cough," "fever," "vomiting," or "diarrhea."

Using these terms can help make them more familiar and less scary for your preschooler when they occur during a real doctor visit.

DEEP DIVE
SET THE EXAMPLE

The best way to teach proper hygiene to young children is to model it yourself. Here are a few obvious suggestions:

- **WASH YOUR HANDS. OFTEN.** Good hand-washing habits are key to good hygiene, and are critical in the prevention of childhood illnesses. Explain to your child that dirty hands spread germs that can cause her to become ill. As you wash your hands, remind your child about the importance of washing her hands before eating, after going to the potty, and, of course, after playing with anything messy. To help your child develop this important practice, sing songs while washing hands and use child-friendly soaps. Have your child help choose the soap she uses; some children are inclined to scrub longer when using foam dispensers or fruit-scented soaps.

- **SNEEZE INTO YOUR ELBOW.** Explain that sneezes and coughs carry germs, and when you sneeze you need to cover your nose and mouth. Catching germs in your hand just spreads them wherever you touch, but directing a sneeze or cough into the crook of your elbow minimizes the spread of germs. After watching "Sesame Street: The Right Way to Sneeze," this song can help you remind your child (and you) to "be like Elmo, use your elbow" next time your child sneezes or coughs.

- **BRUSH YOUR TEETH MORNING AND NIGHT.** Model for your child how you brush your teeth in the morning, during the day (if necessary), and evening before they go to bed after dinner. Sing a song while brushing, so your child learns the importance of brushing for a full two minutes to make sure your teeth are clean and germ-free. Avoid eating gummy fruit snacks, including dried fruits, as these sugary foods cling to your teeth, causing tooth decay. If you can't brush right afterward, swish your mouth with water to remove some of the pieces until you can brush to remove all the sticky particles in between teeth and in the grooves of the enamel. Also avoid drinking soda, sugary carbonated drinks, and juice, as well as eating sugary cereals, crackers, and sucking on lollipops, all of which contribute to tooth decay. Reminder: Have your child brush her teeth after getting medicine, as some contain sugar.

- **IT'S BATH TIME!** Talk to your child about how much you enjoy your own "bath time," and how wonderful it feels to come out of the tub fresh and clean. If your child resists bath time, introduce toys or "bath books" to make bath time more fun.

- **PAY ATTENTION TO POTTY TIME.** Children can become so engaged with their play that they ignore the "gotta-go" signs. Throughout the day, gently cue your child to assess his status: "Do you need to poop or pee?" Perhaps you might adapt a verse from Elmo's potty song to suit your needs: "Is it potty time? Go with the flow! Is it potty time? You can feel it, I know!"

- **"ACCIDENTS HAPPEN" OR "SOMETIMES WE FORGET."** You may consider having a motto ready for when your child doesn't succeed at first in his attempts at establishing a healthy habit. It can be as basic as "It's A-OK. Accidents happen!" Or it can be a quick reminder that we all forget things sometimes, like sneezing into the crook of our arm or washing our hands after going to the potty. Be gentle but consistent.

because I eat all my carrots and they give me strong eyes." Or he might put a bandage on a cut, saying, "This will help keep the germs away."

He also knows that certain grown-ups in the community help us stay healthy. You may see this when your child says she wants to become a dentist someday, "just like *my* dentist, because he helps keep my teeth clean and strong."

Personal Hygiene & Care

Teaching and maintaining healthy hygiene habits, including washing hands, brushing teeth twice a day, and taking baths, takes effort and dedication, especially when children are first learning them. Moreover *transition*s from one activity that a child is enjoying to a different task that might seem less desirable (like taking a bath or going to the potty) can be difficult for young children. One strategy: Provide an alert in advance of that pivot and a clear description of what's coming up next: "When we finish this game, it's time for you to get ready for your bath."

What to Expect from Your Preschooler

AGE 2

- **AT TWO YEARS OLD, YOUR CHILD PROBABLY IS LEARNING ABOUT PERSONAL CARE.** He follows your lead and is starting to practice aspects of self-care routines himself. You may see this when your child uses soap during hand washing when you remind him, "Now that our hands are wet, let's put some soap on them." He tries to create a back-and-forth motion with his toothbrush after you've shown him how.

- **HE IMITATES ADULT BEHAVIORS.** He sees how you cough into your elbow, but might not do it quite right herself.

AGE 3

DOES SOME PERSONAL CARE ROUTINES ON HER OWN. She needs reminders on when and how to do them and may forget some of the steps. You may see this when your child washes her hands after using the potty, but forgets soap. Or she remembers to cough into her elbow *some* of the time.

GOOD STUFF!

Hygiene routines are a popular inspiration for picture books, so it's easy to find ones among the scores of books that use characters or themes that will resonate with your child: dinosaurs, pirates, superheroes, and cuddly animals all brush their teeth, use the potty, and take baths. A librarian or bookseller can recommend one that matches your child's interests, or quickly peruse online resources. Here are a few suggestions:

- *Happy, Healthy Monsters: Squeaky Clean* by Kara McMahon, illustrated by Barry Goldberg

    This ebook for older preschoolers is an early reference book that offers comprehensive, concrete tips and explores the importance of healthy hygiene for battling germs.

- *Time for a Bath* by Phyllis Gershator, illustrated by David Walker

    A sweet story of a little bunny's many days of busy play, always ending in the tub.

- *The Pigeon Needs a Bath*, written and illustrated by Mo Willems

    This story uses humor to make your child giggle helplessly—and head happily to the tub.

- *Brush Your Teeth, Please* by Leslie McGuire, illustrated by Jean Pidgeon

    Featuring friendly bears and smirking sharks, this book also includes pop-ups that invite interaction.

- *Ready, Set, Brush!* by *Sesame Street*, illustrated by Che Rudko

    Produced in consultation with the American Dental Association, this book hits all the key healthy-teeth messages and packages them in an interactive format of flaps, wheels and pop-ups that snare a child's attention.

DEEP DIVE
POTTY TRAINING TIPS

Being ready to use the potty can be an exciting yet challenging time in your child's life. There is no set age to begin toilet training, but children are usually ready between 24 and 36 months of age. Be attuned to your child's cues so that you can be aware of when it is appropriate for her to begin. Observe if she can now follow simple instructions, help undress herself, or give verbal or facial cues that she needs to use the toilet. Remember that your child must also be emotionally ready so it's important to be patient and encouraging. If she keeps resisting, give her more time and continue to stay positive and reassuring as you help her through this process.

You might try these tips to help your child transition from diapers to the potty:

- **MY VERY OWN POTTY!** If possible, take your child to the store with you to choose and purchase the potty together. When you get home, introduce your child to his very own potty, making sure he feels comfortable with it. Help him personalize it by decorating the lid with his name, stickers, or colored markers, which will make him feel more comfortable using it. Point to and label the various parts of the potty, such as the seat and the flusher, as you show your child how the potty works. If needed, reassure your child that he won't fall in by sitting on the potty a few times with his pants on.

- **GOTTA GO!** Help your child listen to her body's signals and recognize the feeling she gets right before she has to go to the bathroom. Whenever she gets that feeling, emphasize that she should stop doing whatever she is doing and say, "Now you know . . . you've gotta go!" To comfort and ease the pressure when your child is waiting on the potty, place books or toys in a basket in the bathroom. Praise your child for even small accomplishments, such as recognizing the feeling that she has to go.

- **WIPE, FLUSH, AND WASH!** Help your child learn a consistent potty routine. Remind him that, after going, he must *wipe* with toilet paper—using only as much paper as he needs. Then he must *flush*. He can help you press the flusher down and then, over time, encourage him to press the flusher on his own. Finally, after using or even touching the potty, make sure he knows to *wash* his hands with soap and water for as long as it takes to sing The Alphabet Song.

- **ACCIDENTS HAPPEN—AND THAT'S OK!** All children have accidents, so remember to stay patient and use gentle reminders to encourage success. Never scold or punish your child while she is learning to use her potty. Help your child regain confidence by saying, "That's okay. Next time, you'll remember to use your potty!" The most important thing is for your child to persist and feel proud of herself when she succeeds.

- **GREAT JOB!** Cheerfully praise your child not only for succeeding, but also for *trying*! After a couple of successful tries, get him excited and motivated by going to buy big kid underpants. Also, encourage your child to keep track of his own progress. He can place reward stickers to decorate a blank notebook or a poster chart. Keep this near the potty. Each time he successfully goes, he can mark his success in his notebook or on the chart himself! When you feel that your child has learned to use the potty on his own, present him with a reward certificate!

AGE 4

DOES MORE PERSONAL CARE ROUTINES ON HIS OWN, but may still need your help to remember all the steps. You may see this when your child remembers to wipe after using the toilet, but forgets to flush.

QUICK TIP

Timers are a handy tool for counting down the recommended two minutes of tooth brushing, persuading your child to stay in the tub long enough to get scrubbed, and transitioning into a healthy habit routine ("You have 5, 10, or 15 minutes left of screen time or playtime until your bedtime routine."). Timers come in cute, kid-appropriate designs, such as penguins, chickens, robots, piggies, cows, ice-cream cones, and ladybugs. Let your child help you choose one to use especially with him.

GOOD STUFF!
POTTY BOOKS AND APP

Potty books, ebooks, and apps, featuring popular characters, abound. Check out your local bookstore, library, or online store. Here are a few excellent suggestions:

– *P is for Potty! Lift the Flap Book* by Naomi Kleinberg, illustrated by Christopher Moroney

Elmo's got you covered with potty-training and toilet-hygiene tips. The book contains over 30 flaps, so it can keep a child occupied while seated on the potty.

– *Potty*, written and illustrated by Leslie Patricelli

This is a very early introduction to the idea of potty training, an option for younger siblings who express interest when an older sibling is establishing a potty routine.

– *Everybody Potties (I Can Do It)* by Cheri Vogel, illustrated by Belinda Strong

Celebrating this milestone with charming illustrations and encouraging rhymes—"Who goes tinkle? Who goes poo? Mommies, daddies, and grandmas, too!"

– *Potty Time with Elmo* app

Appropriate for all app platforms

This app, featuring Elmo and Abby, includes a "sticker" reward chart for tracking a child's growing confidence and success using the toilet.

AGE 5

DOES MANY OF HIS PERSONAL CARE ROUTINES ON HIS OWN. He remembers to brush his teeth each morning and before bed. He might even say to his brother, "You have to wash your hands to get the germs off."

DEEP DIVE

TOOTHBRUSHING TIPS

Teaching your child to brush his teeth properly is a key aspect of good hygiene. Brushing at least twice daily, two minutes each time, is associated in numerous studies with lower risk of tooth decay. Here are some tips to keep kids' smiles healthy for a lifetime:

- **LOOK FOR CHILDREN'S TOOTHBRUSHES THAT HAVE SMALL HEADS** and soft bristles. Get children involved by letting them choose the color, pattern, or character for their brush.

- **KEEP GERMS AWAY** by rinsing toothbrushes after brushing. Stand them up so they can air-dry.

- **CHANGE YOUR CHILD'S TOOTHBRUSH EVERY THREE MONTHS**. If the bristles are no longer straight and firm, or if children have been sick, change their toothbrush right away.

- **HELP YOUR CHILD LEARN TO USE THE RIGHT AMOUNT OF TOOTHPASTE** by putting it on their toothbrushes. Children under age two just need a smear. Children ages two to five need a pea-size amount of toothpaste.

- **SING (OR HUM!) WHILE YOU BRUSH.** "Party Mouth: Brush Your Teeth to This Song!" and Elmo's "Brushy Brush" song are songs timed to match that dentist-recommended two-minute target, plus the happy beats make the time speed past faster, for you and your child. They can be found on the Sesame Studios channel through YouTube.

- **SCHEDULE ROUTINE DENTAL CHECKUPS**, starting within six months of your child's first tooth.

Healthy Eating!

During the preschool years, children (with your guidance and their own food choices) are beginning to learn that foods range from healthy to less healthy options, forming the foundational knowledge for food choices that will last throughout their lives. Through their daily experiences, they build their knowledge of good nutritional habits, such as eating healthy foods gives their bodies energy; eating a healthy breakfast is an important part of the day's routine; and eating "colorful" foods ("eating the colors of the rainbow") offers nutrients that keep their bodies healthy and strong.

Anytime Foods, Sometimes Foods

This is valuable time to reinforce the language that Cookie Monster introduced: that there are *anytime* foods, foods we can eat every day; and *sometimes* foods (those higher in fat and sugars) that are not forbidden foods (which make them more desirable), but are to be enjoyed once in a while, like cookies, chips, and snacks high in sugar, fat, and salt.

Anytime foods include:

QUICK TIP

Talk to your child about the fact that when we wake up in the morning, our energy tanks are empty, and breakfast gives our bodies the boost they need to grow, play, and learn each day. For high-energy breakfasts, choose fruits, low-fat yogurt, or whole-grain bread and cereals as some healthy breakfast choices. For something creative, top a whole-wheat English muffin with low-fat mozzarella and sliced tomato to make a breakfast pizza! Or decorate your child's plate with fruit slices and swirls of yogurt.

- VEGETABLES—fresh, frozen, or (low-sodium) canned.
- FRUITS—fresh, frozen, or canned (in their own juices—no added sugar).
- LOW-SUGAR DRINKS—water, nonfat and low-fat milk, and (no added sugar) juices.
- WHOLE GRAINS—whole-grain or whole-wheat breads, pitas, and tortillas; whole-grain pasta; brown rice; unsweetened oatmeal; hot and cold low-sugar breakfast cereals.
- NONFAT AND LOW-FAT DAIRY PRODUCTS—cheese, cottage cheese, milk, and low-sugar yogurt.

- **PROTEINS AND LEAN MEATS THAT ARE ROASTED, BROILED, GRILLED, OR STEAMED (NOT FRIED)**—Beef and pork (trimmed of fat); extra-lean ground beef; chicken and turkey without skin; tuna canned in water; fish and shellfish; beans; tofu; and eggs.

Sometimes foods include:

- **FOODS THAT ARE DEEP-FRIED IN OIL.**
- **FRUITS CANNED IN SYRUP.**
- **SWEETENED BREAKFAST CEREALS, AND NON-WHOLE-GRAIN BAKERY ITEMS,** like doughnuts, muffins, croissants, sweet rolls, crackers, cookies, chips, cakes, and pies.
- **CANDIES.**
- **ICE CREAM AND ICE POPS.**

Encourage kids to understand the importance of eating a variety of healthy foods. The habits they develop during this time influence their independent food choices when they enter school.

What to Expect from Your Preschooler

AGE 2

At two years old, your child can identify familiar foods and most likely has established food preferences. She might pretend to make a fruit salad with play food and adds strawberries, saying, "Yummy!" or picks the carrots out of her dinner and says, "No like carrots." She probably needs encouragement to try new foods, since it is not unusual for two-year-olds to be picky eaters. Still, she may decide to taste *arroz con leche* (rice with milk) after you tell her "Mmm! Grandpa used to make

QUICK TIP Show gratitude! Even very young children can be taught that we should be grateful for the food we eat, and to appreciate the time and care spent producing and preparing it. We can talk about where food comes from—that it doesn't originate in the grocery store, but is the result of someone's hard work of growing, raising, and tending.

DEEP DIVE

EATING A RAINBOW!

Eat the Colors of a Rainbow" and "Eat Your Colors!" are phrases that support the importance of a balanced diet, which includes eating a variety of fruits, vegetables, and grains. Here are foods to consider to help your child eat a "Rainbow of Colors":

- **RED:** *Fruits:* raspberries, strawberries, red apples (peeled and sliced), cherries (pitted and cut), red grapes (cut), pink grapefruit, pomegranates, red pears, watermelon, fresh cranberries, tomatoes. *Vegetables:* radicchio, radishes, beets, red onions, red potatoes.

- **ORANGE:** *Fruits:* apricots, cantaloupe, mangoes, oranges, tangerines, guava, nectarines, peaches, bell peppers. *Vegetables:* carrots, yams, sweet potatoes, pumpkin.

- **YELLOW:** *Fruits:* bananas, lemons, figs, papaya, pineapple, yellow pears, yellow grapes, yellow tomatoes. *Vegetables:* corn, yellow potatoes.

- **GREEN:** *Fruits:* avocado, honeydew melon, green apples, green pears, green grapes (cut), green tomatoes, kiwi, limes. *Vegetables:* artichokes, arugula, asparagus, broccoli, broccoli rabe, Brussels sprouts, cabbage, cucumbers, endive, leeks, lettuces, green onion, okra, snow peas, sugar snap peas, green beans, celery, spinach, kale, herbs.

- **BLUE & PURPLE:** *Fruits:* blackberries, blueberries, plums, purple grapes (cut). *Vegetables:* purple cabbage, eggplant, blue and purple potatoes.

Other Colors

Of course, white and brown are not part of a "rainbow," but these "color" choices can help in your food planning and selection:

- **WHITE:** *Fruits:* bananas, white peaches, brown pears. *Vegetables:* cauliflower, garlic, kohlrabi, mushrooms, onions, parsnips, white potatoes, shallots, turnips, white corn. *Other Foods:* eggs, bread, cheese.

- **BROWN FOOD:** Brown eggs; meats.
Note: The USDA Food Guide Pyramid recommends five to nine servings of fruits and vegetables every day.

QUICK TIP Use the "Eating the Rainbow" metaphor as a jumping-off thought when you are shopping or cooking with your child. When shopping, suggest that you need three green veggies, two red fruits, or maybe a "white" food or one or two "brown" foods. Turn "eating your colors" into a family challenge. See who can eat at least five different colors (that is, five fruits and vegetables) every day.

DEEP DIVE

HEALTHY SNACKS ON THE GO!

Kids often need a healthy anytime snack to sustain their energy throughout their active day. Here are a few suggestions:

- **FRUIT SLICES:** oranges, seedless clementines, mandarin oranges, skinned apples. Or make fruit sticks with things that are usually considered veggies but (surprisingly!) are really fruits: cucumbers, peppers, zucchini, and summer squash.

- **VEGETABLE STICKS** cut from carrots and celery.

- **CHEESE QUESADILLA OR QUICHE SLICES** make a great to-go snack with protein. Make them for dinner, and then eat the leftovers throughout the week. (**Note**: Pack with an ice pack to keep the food safe.)

- **LOW-FAT YOGURT** is a filling snack that adds protein and calcium. (**Note**: Make sure to pack with an ice pack for safety, and include a spoon!)

- **RICE CAKES** are easy to grab and satisfyingly crunchy. Try adding peanut butter, lean meat, or low-fat cheese.

- **WHOLE-GRAIN CRACKERS** are easy to build into a mini-meal by adding cheese, hummus, or peanut butter.

this for me when I was a little girl." Or she may nibble some lettuce when you say, "I think you'll like this lettuce. It crunches just like your favorite vegetable, celery."

AGE 3

At three years old, your child recognizes more kinds of food and is more open to trying new ones. You may see this when your child includes different foods in his drawings. "It's oatmeal. Yum!" A child who sees a friend choosing carrots from a serving plate might take some, too.

232

QUICK TIP

Although we all live hectic lives, it's important to carve out a few nights a week to have family dinners. These are times to connect and talk about your day, give thanks for the food on the table, and share a healthy meal where new foods can be introduced to the whole family. Remember: Your child is watching what food choices are on your plate. Children who are involved in preparing meals are more likely to try new foods or recipes. Keep in mind that it's natural for a child to be hesitant about trying new foods, but don't give up. Be patient. It takes up to 8-12 attempts of little bites before this new food becomes a new favorite!

AGE 4

At four years old, your child is beginning to understand that some foods are healthier than others and shows this in his pretend play. You may see this when your child tells his sister that they are going to make a "healthy soup" at their pretend restaurant and puts different play vegetables into the pot. He might put the play cookies aside and pick up a banana, saying to his stuffed animal, "Cookies are a 'sometimes' food. Let's have a banana today because it's really good for you." He is more interested in new foods, and may express curiosity about an unfamiliar food on the dinner table and ask, "Is it yummy?" He also asks questions about different foods, fruits, and vegetables he sees when you are grocery shopping.

QUICK TIP

Impress upon your child the importance of drinking lots of water during and after exercise, and to keep her body cool and hydrated. Preschoolers are quick to understand the significance of drinking water during and after exercise. Consider equipping your child with her own water bottle, many of which are designed especially for kids with auto spouts, sippy gizmos, and cool designs.

KIDS IN THE KITCHEN

Cooking together with your child is one of the most rewarding activities you can engage in. Although baking a special birthday dinner or preparing holiday cookies is always a joy, you need not find a "special" occasion to cook together; try to include her as you are preparing dinner on an ordinary day. True, you may be rushed and busy, but it's worth slowing down for just a few extra minutes to introduce your child to healthy food and its preparation.

Children of different ages exhibit varying degrees of skill in the kitchen, but for the most part, the average two-year-old can help:

- Wash and scrub fruits and vegetables.

- Wipe off the work surface.

- Carry safe cooking utensils and small equipment to the work surface.

- Crush crackers and cookies into crumbs.

- Tear up lettuce and spinach leaves.

- Arrange foods on baking sheets and trays.

An average three-year-old can do whatever a two-year-old can do, plus help:

- Cut soft foods with a plastic serrated knife.

- Pour (with assistance) measured liquid ingredients into a bowl of dry ingredients.

- Stir or whisk ingredients together.

- Mix batter.

An average four- and five-year old can do all of the above, plus help:

- Measure (with assistance) dry ingredients.

- Mash soft foods together.

- Peel a banana or an orange if the skin has been loosened for them.

- Crack an egg (with assistance) into a bowl (but have some extra eggs on hand).

- Set the table (with assistance).

The above list of tasks is adapted from the National Network for Child Care's recommendations for cooking with children, and appeared, in part, in *Sesame Street B is for Baking* by Susan McQuillan.

OOPS & AHA

I am the mother of twins, and feeding them has always been a challenge. One was a particularly picky eater, so I often fell into the routine of feeding both of them the things I knew that the picky eater liked. (Oops!) One night I was making escarole and beans, and my non-picky eater asked to try it. She loved it! I learned to be more open-minded as a twin mom and not always assume that just because one doesn't like something doesn't mean the other needs to follow. (Aha!)

—Autumn, educational researcher & mom

FOOD TALK

Enthusiastic language used when shopping, cooking, reviewing menus, and eating healthy foods can help promote in your preschooler greater awareness of various foods, and encourage curiosity that will make him willing to sample new foods. Try these:

- I love fruit. It's yummy! It's so juicy and sweet!

- That's so crunchy and delicious.

- That's a red food! I'm eating part of the rainbow.

- Eat your colors!

- Where does this food come from?

- Healthy food tastes so good.

- Eating fruits and vegetables makes me stronger!

- Eating together makes me happy.

- I think I want to try something new, like . . .

- Want to try a bite? It's scrumptious/delicious/so tasty!

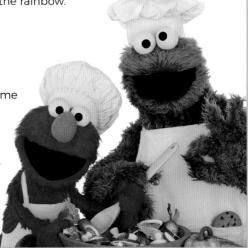

AGE 5

At five years old, your child understands that some foods are healthier than others and why different food choices are made. She might even say, "Milk is good for my bones!" after a grown-up asks her, "Why is milk good for you?"

GOOD STUFF!
KIDS' BOOKS ABOUT FOOD

Scores of books for children on the subject of food are on the market. Here are three very special ones.

– *How to Make and Apple Pie and See the World*, written and illustrated by Marjorie Priceman

This book celebrates a fruit-filled food and also takes children on a whirlwind tour of the origins of its farm-to-table ingredients.

– *I Will Never Not Ever Eat a Tomato*, written and illustrated by Lauren Child

This humorous title will appeal to the picky eater in your family.

– *Eating the Alphabet: Fruits and Vegetables from A to Z*, written and illustrated by Lois Ehlert

This beautifully illustrated title offers a fresh way to learn the alphabet and identify a host of fruits and veggies.

Don't forget about the excellent cookbooks that are readily available in bookstores and libraries. *Sesame Street* offers several that are specifically written for parents or other adults cooking together with preschoolers:

– *C is for Cooking: Recipes from the Street* by Susan McQuillan and Sesame Workshop

– *B is for Baking: 50 Yummy Dishes to Make Together* by Susan McQuillan and Sesame Workshop

– *Let's Cook!* by Susan McQuillan and Sesame Workshop

GOOD STUFF!

PLAYING WITH FOOD

Pretend-play with food offers crossover with so much early childhood learning. Here are some resources that are particularly helpful in prompting play that leads to discussions about food and healthy eating. Look for these and similar kits at toy stores or online.

- *Fruit and Veggie Prep Kit* by Curious Chef
  This six-piece kit will allow children to imagine themselves as a true chefs. Fully functional tools are sized and made as safe as possible for ages five and up; some are fine for younger children, too. The tools include a melon baller; a vegetable scrubber; an apple slicer; a vegetable peeler, a nylon knife, and a silicone spoon.

- *Play Foods & Grocery Items* by Melissa & Doug
  This line of quality toys offers play sets filled with pretend foods, child-size grocery baskets, and small pots, pans, plates, and cups, setting the stage for endless games of grocery store, restaurant, and pretend kitchen.

Moving Our Bodies, Resting Our Bodies

Certainly, as parents, we know that making sure your child is keeping physically active, coupled with ensuring that she is receiving enough rest, helps to keep your preschooler healthy and strong. Most children enjoy being active (if they had ample rest, are hydrated, and ate a nutritious meal or snack) in a variety of ways, from running and jumping, to climbing, dancing, swimming, and biking, to less intensive (but similarly beneficial) activities like stretching, yoga, and walking.

Keeping Active

Preschoolers should be given every opportunity possible to engage in safe, age-appropriate, physical activities. Encourage them to pay attention to the effects of activity and movement on their bodies. You might call your child's attention to the way his heartbeat pounds harder and faster when he moves fast, and slows down as he stops running and walks slowly.

Ask your child how good it feels to stretch up-up-up as "tall" as she can, or reach *waaaay* down low to tickle her toes. Admire the results of your preschooler's jubilant movement by praising how strong she is: "Can you make a muscle? Wow those are BIG muscles! You're so strong because you get up and move!"

When we allow children the time, safe play spaces, and basic tools to access a variety of options, they can explore the many ways to move. Your own child's

GOOD STUFF!
BOOKS ABOUT THE BODY

Although story time is one of those restful periods that a child needs in her day, books can provide inspiration for more active moments at other times. These are a few that will do just that, as well as some tools (a poster and an app) that will make it easy to keep kids moving, then help them get the rest they need.

- *The Busy Body Book: A Kid's Guide to Fitness* by Lizzy Rockwell

    A body is meant to be busy, this book affirms, and it celebrates all the ways it can get that way, as well as explores the parts and actions of the body used in all kinds of kid-happy activities.

- *Go, Go, Go!: Kids on the Move* by Stephen R. Swinburne

    Some children respond more powerfully to photographs of other children than to animal illustrations to incentivize them to get moving.

- *From Head to Toe*, written and illustrated by Eric Carle

    This book for younger preschoolers encourages them to copy a range of body movements first made by an animal, such as wave your arms like a monkey.

- *The ABCs of Yoga for Kids Poster* by Teresa Anne Power, illustrated by Kathleen Rietz

    With colorful illustrations for every letter, identifying simple gestures and yoga moves, this may entice children to begin or end the day with a peaceful pose.

enjoyment might come from bike riding, jogging, swimming, and hiking in nature with you. Perhaps she'll take to particular sports, such as soccer or T-ball, conducted with the appropriate safety measures and a focus on teamwork, rather than competition. Less intense activities move and shape bodies, too, including playing catch, running in and out of the sprinklers on a hot day, climbing the ladders of the slide, running to and away from the incoming waves of the shoreline beach, or flying a kite.

If your child gets in at least one hour of physical movement throughout the day, then you can both rest easy. Check in with her at the end of a busy day, by asking, "How have you used your body and moved today?"

What to Expect from Your Preschooler

AGE 2

At two years old, your child is starting to understand that sleep and rest help him stay healthy. You may see this when your child informs you that "Nap good for me." Or he might cover a doll or a stuffed animal with a blanket and say, "Sleep time!" At the same time, he'll proudly show you how fast he can run!

QUICK TIP Dancing is excellent exercise and something anyone can do, anywhere—including you and your preschooler. Turn up the music and use dance to kick-start mornings, a way to help digest a big dinner, or as a surefire way to release the wiggles before the bedtime routine. You can even dance in a car or a chair, with your arms and upper body. Check out the bouncy rhythms and refrain of *Sesame Street*'s "You've Got a Body" song, which may be just the ticket for a daily family dance party.

AGE 3

At three years old, your child probably more fully understands that both sleep and rest, coupled with being active, help her stay healthy, and that it's good to rest after exercising. You may see this when your child says, "I'm tired. It's time to sleep." She wants to run to make her "legs strong!" and, after running, says, "I need to sit so my legs can rest."

MOVE & LEARN

As you engage in playful physical activities with your child, sprinkle in movement, math, and literacy skills.

Follow My Pattern

Take turns creating dances that repeat patterns—everyone else follows along! For younger children, keep the patterns simple (jump, wiggle / jump, wiggle). For older children, the pattern might be "jump, jump, wiggle, hop / jump, jump, wiggle, hop."

ABC Stretch with Me

Draw a letter on paper, call out its name, and tell children to bend, stretch, and twist to form that letter as best they can. (Challenge older children to think of different words that begin with the letter while they move. Small groups may even spell out a short word, like "cat," with their bodies.)

Move & Count

Invite children to move their bodies in a certain way, a specific number of times ("Hop five times . . . turn three times!"). With younger children, count out loud on your fingers as they follow your directions. With older children, you might use simple number sentences in your directions ("Hop three and two times. How many hops all together did you do? Turn two and one time. How many turns all together did you do?").

Mathematical Obstacle Course

Create an obstacle course either inside or outside, then ask kids to perform the following actions, emphasizing the mathematical terms:

- Crawl *under* the table.
- Jump *over* the cushion or rope.
- Run *around* the chair.
- Skip *between* the pillows or trees.

The fun of physical movement is captured in a rich collection of words and phrases. Use these phrases when commenting on your child's movement games and active play:

- Show me how to . . .
- Let's see how many ways you can . . .
- Do you think you can . . . then . . . ?
- What about doing them *at the same time*?
- Show me a different way to . . .
- When I say "go" then you . . .
- Make believe you are playing. . . / What moves would you make?

PLAY & LEARN

BEDTIME ROUTINES

Once your child is in his PJs, snuggle up and try these ideas to help him transition to sleep:

- **WIND DOWN AND BUILD MEMORIES** by talking about the day together. Go over the things you did together during the day. What was your favorite part of the day? These cozy interactions establish bedtime as a time for sharing and comfort, as well as a time to give thanks and be grateful for all the wonderful things throughout the day.

- **PROVIDE CHOICES TO EMPOWER HIM TO SHAPE THE ROUTINE:** Pick two books and one song you both can sing together. Ask him which of his "friends" (plush toys and dolls) he wants to read a story with.

- **ENCOURAGE KIDS TO SAY GOODNIGHT TO OBJECTS** around the room (clock, toys), and also to the moon and stars. Then, it's your turn: Say good-night to your child's nose, elbows, and belly button!

- **END WITH A CALMING SONG**, such as "You Are My Sunshine" or any special song you share, followed by a good-night kiss and hug, and "I love you, see you in the morning."

AGE 4

At four years old, your child probably shows a slightly more complex understanding of the importance of rest, sleep, and being active. He may have ideas about what people can do to stay healthy; for example, he may encourage his sister to "Have a good rest at naptime so she's not too tired to play at the park later." He may suggest that *you* go outside to run to "get your muscles strong."

AGE 5

At five years old, your child probably shows an even deeper understanding of how rest, sleep, and being active keep us healthy. You may see this when your child reports that "Mommy was feeling sick. Her body needed to rest. She didn't go to the party and felt much better after her quiet day."

GOOD STUFF!

A few favorite books for reading at bedtime:

- *Time for Bed* by Mem Fox, illustrated by Jane Dyer
  Like a storybook lullaby, cozy and calming, this ritual of animal parents putting their young ones to bed will ease the transition into sleep.

- *Llama, Llama, Nighty-Night*, written and illustrated by Anna Dewdney
  This sweet board book is a great story to help young children learn the steps of a bedtime routine that ends with a snuggle and saying "nighty-night."

- *How Do Dinosaurs Go to Sleep?* by Jane Yolen, illustrated by Mark Teague
  With delightfully drawn illustrations, this book features dinosaurs performing traditional nighttime routines. A perfect book for bedtime reading.

- *Maisy Goes to Bed*, written and illustrated by Lucy Cousins
  Younger readers can help a beloved mouse, on her journey toward dreamland, performing routine tasks and more. With flaps and pulls, this mini-size board book is perfect for tiny hands.

- *All Tucked in On Sesame Street!* by Lillian Jaine, illustrated by Mary Beth Nelson
  Elmo, Oscar, Cookie Monster, and the rest of the Sesame Street friends get cozy and comfy—and ready for bed!

The Importance of Rest

Sleep is an essential component of healthy development—in fact, it is "required" for both physical and mental health. While most children have a hard time transitioning from their everyday activities to quiet time or sleep, establishing daily routines that include naps or quiet time and sleep provides a structure that children need.

As your child winds down, talk about how her body needs rest and sleep to recharge, so she has energy to be active again. Help kids to understand the importance of getting enough rest each day—not just through naps, but also quiet activities like sharing story time with you, listening to soothing music, playing a quiet game, or working on a puzzle. During this time, put your cell phone or tablet in its charging station and say it also needs to recharge its batteries to stay active when needed.

242

||||||||||||||||||||||||||||||||||||||||||||||||||||||||||||||||||||||||||||||||||

Conclusions

In response to a growing need to focus attention on nutrition and other healthy habits, *Sesame Street* developed goals and strategies for ensuring that children understand how these good-for-you behaviors support growth and well-being. Our messages to parents and children are about making choices that are healthy for the amazing body your preschooler already inhabits, and building healthy habits for life.

BREATHE, BALANCE, BEND—
A PERFECT WAY TO RELAX

Breathing, balancing, and bending give children (and adults!) a chance to rest their bodies and relax their minds, especially after rigorous exercise.

Breathe

Breathing deeply and slowly is a calming strategy for anytime, anywhere.

* Ask children to place their hands over their mouths and feel their breath. Together, breathe quickly, then slowly, and ask children to compare how each breath feels in their hands.

* Then ask children to pretend that their bellies are balloons. Encourage them to take long and deep breaths to fill the balloons with air, then breathe out through their mouths to let the air out.

Balance

Balancing helps kids focus and relax while building strength and coordination.

* Lay down a piece of string or tape on the ground as a "balance beam"! You can make the beam wide for an easier version of the game and narrower for a challenge.

* Use your imagination. For instance, you might pretend that the beam is high up in the air or over a rocky river—be careful not to fall!

Bend

Bending and stretching help children become more flexible . . . and it feels great!

* Ask kids to bend and stretch their whole bodies—from their head to their toes.

* Give clear directions, starting with the head. (Nod it "yes" and shake it "no." Next, roll the shoulders, twist the stomach, bend at the hips, and so on.) Get creative, and do more of the things that feel good!

From sesamestreetincommunities.org

BODY PARTS & HOW TO CARE FOR THEM

AGE 2	AGE 3	AGE 4	AGE 5
Knows some body parts, inside and out. • Begins to understand the need for self-care to be healthy. • Pats tummy and says, "Tummy hurt!" • Knows the need to visit the doctor when sick.	**Knows some internal parts of the body, and may talk about what they do.** • May talk about ways to stay healthy. • Says, "My bones help me stand up." • Says, "I need to brush my teeth now" after a bedtime glass of milk.	**Knows more about internal body parts.** • Points to chest and says, "My doctor helped me listen to my heart. It's pumping blood in my body." • Says, "My lungs helped me blow out the candle."	**Knows that certain grown-ups in the community help us stay healthy.** • "I want to become a dentist some day, just like my dentist, because she helped me with my toothache."
Is learning about personal care. • Follows a parent's lead and is starting to practice parts of the care routines. • Uses soap during hand washing when you say, "Now that our hands are wet, let's put some soap on them." • Imitates how you cough into your elbow, but might not do it quite right. • Tries to create a back-and-forth motion with a toothbrush after you've shown how.	**Does some personal care routines on own.** • Needs reminders on when and how to do them, and may forget some of the steps. • Washes hands but forgets to use soap. • Remembers to cough into elbow some of the time.	**Does more personal care routines on own, but may still need your help to remember all the steps.** • Remembers to wipe after using the toilet. • Forgets to flush.	**Does many personal care routines on own, and shares why they are important for health.** • Says to sister, "You have to wash your hands to get the germs off." • Remembers to brush teeth each morning and before going to bed.
			Understands how some behaviors keep us healthy. • Says, "I can see a plane way up in the sky. That's because I eat all my carrots and they give me strong eyes." • Puts a bandage on a cut, saying, "This will keep the germs away."

HEALTHY EATING

AGE 2	AGE 3	AGE 4	AGE 5
Identifies familiar foods and has preferences. • Pretends to make a fruit salad with play food and adds strawberries, saying "Yummy!" • Picks carrots out of meal and says, "No like carrots."	**Recognizes more kinds of food and is more open to trying new ones.** • Includes different foods in drawings. "It's oatmeal. Yum!" • Sees a friend choosing broccoli from a serving plate and takes some, too.	**Understands that some foods are healthier than others, and shows this in pretend play.** • Tells sibling that they are going to make a "healthy soup" at their pretend restaurant, and puts different play vegetables into the pot. • Puts the play cookies aside and picks up a banana, saying to a stuffed animal, "Cookies are a 'sometimes' food. Let's have a banana today because it's really good for you."	**Understands that some foods are healthier than others, and why different food choices are made.** • Says, "Milk is good for my bones!" when a grown-up asks, "Why is milk good for you?"
Needs encouragement to try new foods. • Tastes *arroz con leche* (rice with milk) after you say, "Mmm! Grandpa used to make this for me when I was a little girl." • Nibbles some lettuce when you say, "I think you'll like this lettuce. It crunches just like your favorite vegetable, celery."		**Is more interested in new foods.** • Is curious about unfamiliar food on the dinner table and asks, "Is it yummy?" • Asks questions about different foods, fruits, and vegetables she sees when you are grocery shopping.	

MOVING OUR BODIES, RESTING OUR BODIES

AGE 2	AGE 3	AGE 4	AGE 5
Is starting to understand that sleep, rest, and being active keeps one healthy. • Says "Nap is good for me." • Covers a doll or stuffed animal with a blanket and says, "Sleep time!"	**Understands how being active, rest, and sleep keeps one healthy.** • After running, says, "I need to sit so my legs can rest." • Says "I'm tired, It's time to sleep." • Wants to run to make his "legs strong!"	**Shows a better understanding of the importance of being active, rest, and sleep.** • Suggests that you go outside to run and "get your muscles strong." • Encourages his brother to "have a good rest at naptime so he's not too tired to play at the park later."	**Shows a deeper understanding of how being active, rest, and sleep keep us healthy.** • Says, "Mommy was feeling sick. Her body needed to rest. She didn't go to the party and felt much better after her quiet day.

8.
"I AM AN ARTIST"

Creating & Appreciating the Arts

By exposing your children to the arts, you foster an appreciation for the arts and inspire your children to create art. When children acquire the mind-set of " I am an artist," they develop the confidence to express their thoughts, emotions, and imagination through a creative medium. The "arts" include everything from the wide variety of visual arts (drawing, painting, sculpture, and photography), to music, dance and movement, and language-based arts, such as drama and other forms of shared storytelling. The "arts" also encompass many forms for what are commonly known as "crafts," such as sewing, knitting, quilting, and pottery.

The arts are powerful teaching tools, and help children learn a broad range of school-readiness skills. But note that this is the only chapter in this book in which we have not included developmental milestones. It is our belief that artistic development—and

QUICK TIP

Engaging in artistic expression with your preschooler might mean overcoming your own inhibitions or insecurities about being an "artist" yourself. Remember: Your child is not judging your "abilities or performances." They are enjoying with you the process of making art, and they don't care what the end product looks like or sounds like. So, as the classic *Sesame Street* song, "Sing!" says, "Sing, Sing a song"! And remember: It doesn't matter what your voice sounds like, so sing out loud. Together, make art, do crafts, make up dance moves to your favorite songs, retell stories, act out tales using a range of voices for characters, and play musical instruments along with your favorite songs. By doing these activities together, you are bonding with your child and creating lasting memories.

even artistic appreciation—is subjective, and it simply does not matter at what age a child learns to draw a flower, recite a poem, or carry a tune. A child's artistic expertise, whatever form it takes, should not be judged.

As we have shown throughout this book, *Sesame Street* uses the arts as a device to help teach academic skills (language, literacy, and STEM topics);

GOOD STUFF!
CELEBRATING ART IN A STORYBOOK

Illustrated storybooks are often themselves works of art, but these titles are a celebration of museums, finding beauty in mistakes, and other aspects of the fascinating subject of art.

– ***Sesame Street: Grover and The Everything in the Whole, Wide World Museum*** by Norman Stiles, illustrated by Mike Smollin

   This longtime *Sesame Street* favorite is currently only available on most ebook platforms, handy for when traveling to and from your own museum visits. Its compendium of amazing objects and art might encourage your child's own in-home art collection.

– ***Beautiful Oops***, written and illustrated by Barney Salzberg

   An instant "classic," this book celebrates the smears, smudges, and slips that can blossom from mistakes into something magical and marvelous.

– ***I Am an Artist*** by Pat Lowry Collins, illustrated by Robin Brickman

   This book shows how to find art in nature, such as in colored leaves, sea shells, or the shape of a cloud, and, in turn, be inspired to create.

– ***Mini-Masters Series***, by Julie Merberg and Suzanne Bober

   This collection of board books introduces young readers to great art, illustrated with masterpieces from the world's greatest artists, with a rhyming text by Julie Merberg and Suzanne Bober. The series includes: *A Picnic with Monet, In the Garden with Van Gogh, A Magical Day with Matisse, Dancing with Degas, Sharing with Renoir, Painting with Picasso,* and *Quiet Time with Cassatt.*

social skills (turn-taking, collaboration, and making new friends); emotional skills (labeling, expressing, and managing one's emotions); and health lessons (hygiene, healthy eating habits, and the importance of moving your body), *Sesame Street* also fosters an appreciation of the arts by portraying a wide range of accomplished artists, including painters, sculptors, singers, instrumental musicians, dancers, and actors, who demonstrate the various ways they express themselves through their particular art forms.

249

When Julia, a puppet character on the autism spectrum, was introduced on *Sesame Street*, she was paired with an art activity (painting), which she engaged in with her new friends. Julia was originally created as a character for a *Sesame Street in Communities* initiative, titled "See Amazing in All Children." This toolkit of resources was developed for families with a child on the autism spectrum, as well as for the general population to reduce misinformation and destigmatization regarding autism.

Julia, who has limited verbal skills, is a very talented painter who also loves to dance and sing with her friends. Painting provides a universal language for her to communicate with her new friends and for them to learn about Julia. As Elmo, Abby, and Julia paint together, they learn that Julia does things in a "Julia kind of way"—

QUICK TIP

Art exists all around you, not just in museums and books. Search the web for local "sculpture parks" and "public art" in spaces everyone can enjoy and even physically interact with. Also, point out beautiful commercial signs, lovely works of nature, and other sources of art. In turn, ask your child to point out artistic things she may see in her world! These conversations will also help build your child's vocabulary skills. Seeing art through your child's eyes and how they interpret the images and associations will surprise and delight you!

QUICK TIP

Applying the arts to learning can make school-readiness lessons especially memorable. One example: "The Alphabet Song," the most basic of tutorials set to music. Have you recognized that it is the same tune heard in "Twinkle, Twinkle, Little Star" and "Baa, Baa, Black Sheep"? If there's some routine or rule you'd love your little one to remember—how to set the table, follow bedtime rituals, or wait for the WALK sign to cross—make up a little song to that same familiar tune. Or try another melody you like, maybe the tune to "Wheels on the Bus." Through song, it's more likely kids will remember a routine and more happily put their toys away after playing.

A wonderful visual art "supply" that's always around is your child's shadow. Use it in all kinds of artistic ways. On sunny days, take a stick of chalk and trace your child's shadow, which she can fill it in with colorful patterns and designs. An older child might choose to label her body parts (to practice literacy) or fill in the outline with drawings that say something about that person, which cultivates empathy and understanding skills.

meaning that the behaviors Julia exhibits are unique to Julia and are not stereotypical of all children, or even all children with autism. In other words, when you see one child with autism, you see one child with autism. For example, Elmo and Abby like to finger paint, but Julia doesn't like the feeling of the paint on her fingers, so she prefers to paint using a brush. When they finish, they share and admire each other's paintings.

GOOD STUFF!

ART BOOKS FOR KIDS

These titles are just a handful of the many available in libraries, bookstores, and online that can spark your child's creative impulses.

- *Read, Yellow, Blue (and a Dash of White, Too)*, written and illustrated by C. G. Esperanza

    Wildly inventive illustrations leap off the pages of this story about a young artist and her unconventional, inspirational choices.

- *Mix It Up* by Hervé Tullet

    An interactive storybook that teaches how mixing colors makes a new color. Tullet, known by some as the "Prince of Preschool," is also the author of several other imaginative, interactive titles, including *Press Here, Let's Play!* and *Say Zoop!*

- *Perfect Square*, written and illustrated by Michael Hall

    Have paper (origami squares would be perfect!), scissors, and a hole punch handy after reading this book. Your artist won't be able to resist the urge to cut, fold, and imagine. By the author of *The Day the Crayons Quit*.

- *Lines that Wiggle* by Candace Whitman, illustrated by Steve Wilson

    Appropriate for very young preschoolers with its simple text and bold art, this book transitions to older kids with its clever use of line and rhyme.

DEEP DIVE

GUIDE & INSPIRE

For preschoolers, art is about the *process* of making the art, not the end product. Encourage your young artist to experiment with a variety of art tools and supplies, and to express ideas, thoughts, emotions, imagination, and creativity through her art—whatever it is. In short, it's not about aiming for a pretty picture—or even a recognizable image. It's about, among other things:

- OBSERVING what happens when your child moves a crayon to see how she can make a happy or sad face; or uses different brushstrokes to make a tree or a river.

- WONDERING—*TOGETHER* WITH YOUR CHILD—how art can be created. For example, how the paper can change with a fold or a snip; or how a song can change if it is sung slow or fast.

- EXPLORING various materials to see how they might "make art"—molding, rolling, squishing, and pressing clay to design sculptures; finding items in the natural world (leaves, twigs, feathers) and adding them to a picture, collage, or sculpture.

Here are some guidelines for nurturing creativity and art appreciation in your child:

- USE ART AS AN EXPRESSION OF HIS THOUGHTS, FEELINGS, ACTIONS, AND CHOICES. Ask your child to tell you about his artwork, which can range from scribbles (pre-representational) to representational images. Avoid making assumptions, as you may often be wrong, and, if you are wrong, your child may think he made a mistake. Encourage him to extend the process by asking, "What else can you add to that picture to add more to the story behind the picture?" By engaging in these behaviors, you foster his love of art by expressing your interest in his art process.

- FOCUS ON THE PROCESS OF MAKING ART AND NOT ON THE PERFECTION OF THE FINAL PRODUCT. Tell your child that "It's okay to make mistakes." When your child makes a mistake, just say, "Oops! The red paint dribbled! But maybe it adds to the picture!" Reassure your child that it is through mistakes that she is learning, and she should be open to exploring what new idea came from what she thought was a "mistake"!

- USE ART AS A SPRINGBOARD FOR GREAT CONVERSATIONS WITH YOUR CHILD! While you are looking at art together, ask your child what she thinks is happening in a picture or what she sees in a sculpture. Tell stories to each other about what *you* see.

- TALK ABOUT THOUGHTS AND FEELINGS THAT EMERGE FROM A PICTURE. "How is the person in the picture feeling? How do you know?"; "What is the person thinking about?"; "How do you feel when you see . . . ?"; "How does that shape make you feel?"; "How does the color make you feel?"

ART TALK

The visual arts offer so many opportunities to expand your child's vocabulary. Some of the words like the sampling below may appear challenging at first, but they are within the understanding of a child entering kindergarten because of the close association of word with an observable example, which gives them context:

- Artist
- Background
- Brushstroke
- Canvas
- Chalk
- Collage
- Creative
- Design
- Illustrator
- Landscape
- Loom
- Mosaic
- Outline
- Papier-mâché
- Pastel
- Pattern
- Photographer
- Portrait
- Pottery
- Sculpture
- Sketch
- Stencil
- Still life
- Textile

AN ARTIST'S TOOLKIT

Planning in advance for spontaneous play always pays off, in both time and creativity. It's easy to build a robust arts-and-crafts toolkit for kids as you go about your daily routine, so it's ready whenever they are to create some art!

• **BASICS.** In a box (inexpensive plastic boxes work well) or spare drawer, keep such essentials as crayons, chunky colored pencils, chalk, child-safe scissors, and construction paper in various colors, so they are ready the moment your child wants to make art.

• **PAPER SUPPLIES.** Paper is key, of course. Think beyond copy and construction paper, though. Instead of recycling colorful junk mail and holiday cards, add those to a collage-making scraps pile; include the "free" stickers and stamps that come with so many solicitations. Use a lidded tub to corral a handful of paper from your shredder. Collect paper towel, wrapping paper, and toilet paper tubes—essentials for art. Paper bags of all sizes are useful, too.

• **LARGE BOXES.** We can't overstate the simple pleasures of any oversized shipping and appliance boxes you can locate. They morph into stages, puppet theaters, or boats and buildings in dramatic play. Decorated by your child, a large box can become a private hideaway for dreaming, reading, and quiet coloring.

• **FOUND OBJECTS.** Think outside the box. Drop into your art toolkit those inevitable unmatched socks found when doing laundry; they can become hand puppets or be snipped into fabric scraps for mixed-media collages and other works. And, as you're clearing away after dinner, wash and add any empty lidded plastic tubs and bottles in interesting or stackable shapes to make sculptures.

• **SPECIAL INTERESTS.** If your child seems to have a special interest, such as in molding with clay, finger painting, or building things, make sure his "special" tools are put in a separate place, sort of a "toolkit" of their own. Oftentimes, these more specialized art forms require more supervision, especially with younger children.

It's often instinctive to respond with a smiling "That's beautiful!" or "I really like that!" when your child presents his art to you. Instead, talk to him about the specific choices he made. For example, you might say: "I like how you used that color there. Why did you pick that one?" Oftentimes, you can learn more about what's going on in your child's mind when you ask for information, rather than instantly labeling an object. Say, "Tell me about what you drew here." Ask about his inspiration and reaction to his own work: "What do *you* like most about your picture?"

The Visual Arts

The term "visual arts" encompasses many different art forms: drawing, coloring, and painting; photography; collage and mosaics; sculpture, clay play, and pottery making; stenciling and stamping; building structures with blocks, found objects, and other supplies; fiber arts, which include felting, sewing, weaving, and knitting—any method people use to create an object or image. With new media, even more visual art forms are being added to the past century's use of film, animation, and video.

You can guide children to share their ideas through images, especially at times when preschoolers don't yet have the spoken or written vocabulary to express them. Parents can also introduce the concept that appreciation of the visual arts is about observation and thinking skills. When looking at art together with your child, point out the details, think about how the artist expressed an idea, and talk about how each piece of art is unique. This maker/observer relationship expands preschoolers' interpersonal skills as well as developing a child's visual discrimination skills. For example, he gains the ability to notice details and sees how differences make letters, numbers, shapes, and colors unique, which supports his cognitive learning.

GOOD STUFF!

SESAME STREET ART MAKER: AN APP

This app (iOS and Android), which shows parents and kids how to make art, features 24 canvases (that change with the seasons) together with art tools and special effects. A great way to introduce the creative art-making process to kids.

DEEP DIVE

WHY MUSIC?

Music expands your mind, your heart, and your world—reason enough to enjoy music for its own sake! However, there are additional reasons that are important for your child's development.

- **MUSIC ALLOWS YOUR CHILD TO EXPRESS HERSELF IN A UNIQUE WAY.** Music offers a wonderful opportunity to express thoughts, emotions, and creativity. Urge your child to sing or bang on a drum—whatever medium presents itself. Remember: It's the process of making music that's important, not the performance.

QUICK TIP

Encourage your child to sing! Children, even as young as age two, discover favorite songs, which are quickly memorized and sung with expression. Your child may substitute words and make other playful changes to songs she knows well. Children understand that music reflects and inspires different moods (silly songs, playful songs, lullabies), or can tell a story.

- **MUSIC FOSTERS LANGUAGE DEVELOPMENT.** Studies indicate that the rhythmic patterns of music can link to and support language development. It may strain your patience, but hearing the same songs again and again is one of the experiences that builds memorization skills, an integral part of language development.

- **MUSIC PROMOTES EARLY MATH SKILLS.** Math skills, such as counting, relational concepts, and patterns, are all enhanced through an appreciation of music.

- **MUSIC REINFORCES FINE-MOTOR SKILLS.** Playing an instrument—even a pretend one—helps increase the dexterity needed to manipulate a recorder, drumsticks, a ukulele, or a triangle. Playing an instrument also contributes to the same small, muscle movements that children will use in school to write, tap on a keyboard or tablet, and interact with learning toys.

GOOD STUFF!
BOOKS AND MUSIC TOGETHER

Books that you and your child can sing along to or that celebrate the world of music and musicians are plentiful. Here are a few favorites.

- **What a Wonderful World, As Sung by Louis Armstrong** by Bob Thiele and George David Weiss, illustrated by Tim Hopgood
   Based on the 1967 best-selling song by Louis Armstrong "What a Wonderful World." A sweet, optimistic book with lovely illustrations.

- **Trombone Shorty** by Troy "Trombone Shorty" Andrews, illustrated by Bryan Collier
   Winner of both a Caldecott Honor and a Coretta Scott King Award, this beautiful picture book is an inspirational look at overcoming our circumstances to follow our dreams, in this case that of a young musician in New Orleans.

- **Sesame Street: Take Us Out to the Ballgame** by Constance Allen, illustrated by Tom Brannon
   The perfect tune to lure even a non-musically inclined kid (or parent) into a sing-along. The sporty theme proves that music can make any activity even better.

- **Zin! Zin! Zin! A Violin** by Lloyd Moss, illustrated by Marjorie Priceman
   This award winner, an exuberant introduction to the sounds that musical instruments make, is alive with sound itself. Like another classic, **Chicka Chicka Boom Boom**, it's one your child will want read aloud to her again and again.

- **Drum Dream Girl** by Margarita Engle, illustrated by Rafael Lopez
   Lyrical, dreamlike text tells the story of a little girl who refuses to believe she is not good enough to play the drums, and who makes the grown-ups on her island listen.

- **Goodnight Songs** by Margaret Wise Brown, illustrated by a variety of artists
   Offering songs that can help ease an often tricky transition, this book and CD combo provides gentle read-aloud bedtime lyrics from a newly discovered stash of songs written by the author of the beloved **Goodnight Moon**.

QUICK TIP Use music and song as a strategy with young children for calming down from a tantrum, easing the transition from one activity to another, or winding down from an active day and starting the bedtime routine. Music is also a motivator to get your child to move and groove or focus her attention. A quick silly-dance is a wonderful way to get the wiggles out!

256

MUSIC TALK

- **MUSICAL INSTRUMENTS.** Discuss the instruments your child might encounter in preschool (cowbell, chime, drum, horn, recorder, triangle, tambourine, piano), as well as instruments originating from cultures around the world, including conga drum, kettledrum, castanets, rainstick, didgeridoo, and glockenspiel, among many others.

- **PIECES AND PARTS.** Introduce words that describe the materials instruments are made from (wood, metal, plastic, horn, skins, etc.); the parts of instruments (keys, sticks, strings, neck, head); and the ways that children will manipulate them (strum, bang, shake, pluck, etc.).

QUICK TIP

Recordings of *Peter and the Wolf* are a terrific way to introduce some of the key instruments and sections of a classic orchestra: string section, percussion, oboe, bassoon, flute, clarinet, French horn, timpani. The short symphony, a fairy tale where each character is represented by a leitmotif—a recurring musical theme that is always played when they are mentioned in the narration—is a model for the use of music to tell a story, set a mood, and establish a personality.

- **STYLES OR GENRES.** Point out styles of music to your child: rock, pop, J-pop, classical, baroque, reggae, blues, jazz, metal, indie, gospel, R&B/soul, hip-hop/rap, country, electronic. And, of course, introduce children's songs by popular musical artists, such as Laurie Berkner and Raffi, to your child.

- **SOUND WORDS.** Children love to hear and say words that imitate the musical sounds and actions they describe. These include, among many others: clack, hum, hoot, buzz, ding-dong, click, jangle, shhh, swoosh, thud, thump, and zip.

- **MUSICAL TERMS.** Technical words used to describe the changes and variation in music, such as "pitch" (high/low), "tempo" (fast/slow), "rhythm" (pattern), "pulse" (beat), and "timbre" (tone),

MAKING MUSIC

"Let's make music!" Common household objects can make the most wonderful musical instruments: waxed paper folded over the teeth of a comb becomes a kazoo when a child presses it close to his lips and hums a tune; an empty tissue box and a few rubber bands turns into a guitar; and empty oatmeal tubs, plastic containers, and sand pails become drums. As the child in you well remembers, just add some wooden-spoon drumsticks.

Also try the other ideas below, and put on a family concert:

- **WIND INSTRUMENTS.** A long cardboard tube from a roll of wrapping paper can turn into a pretend clarinet or even resemble an Australian didgeridoo, a tube that makes a long, low note when blown.

- **JINGLE BELLS.** Pipe cleaners woven through the loops of holiday jingle bells can be shaped into bracelet-sized circles to shake.

- **SHAKERS.** Plastic bottles with caps can become shakers. Wash them well, peel off any labels, and fill them with lentils, dried peas or beans, orzo, or rice. You might create a whole "rattle orchestra" by filling bottles of different sizes and shapes, each with a different filling! The tubelike containers from chips or raisins, or even toilet paper tubes with their ends sealed by waxed paper, can also be turned into shakers.

QUICK TIP

Music provides excellent opportunities to expose children to different cultures, including your own family's musical background. Look for chances to share diverse music with your child by purchasing or streaming children's songs from around the world. For example, check out the Putumayo Library of Albums, a perennial favorite, which includes *Putumayo Kids World Playground*; *World Singalong*; *Dreamland: World Lullabies and Soothing Songs*; and *Kids World Party*.

Music & Song

Everyone can appreciate music, so expose your child to a range of musical styles and genres. It's not about carrying a tune (a challenge for many preschoolers and even some parents, too!) or symphonic perfection, but about making any kind of purposeful and joyful sound. That means music might take the form of rhyming or rhythmic, sing-song speech ("clean up, clean up, one-two-three!"), and singing lullabies and nursery songs while perhaps even clapping to musical patterns. Also, it's important to point out musical patterns in the environment, such as bird calls or even the beep-beep-beep-whoop-whoop of a car alarm.

Many studies have shown the educational benefits of music, when it comes to math, listening, and language skills; working memory; and social and emotional development, including collaboration and regulating emotions. Music can bond us. It connects children with their peers, of course, as they sing and play together, but it can also cross cultural and generational divides. A child, parent, and grandparent may all have sung some of the same songs as preschoolers ("You Are My Sunshine," perhaps) and are able to share the experience and introduce one another to additional well-loved tunes.

GOOD STUFF!
MUSICAL APP

- **Sesame Street Makes Music** (iOS and Android)
  Preschoolers can play along or make up their own melodies with the easy-to-master instruments in this app. They can follow along to on-screen prompts or enjoy a free-play mode that allows them to become music makers.

Movement & Dance

If you can move your body in any way, you can dance! What's more, dancing is fun! It allows your child to be active and energetic as he joyously expresses himself to the rhythm of the music. Dancing also promotes a range of school-readiness skills, such as self-control, coordination, spatial skills (as you move your body in space), and listening skills, especially through call-and-response songs, such as "Elmo's Slide" and "Hokey Pokey." So, turn on his (or your!) favorite music and dance!

260

QUICK TIP

Children don't need traditional music to move. Be open to the many sounds that can inspire a child to move his body. Together, observe leaves blowing in the wind, willow trees bowing, treetops swaying, or snowflakes drifting. Watch animals galloping, prancing, and pouncing. Listen to the sounds of nature, like falling raindrops. Talk to your child about these beautiful "musical" sounds, then make up a dance by imitating these sounds and movements from nature.

GOOD STUFF!
BOOKS ON DANCE

As with the other art forms, many marvelous books are available that use dance as a central theme. Here are a few favorites.

- ***Angelina Ballerina!*** by Katharine Holabird, illustrated by Helen Craig
  Several variations on Angelina's story (about a feisty little mouse who wants nothing more than to dance) have been published, but ***Angelina Ballerina*** is the original picture book that first introduced Angelina to her adoring fans.

- ***Dinosaur Dance!*** written and illustrated by Sandra Boynton
  The rollicking rhymes combined with the silly pictures of lumbering dinosaurs, are sure to inspire your youngest dancer.

- ***Dance!*** by Bill Jones, photos by Susan Kuklin
  A rare photographic book that features an adult male dancer. This book's clean photos and expressive poses provide great modeling for imitating moves.

- ***I Can Dance***, written and illustrated by Betsy Snyder
  This board book features die-cut holes that allow a child to poke her fingers through, under a tutu, to make legs for the illustrated ballet dancer.

DANCE TALK

As with the other arts, a wealth of vocabulary is associated with dance. Dance words range from the names of body parts, to dance styles, to specific moves. To introduce these words and develop your child's language skills, use them as you comment on her dances. Rather than saying "That was good!," notice and point out specific things, "You spun twice that time!" or "You pointed your toes at just the right time!"

- **BODY PARTS AND DANCE.** Just about every one of the commonly labeled body parts gets involved in dance, as kids follow directions from top to bottom, from "Tap your head" to "Make jazz hands," "Stomp your feet," and "Point your toes."

- **MOVEMENT WORDS.** For younger children, many familiar words can be associated with dance: "stand," "walk," "run," "hop," "jump," "spin," "kneel," "kick," "stretch," "bend," "twist." For slightly older children, more sophisticated movement words can be introduced: "shuffle," "roll," "gallop," "skip," "cross," "change places," "drop," "crawl."

- **DIRECTIONAL WORDS.** Words indicating direction (spatial-relational language) come naturally in dance: "backward," "forward," "up and down," "above," "below," "across," "through," "between." (Many of these are math words, describing relational concepts.)

- **SOCIAL WORDS.** Dance can engage children with words and phrases that help them cooperate in groups, navigate social situations, and strategize: "follow," "copy," "wait," "lead," "take turns," "before," "after," "next," "share."

- **DANCE WORDS.** Many dance styles have words that have wonderful sounds. These might spark curiosity among youngsters to see and learn some of their basic steps, to discover different cultures, or simply to use the rhythms of their music for free-play dance. Try out any that match your child's skill level: "waltz," "cha-cha-cha," "tango," "ballet," "jive," "swing," "tap," "flamenco," "polka," "break dance," "country," "disco,"and "belly dance." With older children, drill down to specific steps that may be challenging but are fun to say and can be demonstrated: "pirouette," "do-si-do," "moonwalk."

FREEZE DANCE

"Freeze Dance" is a fun activity to get your child moving and grooving while also building important school-readiness skills. The dance is simple: Wiggle, tap, jump, leap, and glide, while the music plays; freeze in place when the music stops. Once your child understands the rules of the game, he begins to build executive function skills, such as listening, self-control (controlling both her body and her mind), working memory (remembering the rules), and focusing her attention.

You can also add a few complexities to the game. Try using different songs to indicate different dance moves, such as one tune for leaping, another for twirling. By changing the rules, your child develops cognitive flexibility by holding multiple rules in his mind and being able to shift attention back and forth between the two sets of directions.

QUICK TIP

Elmo's got an endless variety of moves, as a quick search on *Sesame Street*'s curated and kid-safe YouTube channel will attest. His "Elmo's Got the Moves" video and "Happy Dance Tutorial" both walk (and jump and spin and wiggle) kids through simple, exhilarating movements that preschoolers can practice and master. After which, Elmo encourages children in song to show him "what *you've* got!"

DEEP DIVE

BENEFITS OF MOVING AND GROOVING

Dance is a language we all speak and share, even when our languages and customs are different. And, when dancing together, children are developing an array of social and executive function skills, such as turn-taking, collaboration, following directions, flexible thinking, and planning ahead. And, of course, the health benefits of active movement are obvious. Encouraging your child to dance accomplishes many things.

Model and support your child's movement and dance capabilities by:

- **ENCOURAGING ALL FORMS OF DANCING.** Urge your child to engage in silly, structured dances such as the "Hokey Pokey," "Chicken Dance," and "Elmo's Slide," as well as games and songs involving movement like "Ring-Around-the-Rosey." Allow plenty of opportunities for free-form dancing to different tempos of music as a way to explore how to move your body with unique personal style and flair. Remember: There's no correct way to dance, especially as your child explores how to move his body to the rhythm of the music.

- **ADDING SCARVES, BELLS, AND OTHER UNEXPECTED ELEMENTS.** Children enjoy moving their bodies with extra elements. Ask your child to invent a movement using a light, silky scarf or a bracelet of bells. Then, add music to see how her movements expand to the tempo of the music.

- **BREAKING DOWN MOVEMENTS, STEP BY STEP.** When demonstrating new movements and dances for a choreographed dance, break down the sequences into individual movements. Model specific arm and leg movements by moving slowly, and allowing enough time for your child to master each movement before going on to the next. Remember: Children learn best by repetition. Keep the dance patterns simple, as young children may only be able to mimic the pattern of three steps or moves at a time. Learning dance moves helps children build listening and memory skills as well as coordination.

- **ALLOWING DANCE TO EXPRESS HIS EMOTIONS.** Is your child feeling blue? Frustrated? Just plain wiggly? Dance can help your child express his emotions in a safe and fun way. Choose a melody that matches your child's strong emotions and let him dance to the music to get the "ickies" out.

Drama

"Come on, let's think. What if . . ."

Alongside "Once upon a time . . ." that phrase represents the best cue a parent can give a child to spark dramatic role-playing. All forms of theatrical storytelling—everything from pretend play with dolls, action figures, and vehicles, to puppet shows or even "staged" productions in your living room with dress-ups and homemade scenery and props—are essential elements of childhood.

Drama represents a "safe space" where a child can express his imagination and creativity, try out different roles he sees, reenact favorite stories inspired by books and television shows, work through his feelings and concerns, and resolve conflicts.

264

QUICK TIP

Just as visual artists in your family need a crafty toolkit, so do your young actors. Ensure that there's an available supply of stuffed toys, action figures, and toy animals available. When thinking "costumes box," don't get locked into just fantasy elements (crown, cape, wings, wigs) but toss in any discarded shirt, dress, hat, or pair of shoes from your closet, as well as other family members'. Kids love dressing as the grown-ups they know and see. Socks will become all kinds of outfit elements and props. Scarves are a kid's best friend, as are old towels, blankets, and tablecloths. As with your visual artist, never recycle a cardboard box before consulting with your in-home director. Who knows what it could become?

GOOD STUFF!
BOOKS THAT INSPIRE DRAMA

Any storybook on your child's bookshelf can become the spark to reenact part of the story, reimagine a new ending, or create a whole new story inspired by the characters. Here are some suggested titles to add to your collection.

- *Happy, Sad, Grouchy, Glad* by Constance Allen, illustrated by Tom Brannon
    Serving a dual purpose, this rhyming book models *Sesame Street* characters working together to put on a stage production. They act out rhymes about emotions, so the book also provides vocabulary for kids to use in their original works.

- *Mary Engelbreit's Nursery and Fairy Tales Collection* by Mary Engelbreit
    Classic tales are some of children's very first incentives for pretend play. This collection is age-appropriate and chock-full of inspiration.

"LET'S PUT ON A SHOW"

Creating a play, a "pretend" TV show, or a video with your child (and perhaps his siblings or a couple of his friends) can be loads of fun as well as a fertile learning experience for all. Ideas for short dramas are plentiful, through books, favorite TV shows, movies, or your child's own imagination. However, sometimes your imagination needs a jump-start. Try these "What if . . ." questions to help pivot a story that has hit a creative wall, stimulate a dramatic moment for your young actor, or end a squabble between dueling directors.

- What if a tiger escaped from the city zoo?
- What if she could only walk *backward*?
- What if he suddenly shrank and was teeny-tiny?
- What if they all had superpowers?
- What if there was a spell and no one could speak, except by singing? What would happen then?
- What if he was lost at sea / in a forest / on an island?
- What if she helped him?
- What if you could do magic?

Some vocabulary common in classrooms can first be introduced to preschoolers through dramatic play at home. You can talk about what these words mean in an appropriate way through the context of pretend play or when prompting or responding to your child's playacting. Some of these are more complex, theater-specific terms, but even if they seem challenging ("improvise" or "rehearse," for example) they are appropriate to introduce to young children within the context of active pretend play.

- Applause
- Appreciate
- Attention
- Build
- Debut
- Decorate
- Direct
- Enter
- Exit
- Imagine
- Improvise
- Musical
- Performer
- Play
- Practice
- Pretend
- Prop
- Rehearse
- Role
- Scenery
- Script
- Spotlight
- Stage
- Theater
- Wardrobe

Pretend play may appear instinctive for young children, but, in fact, many children need a little help getting role-playing and storytelling started. On *Sesame Street*, we recently modeled how children can set up their pretend play. The following scenarios are simple and expansive to allow for your child's unique creative "voice" to shine through.

- **RESTAURANT / KITCHEN / GROCERY.** As parents know well, the following questions are just about all it takes to get a child off and running with role-play: "How about we set up a bakery / pizza shop / café / ice-cream parlor / supermarket? Who is the customer today?" This role is so popular that it helps to keep the props consistently on hand: clean, empty, food boxes and other food containers (including a small, unused pizza box begged from your local shop); serving pieces, including paper plates, plastic cups, cloth napkins, plastic kitchen utensils; a notepad for "taking orders" or "making grocery lists"; plastic play foods; toy shopping carts; and play money,

- **DOCTOR / NURSE / HOSPITAL.** One of your best investments may be a simple, inexpensive, toy doctor's kit. Look for one with realistic-looking replicas of the tools your child might encounter in a routine visit—and without any gender-specific graphics to avoid stereotypes. You can also use household objects,

QUICK TIP

Because children love playing jobs and careers (doctor, teacher, etc.), watch (together with your child) "Abby's Amazing Adventures" on *Sesame Street*. In their play, children are often limited to only what they see in their own lives, so this show segment features a range of careers. The goal is to inspire young children to aspire—that is, if I can "See It," I can "Play It," and one day I can "Be It." Among the professions introduced on the show are photographer, veterinarian, marine biologist, rancher, dance choreographer, race car driver, volcanologist, and museum curator! If your child singles out a favorite "career," encourage "career" play—perhaps even research the career details together.

such as headphones (stethoscope), flashlight (ear scope, but avoid shining it in your child's eyes), wooden spoon (reflex hammer to lightly tap knees), tongue depressor (thermometer), measuring stick and scale (measure height and weight), and an empty water bottle (medicine). Augment with true-life supplies that will make your young actor feel even more empowered, like real bandages, gauze, cotton balls, etc. When a doll or toy gets broken, hold onto it—it can become a prop in a hospital scene that your preschooler directs. Prompt with "Oh no! This baby has spots AND STRIPES! What do you think is wrong, Doctor?" Another popular variation is to play "Veterinarian" or "Animal Trainer."

- **VEHICLE DRIVERS.** Cars, trucks, buses, taxicabs, airplanes, helicopters, railroad trains, boats—vehicles of all sorts—stimulate the imaginations of children. Kids love to pretend they are the masters of any sort of vehicle; even very young children, when simply sitting in a cardboard box, can imagine they are driving a car. Older kids will enjoy pretending to pump gas, fix an engine, or organize a road trip in an SUV or a long-haul truck. They will also enjoy turning vehicle driving into a full-blown profession, such as bus driver, ambulance driver, taxi driver (including a water taxi), train engineer, firefighter, airplane pilot, even an astronaut. Suggest that she tie a small wagon to her tricycle to create a truck rig, a train, or a bus, then fill the wagon with stuffed animal "passengers." Fit your child for her chosen vehicle with relevant accessories: an appropriate hat, sunglasses, toy cell phone, maps (or GPS), and maybe a tool or two to make repairs. Talk to your child about "driving" safety, including wearing a seat belt (or a floatation device, should the vehicle be a boat), reading signs (even nonreaders will recognize STOP), and following the rules of the road, water, or air.

Imaginary play and storytelling help build essential school-readiness skills, among them:

- **IMAGINATION.** The dramatic arts broaden children's thinking, planning, and imagination as they develop the roles and scenarios while creating their story.

- **LANGUAGE.** By talking through their ideas and often narrating their play, children are adding new and expressive words, many of which include emotional language. The recognition, labeling, and expression of emotions are the heartbeat of dramatic play. Such storytelling provides a glimpse into your child's worries, joys, and growing awareness of themselves as independent thinkers.

- **EMPATHY.** By acting out a role in a story, a child puts himself in "someone else's shoes." When your child thinks *as* his character and acts out that character's emotions and behaviors, he is taking on the perspective of another. This is an important skill in the development of empathy and compassion.

- **SOCIAL SKILLS.** When dramatic play involves an ensemble, your child is building important skills, such as focused attention (staying in character), turn-taking, listening, sharing, communication, and conflict resolution, especially as they negotiate their roles.

- **SELF-CONFIDENCE.** The flexibility to adapt to the improvisations and plans of other children and to express themselves freely helps your child to think outside her normal comfort zone.

QUICK TIP Children will act out familiar routines, especially ones that involve their slightly younger selves, like bottle-feeding and changing diapers. They'll pretend to talk on the phone and mimic other actions, so have plenty of real and symbolic items—such as a block to be used as a telephone—handy for these tiny dramas. As with the other arts, your participation as audience or co-performer is key to your child's development.

|||||||||||||||||||||||||||||||||||||||||||||||||||||||||||||||||||||||||||||||||||||||||||||||||||||||

Conclusions

The arts are an integral part of every aspect of *Sesame Street*'s preparations for school readiness. All facets of the arts, including visual arts, music, dance, and drama, play a role in enhancing your child's literacy, math, science, health, social, and emotional skills. What's more, every aspect of the arts inspires joy, both for you and for your child.

FURTHER INFORMATION

A lthough hundreds of books are available that provide excellent advice, here are a few resources that we found particularly useful for parents of preschool-aged children.

SESAME STREET IN COMMUNITIES (SESAMESTREETINCOMMUNITIES.ORG)

Sesame Street in Communities is a model that provides national and local partners and providers with resources to help children and their families. In addition, it's a constantly growing and evolving website that builds on *Sesame Street*'s 50-year commitment to addressing kids' intellectual, developmental, physical, and emotional needs. The program provides hundreds of bilingual, multimedia tools to help kids and their families (including parents and caregivers) enrich and expand their knowledge during a child's early years, from birth through six, a critical window for brain development. These resources engage kids and adults in everyday moments and daily routines relating to scores of subjects—from teaching early math and literacy concepts, to encouraging families to eat nutritious foods, to dealing with serious life issues, such as divorce and food insecurity.

BORBA, MICHELLE, EDD. *Unselfie: Why Empathic Kids Succeed in Our All-About-Me World.* New York: Touchstone (reprint ed.), 2017.

With easy-to-implement techniques, engaging stories, and practical advice, *UnSelfie* shows parents how to make sure your children learn one of the most useful lessons in life: empathy. Hailed by experts as an "absolute must-read for parents."

CONNER, BOBBI, AND ILLUSTRATED BY DENISE HOLMES. *The Giant Book of Creativity for Kids.* Boston: Roost Books, 2015.

A guide to being a creative parent or caregiver, with over 500 arts, crafts, writing, singing, and dancing activities, designed to encourage children to discover their imaginative selves. This book is for kids ages 2 to 12, but scores of activities are created especially for preschoolers.

GALINSKY, ELLEN. *Mind in the Making: The Seven Essential Life Skills Every Child Needs.* New York: William Morrow, 2010.

A guide to raising children to be well-rounded and achieve their full potential, helping them learn to take on life's challenges, communicate well with others, and remain committed to learning. Ellen Galinsky is president and co-founder of the Families and Work Institute, and was on the faculty of Bank Street College of Education for 25 years.

GOLINKOFF, ROBERTA MICHNICK, PHD, AND KATHY HIRSH-PASEK, PHD. *Becoming Brilliant: What Science Tells Us about Raising Successful Children.* Washington, D.C.: American Psychological Association, 2016.

These authors provide a science-based framework for how we should be teaching children in and outside of school. The authors introduce the six Cs—collaboration, communication, content, critical thinking, creative innovation, and confidence—the skills that ensure a child's academic and social success in our world. Each chapter includes tips to optimize children's development in each area.

JANA, LAURA, MD. *The Toddler Brain: Nurture the Skills Today That Will Shape Your Child's Tomorrow.* New York: Lifelong Books, 2017.

This book offers fresh, practical, and innovative thinking about how 21st-century parents can help their young children thrive and achieve future success. Lots of advice and tips to empower parents.

KLEIN, TOVAH, PHD. *How Toddlers Thrive: What Parents Can Do Today for Children Ages 2–5 to Plant the Seeds of Lifelong Success.* New York: Touchstone, 2014.

This book is unique in that it is written from the point of view of the child. Dr. Klein's experience with young children gives parents an understanding of child development within the context of family dynamics. She empowers parents with knowledge about the whys behind their children's behaviors.

KAMENETZ, ANYA. *The Art of Screen Time: How Your Family Can Balance Digital Media and Real Life.* New York: Public Affairs, 2018.

Anya Kamenetz, an expert on education and technology and mother of two young children, takes a practical, even critical, yet supportive look at the subject of technology in the home. Surveying hundreds of fellow parents on their practices and ideas, she hones a simple message, a riff on Michael Pollan's well-known "food rules": Enjoy screens. Not too much. Mostly with others.

PRUETT, KYLE D., MD. *Fatherneed: Why Father Care Is as Essential as Mother Care for Your Child.* New York: The Free Press, 2000.

A how-to guide for fathers that gives children skills needed to develop into happy, healthy adults. The book covers childhood, from birth to late adolescence; the preschool years are covered extensively. It offers useful information for mothers and other caregivers, as well as fathers. Dr. Pruett is also the author of several other useful books, including *Me, Myself, and I: How Children Build Their Sense of Self*, and *Partnership Parenting* (with Marsha Kline Pruett).

SANTOMERO, ANGELA, MA. *Preschool Clues: Raising Smart, Inspired, and Engaged Kids in a Screen-Filled World.* New York: Touchstone, 2018.

By the co-creator of *Blue's Clues,* and creator of *Daniel Tiger's Neighborhood,* this book shows parents (and educators) eleven research-based, foundational "clues" that lay the groundwork for preschooler's academic, social, and emotional growth.

SIEGEL, DANIEL J., AND TINA PAYNE BRYSON. *The Whole-Brain Child: 12 Revolutionary Strategies to Nurture Your Child's Developing Mind.* New York: Bantam Books, 2012.

Erudite (based on the latest neuroscience), tender, and even funny, this reader-friendly book helps parents nurture kind, happy, emotionally healthy kids. The book examines parenting from birth through adolescence.

SUSKIND, DANA, MD. *Thirty Million Words: Building a Child's Brain.* New York: Dutton, 2015.

The founder and director of the Thirty Million Words Initiative, Dr. Suskind explains why the simplest thing you can do for your child's future success in life is to talk to him or her. This book reveals the recent science behind this truth, and outlines precisely how parents can best put it into practice.

271

ACKNOWLEDGMENTS

Ready for School! is based on Sesame Workshop's 50 years of research and development in early childhood education, including the *Sesame Street Whole-Child Curriculum* and the *Sesame Street Framework for School Readiness*. The *Framework* was guided and informed by the key standards and best practices in early childhood education, including The Head Start Child Development and Early Learning Framework, Teaching Strategies Gold Objectives for Development and Learning (ODL) assessment tool, and external advisors.

We could not have written this book without help of these esteemed professionals:

ACADEMIC CONTRIBUTORS TO THE *FRAMEWORK FOR SCHOOL READINESS*: Arthur Baroody, Ph.D.; Karen Bierman, Ph.D.; Nancy Brasel, M.Ed.; Sue Bradekamp, Ph.D.; Jeff Capizzano, M.P.P; Stephanie Carlson, Ph.D.; Douglas Clements, Ph.D.; Kathy Conezio, Ph.D.; Anne Culp, Ph.D.; Emily DeGroof, M.A.; Mia Doces, M.Ed.; Ellen Frede, Ph.D.; Sumi Hagiwara-Gupta, Ph.D., Judith Levin, Ph.D.; Joan Lombardi, Ph.D.;. Sara Sweetman, Ph.D.; Barbara Tinsley, Ph.D.; and Hiro Yoshikawa, Ph.D.

SESAME WORKSHOP EDUCATION CONTRIBUTORS TO THE *FRAMEWORK FOR SCHOOL READINESS*: Lewis Bernstein, Ph.D., Jeanette Betancourt, Ed.D., Mindy Brooks, M.A., Jessica DiSalvo, Maria del Rocio Galarza, M.A., Nancy Garrity, M.A., Akimi Gibson, M.A., Jennifer A. Kotler, Ph.D., Alicia Narvaez, M.P.A., Michelle Newman-Kaplan, M.A., Jennifer Schiffman-Sanders, M.A., Susan Scheiner, M.A., and Autumn Zitani, M.A.

SESAME WORKSHOP CURRICULUM AND EDUCATION EXPERTS: We are truly grateful to work with a dedicated and talented team of educators. This book would not be possible without their collective knowledge and hard work as co-keepers of the ever-evolving *Sesame Street Whole Child Curriculum*.

Specifically, we would like to thank: Lewis Bernstein, former Executive Vice President of Education, Research, and Outreach, for his leadership in the development of curricula over the years and for initiating the *Sesame Street Framework for School Readiness*; Alicia Narvaez for leading the team in transforming the original *Framework* into parent-friendly language; Jen Schiffman-Sanders for reading drafts of every chapter of *Ready for School!,* and ensuring that we reflected the busy lives of parents; Jessica DiSalvo for her unwavering patience in response to endless requests for documents and her incredible memory regarding show content; and Susan Scheiner for graciously researching the content library for illustrative show segments.

SESAME WORKSHOP PUBLISHING TEAM: We were helped in myriad ways by our colleagues in the publishing division. Infinite thanks go to Vice President and Publisher Jennifer A. Perry and Editorial Director Karen Halpenny, invaluable guides and champions from start to finish—their contributions to this book are immeasurable.

Executive Editor Betsy Loredo earns special kudos for stepping in to write first drafts of several chapters when we were under tremendous pressure to deliver our manuscript. We are very grateful for her swiftness, unique brand of creativity, deep knowledge of the *Sesame Street* art and photo archives, and unflagging teamwork.

Speaking of speedy, we also express our gratitude to Caitlin Reynolds, who pulled together countless bits of art and photography with lightning speed; we would have been lost without her help. And, too, the rest of the team—Jenna Fishner, Leslie Kimmelman, Lili Lampasona, Bridget Miles, Paul Roberts, and Jonathan Shaw—thank you for your support.

SESAME WORKSHOP CREATIVE TEAM: Special thanks go to the Creative team which generously helped out with advice and expertise, including Vice President & Creative Director Theresa Fitzgerald; Senior Design Director Vanessa Germosen; Senior Director Production Pam Aviles; Design Director Molly Hein; and Creative Director, Character Design Louis Mitchell.

OTHER CONTRIBUTORS: Others inside and outside the Workshop offered valuable help in many ways and have earned our deep gratitude: Glace Chou, Kerri Conti, Sara Drake, Kama Einhorn, Bobbi English, Sheila Funaro, Conrad Lochner, Jane Nash, Jerry Nash, Jessica Sullivan, and Ann Thomas.

FRIENDS AT RUNNING PRESS: Throughout the book publishing process, the team at Running Press was a pleasure. We greatly appreciate their commitment to preschool education, which allows us the opportunity to reach parents and caregivers with this book. We especially offer thanks to Publisher Kristin Kiser, Editorial Director Jennifer Kasius, Managing Editor Hannah Jones, Marketing and Publicity Director Jessica Schmidt, Digital Manager Cassie Drumm, Publicist Seta Zink, and Creative Director Frances Soo Ping Chow.

From Rosemarie Truglio

In my role as Senior Vice President of Curriculum and Content, I have had the distinct joy of working with a talented staff, many of whom participated in the creation of the *Framework*. Together we have learned a tremendous amount about children's needs and the best educational approaches to address those needs. I am particularly grateful to all our educational advisors through the years for lending their expertise and guidance. Special thanks go to Autumn Zitani for being my other right hand so that I could carve out time to write this book, and to Brown Johnson, EVP and Creative Director, for her commitment to reaching and teaching children, and for all her support and help, making it possible for me to write this book.

To my husband Steve and son Lucas, thank you for all the encouragement and love that not only inspired me throughout the writing process but sustains me each waking day! I am truly blessed and grateful for your patience, especially when I was stressed and sleep-deprived and when deadlines interfered with weekend plans and family vacations. Lucas, you taught me the importance of following your lead, and our experiences (both joyful and challenging) helped me be a better mom, educator, and person. Steve, my parenting partner, biggest fan, best friend and gifted editor, your love and support grounds me and inspires me to be the best person, wife, and mother.

To Pam Thomas, my co-writer and editor: I have truly enjoyed our writing journey together, all the talks we shared about child development, personal histories, and *Sesame Street* stories. I am grateful for your tireless dedication to translating theory into practice and for the thoughtful design of this book, for your patience, encouragement, and most of all, friendship.

From Pamela Thomas

My work as a children's book editor at Sesame Workshop has been one of the proudest achievements of my professional life. I had been an editor of adult books for many years when Jennifer Perry took a chance and hired me to write children's books. That was 13 years ago, and I never looked back. I am so fortunate to work with an incredible group of intelligent, curious, and endlessly witty people. Frankly, I thought a job couldn't get much better, but it did!

Working with Rosemarie Truglio to create *Ready For School!* surpassed even my already-amazing Sesame Workshop experiences and expectations. Rosemarie's expertise, professionalism, intelligence, kindness, and warmth have been a tremendous learning experience for me, and her humor has been a delight. Best of all, I made a new friend!

Finally, I want to acknowledge Sedgwick Ward, who appeared in my life in the midst of this book's writing process, and turned it upside down. Among many special things he is and does, I am grateful for his patience, generosity, good humor, and, most of all, his willingness to dine many-a-night at Memo's.

INDEX

SESAME WORKSHOP™

About Sesame Workshop

Sesame Workshop is the nonprofit media and educational organization behind *Sesame Street*, the pioneering television show that has been reaching and teaching children since 1969. Today, Sesame Workshop is an innovative force for change, with a mission to help kids everywhere grow smarter, stronger, and kinder. We're active in more than 150 countries, serving vulnerable children through a wide range of media, formal education, and philanthropically-funded social impact programs, each grounded in rigorous research and tailored to the needs and cultures of the communities we serve. For more information, please visit sesameworkshop.org.

THEY'RE FAMOUSE . . .
THEY'RE FABUMOUSE . . .
AND THEY'RE HERE
TO SAVE THE DAY!
THEY'RE THE

HEROMICE

AND THESE ARE THEIR
ADVENTURES!

Geronimo Stilton

HEROMICE

CHARGE OF THE CLONES

Scholastic Inc.

www.geronimostilton.com

Published by Scholastic Inc., *Publishers since 1920,* 557 Broadway, New York, NY 10012. SCHOLASTIC and associated logos are trademarks and/or registered trademarks of Scholastic Inc.

Stilton is the name of a famous English cheese. It is a registered trademark of the Stilton Cheese Makers' Association. For more information, go to www.stiltoncheese.com.

This book is a work of fiction. Names, characters, places, and incidents are either the product of the author's imagination or are used fictitiously, and any resemblance to actual persons, living or dead, business establishments, events, or locales is entirely coincidental.

ISBN 978-1-338-11660-1

Text by Geronimo Stilton
Original title *Superallarme, supertopo in fuga!*
Original design of the Heromice world by Giuseppe Facciotto and Flavio Ferron
Cover by Giuseppe Facciotto (design) and Daniele Verzini (color)
Illustrations by Luca Usai (pencils), Valeria Cairoli (inks), and Serena Gianoli and Daniele Verzini (color)
Graphics by Francesca Sirianni and Chiara Cebraro

Special thanks to Kathryn Cristaldi
Translated by Julia Heim
Interior design by Kevin Callahan / BNGO Books

10 9 8 7 6 5 4 3 2 1   17 18 19 20 21

Printed in the U.S.A.   40

First printing 2017

When darkness falls over Muskrat City, the Sewer Rats slither into the alleys to cause chaos aboveground. But the citizens of Muskrat City know that there are mysterious figures watching over them, ready to fight evil at all costs.
They are strong, they are invincible, they are fearless — well, almost . . .
They are the Heromice!

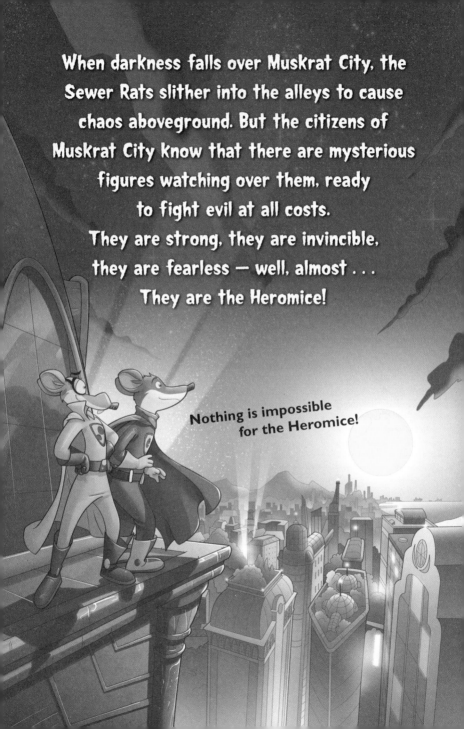

Nothing is impossible for the Heromice!

MEET THE HEROMICE!

GERONIMO SUPERSTILTON

The strongest hero in Muskrat City . . . but he still must learn how to control his powers!

SWIFTPAWS

Geronimo Superstilton's partner in crimefighting; he can transform his supersuit into anything.

LADY WONDERWHISKERS

A mysterious mouse with special powers; she always seems to be in the right place at the right time.

TESS TECHNOPAWS

A cook and scientist who assists the Heromice with every mission.

ELECTRON AND PROTON

Supersmart mouselets who help the Heromice; they create and operate sophisticated technological gadgets.

AND THE SEWER RATS!

TONY SLUDGE

The undisputed leader of the Sewer Rats; known for being tough and mean.

TERESA SLUDGE

Tony's wife; makes the important decisions for their family.

SLICKFUR

Sludge's right-hand mouse; the true (and only) brains behind the Sewer Rats.

ELENA SLUDGE

Tony and Teresa's teenage daughter; has a real weakness for rat metal music.

ONE, TWO, AND THREE

Bodyguards who act as Sludge's henchmice; they are big, buff, and brainless.

I'M AN EXPERT!

It was a beautiful spring **morning**. The sun was shining, the birds were **SINGING**, and the flowers were **BLOOMING**. It was a perfect day outside, but I was sitting in my office. The night before, two messengers had delivered the **TURBOCOPIER 9000**, our new high-tech photocopier. It was sleek, sophisticated, and **SUPERCOMPLICATED**!

I was reading the instructions manual when . . .

Oops! I'm sorry—I haven't introduced myself yet. My name is Stilton, *Geronimo Stilton*, and I am the *publisher* of *The Rodent's Gazette*, the most famouse **newspaper** on Mouse Island!

Anyway, as I said, I was reading away when my cousin Trap **BURST** in.

"Trap!" I exclaimed. "What are you doing here?"

"Oh, not much, Germeister," he squeaked. "I just stopped in to say hi!"

Then he noticed the new superphotocopier. "Wow! Is

Hey, Cousin!

Huh?

that the Turbocopier 9000?" he asked. "I've always wanted to get my paws on one of those."

"Well, I haven't quite figured out how it works," I said.

"Ah, don't worry about reading the instructions, Cuz!" Trap replied, waving his paw dismissively. "I'm an **expert** on all things **electronic**!"

Before I could protest, he began **HITTING** buttons on the copier.

Nothing happened.

Then Trap's eyes lit up. "This might do the trick!" he exclaimed. With a loud smack, he hit a giant **RED** button on the side of the copier.

SSSQUiRttt!

A stream of ink shot out of the copier, staining my favorite green jacket.

Holey cheese, what a huge **DISASTER**!

"Oops, sorry, Ger." Trap giggled. "Hee, hee, hee! I was sure that was going to be the right button!"

Aaaack!

I was about to yell at him when the phone rang.

Riiiing! Riiiing! Riiiing!

Now what?

I picked up the phone.

"What took you so long, Geronimo?!" A familiar voice squeaked. It was my friend **HERCULE POIRAT**. He is also known as Swiftpaws, my Heromouse partner!

"Get your tail in gear, Geronimo! The Heromice are needed in Muskrat City! I'll be waiting for you at the Central Bank! Now *hurry, hurry, hurry*!"

"Um, what? I mean, how? I mean, why?" I babbled.

But it was too late. My hero partner had already hung up on me!

How rude!

Meanwhile, Trap was still PUNCHING buttons on the Turbocopier.

"Ahem, Trap, I need to run out," I squeaked as I headed for the door.

"No worries, Geronimo!" my cousin cried. "I'll handle the Turbocopier 9000. When you get back, it will work perfectly!"

I doubted it, but I couldn't worry about Trap or the copier. I had **BIGGER** problems!

Once I was outside, I ducked behind a lamppost and pressed the secret button on my Superpen.

Swoooooshhhh!

In an instant, I had transformed into my alter ego, Superstilton. The **green** super-ray surrounded me from my whiskers to my tail. Soon, I was flying through the air with my supercape BILLOWING behind me.

Too bad there was a hot air balloon festival taking place that day.

I bumped into one hot air balloon with my snout. *Bonk!*

Then I bounced into another balloon and landed on my tail. **Boing!**

Next, I crashed into a third balloon. **SMACK!**

Finally, I slammed into a fourth. CRASH!

Holey cheese balls, what a superblooper!

Help!

PAWS UP, SLUDGE!

Before long, I arrived at the Central Bank of Muskrat City. **Swiftpaws**, **Tess Technopaws** (the genius scientist and cook for the Heromice), and helpers **ELECTRON** and Proton were waiting for me.

Commissioner Rex Ratford was also there, yelling into a bullhorn, "Come out with your paws up, Tony Sludge!"

Immediately, my paws began shaking. Tony Sludge was the

Paws up, Sludge!

leader of a crew of **criminal** Sewer Rats. Whenever Tony appeared, trouble followed.

"Tony is in the b-b-bank?" I stuttered.

"Yep," Swiftpaws confirmed. "He's in there! The Sewer Rats were **robbing** the bank when the bank manager hit the **alarm**."

"Catching those cheeseheads will be a snap for us Heromice!" a voice added.

I **whirled** around and came snout-to-snout with the smart, **STRONG**, and beautiful **Lady Wonderwhiskers**! My heart began to **POUND WILDLY**. Oh, what a fascinating hero-rodent!

I was staring **dreamily** at my crush when Swiftpaws exclaimed, "**HEROMICE IN ACTION!**"

Then my hero colleagues raced into the bank, **DRAGGING** me along with them!

Inside the bank, the manager and the tellers were in a corner, gagged and tied up.

The safe was open, and the Sewer Rats were loading up bags of money!

Tony Sludge; his assistant, SLICKFUR; and his bodyguards, ONE, TWO, and THREE, didn't even notice us.

Swiftpaws snuck up behind them.

"Drop it, Sewer Slime!" he exclaimed.

The head of the Sewer Rats shot us an annoyed look. Then his henchmice, One, Two, and Three, came at us.

But with a series of super *agile* acrobatic jumps, Lady Wonderwhiskers fended off the rats and flipped to safety!

BONK! **POW!** **FLIP!**

Unfortunately, I was so distracted by my hero partner's *amazing* maneuvers that I didn't notice Two heading right for me! I turned suddenly, but it was too late!

"**Leaping liters of liquid Gorgonzola!**" I managed to squeak. "Get those paws off me!"

At those words, my superpowers activated.

Splaaaash!

Two was hit by a **WAVE** of

Huh?!

Ooooooh . . .

SUPERPOWER:
A WAVE OF MELTED GORGONZOLA
ACTIVATED WITH THE CRY:
"LEAPING LITERS OF LIQUID GORGONZOLA!"

Hee, hee, hee!

liquid Gorgonzola!

At the same time, Swiftpaws shouted,

"Costume: Super-Top Mode!"

In a flash, his costume transformed into a spinning yellow top that struck One and Three, sending them running in the opposite direction with their paws in the AIR.

Now that the three bodyguards were out of the picture, Tony and Slickfur looked around, confused.

"Give up, Sewer Rats!" Lady Wonderwhiskers ordered them.

"It's over, sewer slime!" Swiftpaws

chimed in. "This h℮ist is history!"

Then something **incredible** happened. Tony Sludge and Slickfur **surrendered**!

Is It True?

Commissioner Ratford and the police strode into the bank. In the **BLINK** of an eye, Tony and the Sewer Rats were arrested, loaded into a van, and taken to the police station.

"Holey ham and Swiss!" Swiftpaws exclaimed. "That was as easy as drinking a super **cream cheese** smoothie!"

As we left the bank, we were greeted by **loud** shouts and cheers.

A huge crowd of excited rodents had gathered around the police barricade. There was even a television crew led by **Blabberella**, the famouse Muskrat TV anchormouse!

"And now, breaking news coming to you

live from the Central Bank of Muskrat City!" she squeaked, pointing the camera at Swiftpaws and me. "The **amazing** and superheroic Heromice have just captured the infamouse Sewer Rat gang!"

A group of photographers began **snapping** our pics as if we were celebrities on a **RED CARPET**! I turned as red as a tomato. Did I mention I'm a shy mouse at heart? Meanwhile, Swiftpaws struck a pose. Unlike me, my Heromouse partner LOVES being the center of attention!

"Is it true?" a voice squeaked from the crowd. It was Tess Technopaws. She pushed her way through the crowd to reach us. "Were the Sewer Rats really captured?!"

"They were!" Commissioner Ratford confirmed. "There's a cell waiting for them at **MOUSECATRAZ PRISON**!"

Electron and Proton joined us as well. "Superstilton, your *mouserific cheesy powers* were supercool!" said Proton.

"Superspectacular!" agreed Electron.

As everyone celebrated, I started thinking. With Tony in prison, my life would be completely transformed. **Good-bye**, phone calls from Swiftpaws at inconvenient times. **Good-bye**, flying at supersonic speeds to get to Muskrat City. **Good-bye**, hero friends.

Good-bye, Swiftpaws. **Good-bye** Lady Wonderwhiskers. **Good-bye**, Tess Technopaws, Electron, and Proton.

Sniff!

The more I thought about it, the sadder I became. I chewed my whiskers to stop myself from **bawling** like a newborn mouselet.

I glanced at Lady Wonderwhiskers and saw that she had a strange expression on her snout. Was she thinking what I was thinking? Was she going to miss being a Heromouse, too?

I was about to suggest we hold a yearly **Heromouse reunion** to keep in

Yay!

Sniff! Sniff!

Great work!

touch when Lady Wonderwhiskers let out a squeak first.

"Something's not right about this, Superstilton," she said. "Tony and Slickfur didn't even try to *flee*! It was much too easy to catch them!"

Commissioner Ratford was muttering into his cell phone. He looked serious. Suddenly, he yelped in shock. Then he ran toward us, a frightened look on his snout.

"You're not going to **believe** this, Heromice!" he cried. "But it seems as though there has been another burglary. This time it was at Muskrat Gems, the most famouse jewelry store in Muskrat City!"

Immediately, my whiskers began to *tremble* with fear.

Swiftpaws smiled SMUGLY.

"Don't worry, Commissioner," he said.

"Compared to capturing the Sewer Rats, stopping these thieves will be as easy as taking cheese from a **BLIND** rat!"

"But that's the problem," Ratford explained. "According to witnesses, the *Sewer Rats* were the thieves!"

ANOTHER GANG OF SEWER RATS?!

Swiftpaws's jaw nearly HIT the ground. "Tony Sludge is robbing a jewelry store?" he cried. "But that's impossible. He was just captured!"

The commissioner was as baffled as the rest of us. No one squeaked.

Lady Wonderwhiskers broke the silence. "We have to get to Muskrat Gems immediately!" she exclaimed.

Swiftpaws SPRANG into action. "Costume: Flying Scooter Mode!" he ordered.

ZAAAPPP!

Instantly, Swiftpaws had transformed himself into a **flying** scooter. Lady Wonderwhiskers jumped on. "**Come on, Superstilton!**" she urged.

I gulped. "Well, I, um . . ." I stalled. Did I mention I'm afraid of **heights**?"

"Stop **babbling**, hero partner!" Swiftpaws commanded. "Jump on!"

Oh, how do I get myself into these superscary situations?! Of course, I had no choice. I closed my eyes and jumped.

In a FLASH, we arrived at Muskrat Gems. The window was broken and the alarm was shrieking. We could see suspicious figures scampering around inside.

"Come out, Fontina Faces!" Lady Wonderwhiskers shouted.

At that moment, Tony, Slickfur, One, Two, and Three appeared before us.

"Galactic Gouda! I don't believe my eyes!" yelled Swiftpaws.

I couldn't believe mine, either! The Sewer Rats had just been taken to prison. But now they were standing right in front of us!

Without missing a beat, the amazing Lady Wonderwhiskers charged ahead. Ah, what a **COURAGEOUS** super-rodent!

One, Two, and Three blocked her path as Tony and Slickfur dropped the jewels and ran.

Swiftpaws raced forward. "Hold it, **Sewer Slimeballs**!" he yelled.

B-but . . .

Heromice in action!

I was **FROZEN** with fear.

All of a sudden, I realized Two was about to hit Lady Wonderwhiskers! "**Whirling web of string cheese!**" I squeaked. "Watch out, hero partner!"

At those words, my superpowers activated.

Two webs of **SUPER-ELASTIC** string cheese fell over the Sewer Rats, trapping them!

"Great work, Superstilton!" cheered Lady Wonderwhiskers.

ZIIIIIP!

Nooooooo!

Ahhh!

SUPERPOWER:
SUPERSTRONG WEB
OF STRING CHEESE
**ACTIVATED WITH
THE CRY:**
"WHIRLING WEB OF
STRING CHEESE!"

Right at that moment, we heard police siɛns approaching. At first I was relieved to see the commissioner. But when he jumped out of the car, I could tell something was wrong. His fur was as WHITE as a ball of mozzarella!

"Heromice, you'll never believe this," he squeaked. "An art gallery in Muskrat Plaza filled with priceless works has just been raided! And witnesses say the thieves are Tony and his gang!"

My eyes **POPPED** out of my fur. Well, okay, my eyes didn't really pop out, but you get the picture. Once again, I was shocked!

How could the **Sewer Rats** be in several places at once?

Then Commissioner Ratford told us some even more disturbing news. It seemed that the Sewer Rats had also been seen lurking

around **Precious Cheeses**, Muskrat City's premier cheese shop!

Good gravity! This case was getting **stranger** by the minute!

Bzzzz!

"*Supersonic Swiss slices!*" Swiftpaws exclaimed. "It sounds like Tony and his henchmice have a bunch of clones running around the city. We've got to stop them. I just wish I knew—"

BZZZZ!

My hero partner was interrupted midsentence by a **loud** sound. The sound seemed to be coming from the appliance store next to Muskrat Gems.

In the window, a display of different-sized television monitors was broadcasting a loud static humming sound along with a **fuzzy** image.

As we stood staring at the screens, the clear face of **Tony Sludge** appeared.

"Whoa! Way too much Tony!" Swiftpaws commented, holding up a paw.

"Good day, citizens of Muskrat City!"

Tony sneered. "I interrupt your regularly scheduled programming to give you this special announcement from your favorite rodent—me!" Tony cackled wildly.

"HA! HA! HA! HEE! HEE! HEE!"

The image on the screen changed.

Now it showed a large piece of equipment with a lot of buttons and flashing lights. Sludge's right-hand mouse, Slickfur, tinkered with the device, pulling levers and PUSHING buttons.

"And now I am happy to introduce to

you Slickfur's supergenius invention: the RATOCOPIER!" Tony announced.

Slickfur pressed a red button, and the machine began to run.

(1) First, a really powerful ray lit up Tony . . .

(2) Then two flashes SPARKED, surrounding him from the tip of his whiskers to the end of his tail . . .

(3) Finally, a large tube spit out not just ONE but two more Tonys! It deposited them on a conveyer belt right before our eyes!

"Thanks to the Ratocopier," the original Tony explained, "we can now create identical Sewer Rats!"

I gulped and glanced at Lady Wonderwhiskers and Swiftpaws. They looked very WORRIED. Now we knew

how **MULTIPLE** Sewer Rats were wreaking havoc on Muskrat City! We had to **stop** them!

Tony's sinister smile **SPREAD** from whisker to whisker. "Soon, thousands of my Ratocopies will invade Muskrat City! So, citizens, it's time to throw in the *cheesecloth*. You heard it here

first — Tony Sludge is taking over the city, and **no one** can stop me!"

And then Tony's snout disappeared.

"*Blistering, blue cheese!*" Swiftpaws yelled at the **blank** screen, shaking his paw defiantly. "I will stop you!"

"And so will I!" Lady Wonderwhiskers chimed in.

I chewed my whiskers. Taking on one pack of Sewer Rats was hard enough. How were we going to handle *multiple* gangs? Still, I didn't want to seem like I wasn't a ***team player***.

"Um, well, I guess, maybe I might be able to help, too . . ." I muttered under my breath.

"That's the **spirit**, Superstilton!" Swiftpaws cheered. "We will find Tony and destroy the Ratocopier! Isn't that right, hero partner?"

. . . a total mouserific disaster!

I glanced down the street. There were at least **ten** Ratocopied Tonys headed our way! And they were followed by about thirty Ratocopies of One, Two, and Three!

It all added up to a total mouserific disaster!

The Ratocopies advanced **threateningly**

as my whiskers **tRemBLeD** with fear. I wanted to turn tail and run, but not my hero partner. Swiftpaws nodded at Lady Wonderwhiskers and then at me.

"We can do this!" he squeaked. Then he shouted our battle cry:

"HEROMICE IN ACTION!"

MULTIPLYING MONSTER RATS!

The **Ratocopies** continued their march toward us. Together, they looked like one **massive**, **MENACING** mouse army. In fact, there were so many of them, they took up the whole street!

Multiplying monster rats! How could three Heromice take on an entire army? We needed an idea . . . and fast!

Suddenly, Swiftpaws yelled, "**Costume: Rubber Band Mode!**"

Within seconds, he had transformed into a super rubber band that **stretched** across the street.

As soon as the first line of Sewer Rats

reached the band, they **tripped**, ROLLED, and fell flat on their snouts! The second row fell on top of the first. And the third **fell** on top of the second! Pretty soon, the whole army lay in an enormouse heap on the ground!

Ratford and his mice arrested them at once.

While the Ratocopies were being taken to

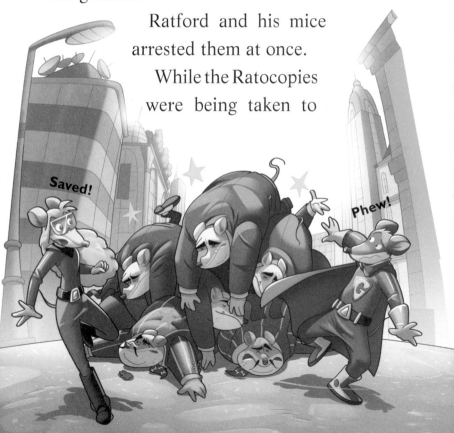

Saved!

Phew!

the police station, Swiftpaws puffed up his fur. "I told you, dear Heromouse partners, nothing is impossible for the HEROMICE!" he boasted.

I have to admit, I was feeling super good about everything when disaster struck. A second group of Ratocopies POPPED up from around the corner!

"Good gravity! Let's get out of here!" Swiftpaws yelled as he ducked into an alley.

We followed him, paws flying as quickly as possible. But the Tony Sludge Ratocopies were right behind us!

Swiftpaws turned RIGHT, then left, then RIGHT again. *Where, oh, where was he going?*

"I don't know if I can make it!" I wailed, **huffing** and puffing. I knew I shouldn't have quit that scamperobics class I had signed up for at the gym. My paws were aching and my heart was *POUNDING* out of my fur!

Still, Swiftpaws kept going. "Come on, hero partners! Follow me!" he shrieked, racing off.

But after a few more turns, Swiftpaws slowed down. "I thought we were close, but . . ." he muttered.

Just then we turned the corner and found ourselves at a dead end. At the far end of the street was a PHONE BOOTH. How strange.

"Quick, everyone inside!" Swiftpaws squeaked, slipping into the booth.

Which way?

"All **three** of us won't fit!" I cried.
But my superpartners yanked me in
behind them.

When all three of us were in the
booth, Swiftpaws began to press
a **SUPERLONG** sequence of
numbers into the phone.

5 . . . 6 . . . 1 . . . 6 . . .

Get them!

Get them!

Get them!

7 . . . 3 . . . 2 . . . I gulped. The Ratocopies were almost at the booth!

Still, my hero partner calmly continued to punch in numbers.

Who was he calling?! "Um, Swiftpaws, this probably isn't a great time to make a phone call," I commented.

"SHHHH!" he replied,

Hooray!

Here it is!

A phone booth?

annoyed. "Don't make me lose count!"

7 . . . 4 . . . 3 . . . 5 . . .

BLAM!

The strangest thing happened. The floor of the booth opened and we **slid** down a steep UNDERGROUND tunnel!

"You see?" Swiftpaws said, chuckling.

"But where

Wahoo!

Hee, hee!

Help!

are we goooooiiiinnngg?" I yelled, terrified.

We continued to fall down, down, down at rattastic speeds until . . . bonk!

We landed in a small, windowless room.

I looked around in a panic. Was it my imagination, or were the walls CLOSING in on us? Have I mentioned that I'm afraid of TIGHT spaces?

Lady Wonderwhiskers was the first to stand up. "Where are we?" she asked.

Swiftpaws grinned. "Don't worry, hero partners! It's all under control! Let me explain . . ."

It turns out the phone booth led to a secret passage. It had been built by Swiftpaws's grandfather Pierre Poirat, the first supercourageous Heromouse of Muskrat City!

"By dialing the **SECRET CODE**, we gained access to this room," Swiftpaws explained. "We're just steps away from the basement of **Heromice Headquarters**!"

"Well, what are we waiting for?" Lady Wonderwhiskers replied, grinning. "Let's go!"

SUPER INFRAMOUSE RAY GLOVE!

We left the secret room using a door hidden in a wall. The door led to a long, NARROW corridor, which led to Heromice Headquarters!

Electron and Proton came to greet us. "*WELCOME, HEROMICE!*" they squeaked excitedly.

As we entered the control room, Tess Technopaws rushed over. "*Great gobs of Gouda!*" she exclaimed. "It's good to see you. Come look at this!"

The screens of the supercomputer were transmitting the news. *Melted mozzarella!* The images passing

before our eyes confirmed our worst fears. Muskrat City had fallen into complete **chaos**!

The police were trying to block the Ratocopies, but they were everywhere!

"**Twisted cat tails!**" I wailed. "We'll never be able to stop all of them!"

"Unless we manage to find their weakest point . . . " Lady Wonderwhiskers wondered aloud, her voice *trailing* off.

Electron smiled mischievously. "Well, I think we may have found out an important **SECRET** about the Ratocopies that just may prove useful," he squeaked.

"What is it?" Swiftpaws demanded.

"We did some studies of the Ratocopies that were captured at the bank," Electron explained.

"The Ratocopier is a **3-D** printer.

It's making three-dimensional copies of the Sewer Rats. But they're just copies. They obey Tony's orders, but they can't think for themselves."

"And it appears that the Ratocopies are sensitive to the light of the **inframouse ray**," Tess Technopaws chimed in.

She held up a *strange-looking* glove. It was her latest invention, the Super Inframouse Ray Glove. "One flash from this glove and the Ratocopies should *disappear*! I haven't been able to test it out yet. That will be your job, Heromice!"

Blistering blue cheese!

"Um, w-well, b-but . . ." I stammered, protesting.

But my hero partner was already on his way out the door with one of Tess's prototypes.

"We'll do it!" he cried. "Now let's get to the police station. There's no time to waste!"

When we arrived, the commissioner was trying FRANTICALLY to respond to all the emergency calls from citizens.

"The jail cells are already PACKED with Ratocopies!" Ratford lamented.

What can we do, Heromice?

Umm . . .

"It's okay, Commissioner!" Swiftpaws said. "We've got a **plan**!"

My hero partner held up Tess's invention.

"This glove can defeat a Ratocopy faster than you can say 'super Swiss slices'!" he gloated.

Swiftpaws approached a **cell** with two Tony Ratocopies locked inside.

"Let's try taking a PICTURE of this

We've got a plan!

no-good Sewer Rat!" he said.

Then he pointed Tess's glove at the Ratocopy.

Flash!

Ahhh!

Within seconds . . . poof!

The Ratocopy had DEMATERIALIZED before our eyes!

SWIRLING TORNADO OF SWISS ROLLS!

"Super Swiss rolls!" Swiftpaws rejoiced. "This thing really works!"

Then he pointed the glove at another jail cell full of Ratocopies.

Flash! **Flash!** **Flash!**

After a few minutes, there wasn't a single Ratocopy left at the police station.

"**FABUMOUSE!**" Ratford exclaimed.

At that moment, my wrist communicator began to beep.

It was a call from **HEROMICE HEADQUARTERS**.

Lady Wonderwhiskers appeared on the screen. "Base to Superstilton, is everything okay?" she asked. "Did you try Tess's iNVENTiON?"

"We sure did, Lady Wonderwhiskers!" Swiftpaws said. "It worked like a charm!"

The hero-rodent of my dreams beamed. Then she asked us to meet her at **City Hall**. "I have a plan to get **RID** of all the Ratocopies at once!"

"B-but how will we g-get there?" I stammered. "The streets are full of R-r-r-ratocopies!"

"Nothing is impossible for the Heromice!" she replied, winking at me.

Then the image disappeared.

I cringed. How many times did I have to say it? **I'm not cut out to be a Heromouse!**

Still, I couldn't let Lady Wonderwhiskers down. Too bad the **FASTEST** way to City Hall was flying. Oh, how I hate to fly! Luckily, my Heromouse partner had a solution.

He transformed himself into a **supercatapult** and . . .

Swoosh!

He launched me toward the roof of City Hall!

From above, we could see all the streets that had been invaded by Ratocopies. Good gravity!

Gulp!

Get ready, Superstilton!

There were tons of Slickfurs and Tonys!

Then we saw the athletic and courageous Lady Wonderwhiskers. She wasn't ALONE, and she had one of Tess's prototypes, too. Proton and Electron were with her in front of City Hall.

As we watched, a group of Ratocopies of **ONE**, **TWO**, and **Three** set out to capture them. The Ratocopies surrounded our friends, but Lady Wonderwhiskers pointed the **Super Inframouse Ray Glove** at them and . . .

Flash!

Flash!

Flash!

The Ratocopies dematerialized, leaving behind a bunch of colorful sparkles. But seconds later, at least **thirty**

Ugh!

Stay back!

Ratocopies of Tony entered the square.

"Superstilton! Swiftpaws! Help!" shrieked Electron and Proton.

Swiftpaws flew toward our friends. "HEROMOUSE NOSEDIVE!" he yelled.

He grabbed the two *mouselets*, pulling them to safety.

I followed my hero colleague's example and darted downward.

WHOOOSH!

I flew toward Lady Wonderwhiskers like a real Heromouse. "Hold on, Lady Wonderwhiskers!" I exclaimed, grabbing the hero-rodent's paws. But just before I could take off, a Tony Ratocopy managed to grab on to Lady Wonderwhisker's **boot**!

"Help!" she shouted.

"**Swirling tornado of Swiss rolls!**" I squeaked. "Let go of her!"

At those words, a **TORNADO** of Swiss rolls hit the Ratocopy. He immediately let go of Lady Wonderwhiskers and landed with a splash in the fountain in the middle of the square.

SPLAAAASH!

"*Nice work, Superstilton!*" cheered Swiftpaws as we landed on the roof of City Hall.

SUPERPOWER:
A TORNADO OF SWISS ROLLS
ACTIVATED WITH THE CRY:
"SWIRLING TORNADO OF SWISS ROLLS!"

Wow!

Oof!

Hang on!

THE
SUPERMEGAFLASH

Lady Wonderwhiskers's lovely blue eyes **SHONE** with admiration.

"You saved me, Superstilton!" she squeaked. "I would have never escaped without your help!"

It was nothing!

Thank you!

turned as RED as a
. "Oh, it was nothing, Lady
n, **Lady Wonderful**,
ady Wonderwhiskers," I
.

rrassing. Just once, I wish
to a **stammering**
avorite Heromouse.
k of something clever
nd Electron arrived.
Supermegaflash,
a   ss's fabumouse
inventions.   It   can
transform electric light
into   **inframouse**
rays!" Proton said. He
showed us a contraption
full of levers, lights,
and buttons.

"Now all we have to do is hook it up to Muskrat City's electricity," Electron explained. "Then every streetlight in the city will become a super potent ray capable of DESTROYING the Ratocopies!"

"Perfect!" Lady Wonderwhiskers said, putting her arms around the two mouselets.

We decided that Lady Wonderwhiskers would go with Electron and Proton to set up the Supermegaflash. "We'll attach it to the **electricity transmitter tower** at the top of the great **hill** that overlooks Muskrat City," Electron said.

"That's a fantastic idea," agreed Lady Wonderwhiskers. Then she turned to Swiftpaws.

"While we're busy setting up the **SUPERMEGAFLASH**," she said, "you and Superstilton can get to work on the second part of the plan. It will be superdangerous and superscary, but you two can handle it."

Superdangerous? Superscary? Immediately, my heart began to pound so hard I thought it might POP right out of my fur! Well, okay, I didn't *really* think it would *POP* out, but you get it. I was scared silly!

"Of course!" Swiftpaws agreed. "Nothing is too difficult for us Heromice! So what's the plan?"

"You two will need to locate and destroy the Ratocopier!" said Lady Wonderwhiskers.

I blinked. "B-b-but how will we find it?" I stammered.

"We have some idea, Heromice!" Electron exclaimed. "Do you remember Tony's message on TV this morning? The one where he was showing off Slickfur's new invention? Well, we managed to locate the origin of the TV SIGNAL. The Sewer Rats transmit from somewhere on the outskirts of Muskrat City!"

Swiftpaws winked at me. "Super Swiss slices! That'll save us a nice trip to the sewers!"

I nodded. I was thrilled we didn't have to brave the stinky sewers. Still, I wasn't looking forward to *prowling* around the outskirts of Muskrat City, either. Who knew what other dangers lurked there?

I was trying not to think about the scary possibilities when my **Heromouse watch** activated. Tess's smiling face appeared on the screen. "Good news, Heromice! I have an idea of where the Sewer Rats may have hidden the Ratocopier. There are some abandoned *warehouses* on the outskirts of Muskrat City that are big enough to hide the contraption!"

"**LET'S GO!**" cried Swiftpaws.

Don't get me wrong. I was terrified. But with the moon **GLOWING** and my cape flapping in the wind, I also felt superspecial.

What an adventure!

Bonk! Pow! Bop!

While Swiftpaws and I took off in search of the abandoned warehouses, Lady Wonderwhiskers and the mouselets made their way toward the **transmitter tower**.

Suddenly, a Ratocopy POPPED out of an oversized trash bin. "Look out!" yelled Electron.

Lady Wonderwhiskers pointed the glove at the Ratocopy and . . .

Flash!

Flash!

Flash!

Grunt, grunt!

The Ratocopy vanished in a cloud of **golden sparkles**.

"Yes!" Proton exclaimed.

Dusk was falling as Lady Wonderwhiskers, Electron, and Proton continued their hunt for Ratocopies. Before long, it was **COMPLETELY DARK**. Suddenly, Proton felt someone grab him from behind.

"**Help!**" he screamed. "**THEY GOT ME!**"

Lady Wonderwhiskers turned on her **flashlight** and pointed it at Proton.

Hey!

Everything okay, Proton?

Electron burst out laughing. "Ha, ha!" she giggled. "A branch just got caught on your backpack! You're not scared, are you, Proton?"

Proton tried to laugh, too, but a minute

Help!

later his eyes **widened** in alarm.

"What is it now?" Electron asked, still chuckling. Then she looked up and turned as *pale* as a slice of provolone.

Nine **Ratocopies** of Tony had just popped out from behind some bushes.

Lady Wonderwhiskers turned on the SUPER INFRAMOUSE RAY GLOVE and made the first of the Ratocopies disappear.

Flash! **Flash!** **Flash!**

"Yes!" Proton cheered, PUMPING his paw in the air.

Lady Wonderwhiskers **zapped** more Ratocopies.

Flash! **Flash!** **Flash!**

But then . . .

Stop them . . .
Stop them . . .
Stop them . . .
Stop them . . .
Stop them . . .
Uh-oh!
Get ready!
Stop them . . .
Aaaahhh!
Stop them . . .
Huh?

Bzzzzoootttt!

"What happened, Lady Wonderwhiskers?" asked Electron.

"Hmm . . . it looks like the **glove** needs to be recharged," the Heromouse said calmly.

"W-w-what do we d-d-do n-n-now?" stammered Proton.

There were still four Ratocopies left in the clearing.

"I'll just have to use more traditional methods with these pests!" Lady Wonderwhiskers replied confidently.

Then she took one **super-agile**, *superspeedy*, super-elegant jump . . . and knocked all the Ratocopies out in one go!

BONK!   **POW!**   **BOP!**

76

Lady Wonderwhiskers pulled a rope out of her belt and wrapped it around the Ratocopies, tying them up like the perfect cheese enchilada.

"Wow! That was *awesome*, Lady Wonderwhiskers!" Proton exclaimed with

admiration. "Maybe someday you could teach me how to **TIE** up criminals like that!"

Lady Wonderwhiskers grinned. "Sure! **Nothing to it!**" she declared.

Electron giggled. "First you'd have to teach him the difference between a **TREE BRANCH** and a criminal," she snorted.

Lady Wonderwhiskers put her arms around the two mouselets. "Come on," she squeaked. "We'd better get to the tower as quickly as we can. **Time's ticking!**"

Don't Look Down!

As Lady Wonderwhiskers and the mouselets climbed the hill to set up Tess's SUPERINVENTION, Swiftpaws and I landed in the outskirts of Muskrat City after a superclose flight between skyscrapers.

Aside from the houses, there was a stretch of abandoned factories, WAREHOUSES, and storage facilities, just as Tess had said. It didn't take long to find the Sewer Rats' **hideout**. There were dozens of Ratocopies of **ONE**, **TWO**, and **Three** keeping guard in the courtyard of one of the buildings!

Luckily, the **RATOCOPIES** weren't the sharpest cheese knives in the drawer. As soon as the Sewer Rat guarding the entrance was distracted, we entered the building.

Holey aged gorgonzola!

The warehouse was jam-packed with Ratocopies!

There were a hundred Tonys and an equal number of Slickfurs! In the middle of the warehouse, the Ratocopier churned

away. Every few minutes, another Ratocopy joined the others!

As we watched, the real Sewer Rats (not the Ratocopies) congratulated themselves.

"Tomorrow will be the final showdown!"

CLACK! CLACK!

CLACK! CLACK! CLACK!

... Go! ... Go! ... Go! ... Go! ... Go!

eady ... Ready ... Ready ... Ready

Tony snickered. "Then Muskrat City will be mine, mine, mine!"

How did we know who the *real* Sewer Rats were? By now, we had discovered a difference between the two. The Ratocopies never **BLINKED**!

"What a cosmic catastrophe!" Swiftpaws whispered. "We need to stop Slickfur's machine right away!"

"B-b-but how?" I stammered.

Swiftpaws had an idea. He pointed to a rusty ladder. It led to a walkway that **HUNG** directly over the Ratocopier.

"We'll climb over!" he announced.

My heart pounded under my fur. Did I mention I'm afraid of heights?

"Are you sure, hero partner?" I stammered, twisting my tail. "That ladder looks rusty—"

"Are you or aren't you a
HEROMOUSE?"
Swiftpaws interrupted me.

I tried to explain that I
am not cut out to be a
Heromouse, but as usual
my hero partner didn't
seem to hear me.

Instead, he dragged
me over to the
ladder. What could
I do? I began to
CLIMB...

As I climbed, I gave
myself a pep talk. It
went like this:
**Don't look down!
Don't look down!
Don't look down!**

Gulp!

Keep going!

Far below us, we could hear One, Two, and Three talking to Slickfur.

"Um, Boss?" asked One. "Do you think we could get our **Ratocopies** now?"

"You *PROMISED* we could each have one," added Two.

"That's right," agreed Three.

"I'm going to call mine FOUR!" said One.

"I'm calling mine *Five*!" added Two.

"And I'm calling mine . . ." began Three.

But he never finished. Slickfur had flown into a rage. "Forget it, you fools!" he shrieked. "The Ratocopies aren't toys!"

Meanwhile, Swiftpaws and I had arrived on the walkway that hung in MIDAIR. Holey cheese! We were so HIGH up, my head began to feel light. Oh no! Was I going to faint? Suddenly, the whole walkway began

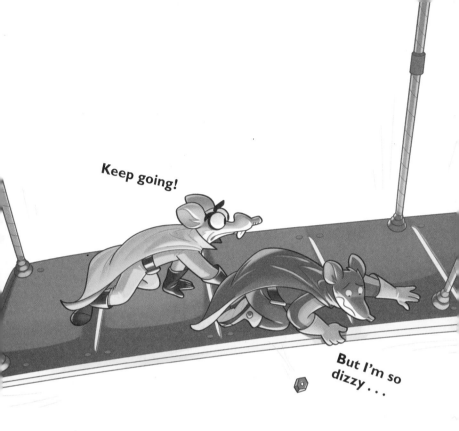

Keep going!

But I'm so dizzy . . .

to **wobble** and **SHAKE!**

I reached for the side to steady myself and accidentally knocked off a loose bolt. **Clonk!**

The bolt rolled toward the edge of the walkway and fell down . . . down . . . down . . . To my horror, it landed right on

Tony's head. It **BOUNCED** off his fur and rolled to the ground.

Boing! Boing! Boing!

"Hey! What was that?" he growled.

Then Tony, Slickfur, One, Two, and Three looked up and **SPOTTED** us.

"**Intruders!**" the head of the Sewer Rats **tHUNDeReD**.

Swiftpaws and I looked at each other in a panic. Getting discovered was not part of our plan! What a superdisaster!

Stop That Machine!

After a really strong initial case of the supertrembles, Swiftpaws took control of the situation. "That's it, Sewer Slimes! STOP that machine at once or you'll have to deal with the Heromice!" he squeaked.

"Ooooh, I'm so scared!" Tony snickered.

He ordered his henchmice to capture us. Dozens and dozens of ONES, TWOS, and THREES approached the ladder, trying to reach us.

"You're finished now, superpests!" the head of the Sewer Rats yelled, eyes FLASHING wickedly.

The Ratocopies began to climb up the

RUSTY ladder. The ladder groaned with every step. I closed my eyes. **Blistering blue cheese!** Is this how it would all end?

"I am *so* not cut out to be a Heromouse!" I sobbed.

But, just then, the most amazing thing happened. I heard a loud screeching sound, so I opened my eyes. GREAT BALLS OF MOZZARELLA! The ***rusty*** metal ladder had become detached from the wall. It **crashed** to the ground, taking the Ratocopies with it!

Ka-blam! Ka-blam!

"Ratocopies, get into **PYRAMID FORMATION**!" Tony thundered.

Uh-oh. That didn't sound good!

The Ratocopies climbed onto one another's backs, forming a super rat pyramid!

Get ready!

"Costume: Bouncing Ball Mode!"

I was ready to give up when Swiftpaws shouted,

He transformed himself into a gigantic rubber ball and bounced through the air.

BOING!

BOING!

BOING!

He crashed into the pyramid, toppling it!

But more Ratocopies quickly formed another pyramid!

Rotten cheddar rinds! It seemed like things couldn't get any worse.

And then they did!

One of the chains LINKING the walkway to the roof suddenly snapped!

Craaaaack!

I lost my balance, slipped, and found myself dangling in midair!

"Help!" I squeaked at the top of my lungs. I was about to become one FLATTENED rodent!

"HOLEY HAILING CHEDDAR BITES!"

At those words, my Heromouse superpowers activated. A HAILSTORM of *cheddar bites* crashed down from above.

The Ratocopies ran for cover.

"Look out!" yelled the Ones.

"They're **ATTACKING**!" screeched the Twos.

"Mmmm . . . tasty!" commented the Threes.

While the Ratocopies were **pelted** with cheese bites, Slickfur and Tony hid in a corner of the room.

"Give it up, superfools!" Slickfur snorted. "Do you really think this cheesy little **HAILSTORM** is enough to stop us?"

"The Ratocopier is made of super-reinforced steel! Cheddar bites won't shut it down!" added Tony.

Right at that moment, I noticed a cheddar bite had rolled into the Ratocopier. A minute later, the machine began to hum.

First there was a strong RAY OF LIGHT that lit the cheese.

Then a short while later . . .

Splutt! Splutt! Splutt!

Thousands of cheddar cheese bites began to tumble out of the Ratocopier, filling up the entire warehouse and crushing the Ratocopies!

Sweet cherry chunk cheesecake! What a super sight!

As the Sewer Rats (the real ones) tried to scramble to safety, I let myself fall from the walkway. I landed on a nice, soft mountain of cheese bites.

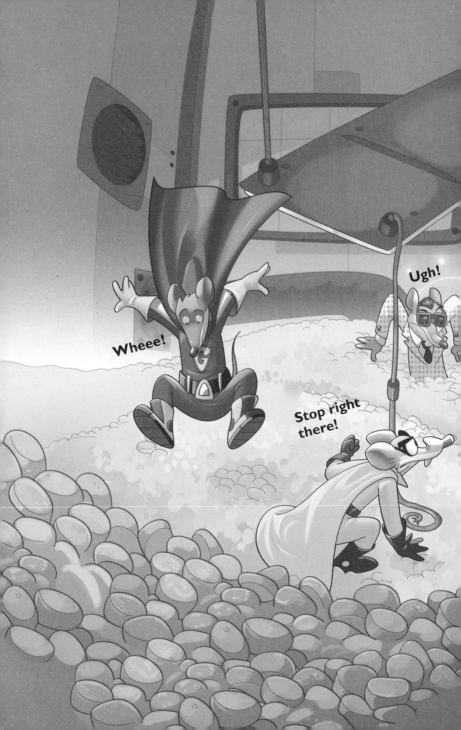

Super Lights!

Swiftpaws high-fived me. "Great **GOBS** of Gruyère! Nice move, hero partner!"

"Er, thanks," I mumbled. I was glad my **superpowers** had stopped the Ratocopies. Still, it's hard to take credit for something you did when you're not really sure how you did it! Maybe one of these days I'd figure out exactly how my superpowers worked . . .

A **SHOUT** from Tony Sludge broke into my thoughts. He was standing on the top of a mound of cheese.

"You'll never get us!" he cried, hitting the button on a remote control.

Immediately, the Sewer Rats' armored limousine, the Drillmobile, popped out of the cheese.

"So long, superfools!" Tony sneered as he climbed aboard. "You *destroyed* the Ratocopier but not the Ratocopies that have taken over the city!"

A moment later, the Drillmobile *disappeared* underground.

"Let's follow them!" Swiftpaws exclaimed, super determined.

I really wanted to take a CHEESE BREAK. (Those cheddar bites looked delicious!) But I knew what we had to do.

"Wait!" I told my Heromouse partner. "We need to deal with the other Ratocopies and save Muskrat City!"

So, in the end, we returned to the city, where we were approached by a group

of Ratocopies. Luckily, we managed to
FLASH them with the *inframouse rays*
from Tess's superglove.

FLASH! FLASH! FLASH! FLASH!
FLASH! FLASH! FLASH! FLASH!

Still, it wasn't long before more Ratocopies appeared. After a few minutes, we were surrounded once again!

Rancid Rat Hairs!

While we were battling the Ratocopies, Lady Wonderwhiskers, Proton, and Electron were gathered on the other side of town. They had just arrived at the transmitter tower.

Proton carefully opened the electrical box and began hitting buttons.

"Do you remember the **numeric code** so we can activate the SUPERMEGAFLASH?" asked Electron.

Proton gave him the code, and a second later the connection was complete! All the streetlamps of Muskrat City lit up with a super bright, **BLINDING** light!

BZZZZZZTTT!

A flash LIT UP the night and hit the Ratocopies, dematerializing them into millions of tiny **colorful** sparkles!

We've almost got it . . .

Great work!

Bzzzagappp!

"Super Swiss slices!" Swiftpaws exclaimed. "What just happened?" We watched in amazement as the Ratocopies **disappeared** before our eyes.

I pointed to the lights coming from the transmitter tower. "Lady Wonderwhiskers and the mouselets have done it!" I squeaked happily. "They must have hooked up the **Supermegaflash** and activated the lights.

As I spoke, the FLASHiNG continued. One by one, the Ratocopies were ZAPPED into oblivion! In fact, by now, the entire city was lit up in that fabumouse anti–Sewer Rat light!

MISSION ACCOMPLISHED!

When we got back to the base, we were in for a **treat**. And I mean, a *real* treat! Tess greeted us with a tray of her *super-fried mozzarella balls*. They were **hot**, crispy, and whisker-licking delicious!

"**Welcome back, Heromice!**" she exclaimed, giving us each a **hug**.

Lady Wonderwhiskers, Proton, and Electron were gathered around the television watching the news.

"Thanks to the Heromice, the Ratocopies

have been dematerialized," the reporter announced with a grin. "And just look at that amazing **fireworks** display! Muskrat City is **SAFE** at last!"

I smiled. **Mission accomplished!** It was time to return to New Mouse City.

Back to you in the studio!

I said good-bye to my friends and prepared to fly back home.

"I'm sure those rotten Sewer Rats will be back again," Electron said, wrapping her paws around me. "But at least we know that the **HEROMICE** will always be here to protect us!"

Swiftpaws chuckled. "You got it!" he agreed. "Like I always say, nothing is impossible for us **Heromice**! Right, Superstilton?"

Aww!

Thanks!

"Um, er, well, yes, I guess . . ." I mumbled. What could I say? I'm afraid to fly, and I don't quite understand my own superpowers. Still, no one ever listened when I explained I'm not cut out to be a Heromouse. So I just smiled and **waved** good-bye.

Then, without any warning, my **supercostume** suddenly took off, taking me with it! I was racing through the sky at full speed toward NEW MOUSE CiTY!

I landed not far from *The Rodent's Gazette*. A second later, my costume switched back to my usual green suit. Even though it was late, I decided to go to the office to check on things. When I opened the door, I heard a *buzzing* sound.

BzZZZZZZZZ!

How strange. What was that?

Then I remembered . . .

When I left for my hero ADVENTURE, Trap had been in charge of figuring out how to work the new photocopier! Now the **TURBOCOPIER 9000** was up and running, and it was shooting out copies at *full speed*!

HOLEY CHEESE BALLS! The machine was **out of control**! It was **Spitting** out copies as fast as Tony's terrifying Ratocopier!

Luckily, they were just paper photocopies and not dangerous copies of the Sewer Rats. In fact, the only **SCARY** thing about these copies was that they had my cousin's snout **plastered** all over them!

I looked around, but there was no sign of Trap anywhere.

I searched for the OFF SWITCH on the copier, but I couldn't find it. I decided I had only one choice—I **PULLED** the plug!

Finally, there was peace and quiet!

A minute later, I noticed a **BLUE** piece of paper taped to my desk lamp. It was from Trap.

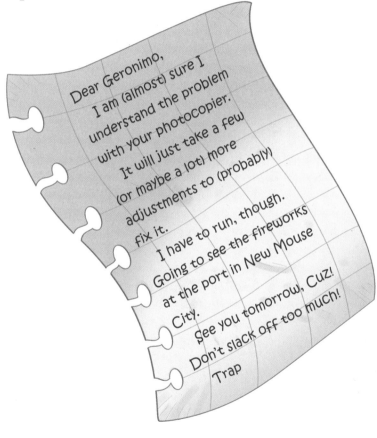

Dear Geronimo,

I am (almost) sure I understand the problem with your photocopier. It will just take a few (or maybe a lot) more adjustments to (probably) fix it.

I have to run, though. Going to see the fireworks at the port in New Mouse City.

See you tomorrow, Cuz! Don't slack off too much!

Trap

I rolled my eyes. Why was I not surprised? I was used to cleaning up my cousin's big messes. I scooped up all the sheets with Trap's face on them. Then I sat down at my desk and pulled out a trusty piece of literature.

"Here we are!" I exclaimed. "The good old instruction manual!"

I had just started reading when . . .

the fireworks started.

I went to the window to enjoy the show. The sky was beautiful, lit up by COLORful sparkles.

How beautiful!

As I watched the fireworks, I couldn't help but think of my adventure in Muskrat City. The colorful sparkles looked just like the sparkles from the Ratocopies when they were hit with the Supermegaflash.

See you later, Sewer Rats! I chuckled to myself.

NOTHING IS IMPOSSIBLE FOR THE HEROMICE!

Be sure to read all my fabumouse adventures!

#1 Lost Treasure of the Emerald Eye

#2 The Curse of the Cheese Pyramid

#3 Cat and Mouse in a Haunted House

#4 I'm Too Fond of My Fur!

#5 Four Mice Deep in the Jungle

#6 Paws Off, Cheddarface!

#7 Red Pizzas for a Blue Count

#8 Attack of the Bandit Cats

#9 A Fabumouse Vacation for Geronimo

#10 All Because of a Cup of Coffee

#11 It's Halloween, You 'Fraidy Mouse!

#12 Merry Christmas, Geronimo!

#13 The Phantom of the Subway

#14 The Temple of the Ruby of Fire

#15 The Mona Mousa Code

#16 A Cheese-Colored Camper

#17 Watch Your Whiskers, Stilton!

#18 Shipwreck on the Pirate Islands

#19 My Name Is Stilton, Geronimo Stilton

#20 Surf's Up, Geronimo!

#21 The Wild, Wild West

#22 The Secret of Cacklefur Castle

A Christmas Tale

#23 Valentine's Day Disaster **#24 Field Trip to Niagara Falls** **#25 The Search for Sunken Treasure** **#26 The Mummy with No Name** **#27 The Christmas Toy Factory**

#28 Wedding Crasher **#29 Down and Out Down Under** **#30 The Mouse Island Marathon** **#31 The Mysterious Cheese Thief** **Christmas Catastrophe**

#32 Valley of the Giant Skeletons **#33 Geronimo and the Gold Medal Mystery** **#34 Geronimo Stilton, Secret Agent** **#35 A Very Merry Christmas** **#36 Geronimo's Valentine**

#37 The Race Across America **#38 A Fabumouse School Adventure** **#39 Singing Sensation** **#40 The Karate Mouse** **#41 Mighty Mount Kilimanjaro**

#42 The Peculiar Pumpkin Thief **#43 I'm Not a Supermouse!** **#44 The Giant Diamond Robbery** **#45 Save the White Whale!** **#46 The Haunted Castle**

#47 Run for the Hills, Geronimo! **#48 The Mystery in Venice** **#49 The Way of the Samurai** **#50 This Hotel Is Haunted!** **#51 The Enormouse Pearl Heist**

#52 Mouse in Space! **#53 Rumble in the Jungle** **#54 Get into Gear, Stilton!** **#55 The Golden Statue Plot** **#56 Flight of the Red Bandit**

The Hunt for the Golden Book **#57 The Stinky Cheese Vacation** **#58 The Super Chef Contest** **#59 Welcome to Moldy Manor** **The Hunt for the Curious Cheese**

#60 The Treasure of Easter Island **#61 Mouse House Hunter** **#62 Mouse Overboard!** **The Hunt for the Secret Papyrus** **#63 The Cheese Experiment**

#64 Magical Mission **#65 Bollywood Burglary** **The Hunt for the Hundredth Key** **#66 Operation: Secret Recipe**

Check out these very special editions!

**THEA STILTON:
THE JOURNEY
TO ATLANTIS**

**THEA STILTON:
THE SECRET OF
THE FAIRIES**

**THEA STILTON:
THE SECRET OF
THE SNOW**

**THEA STILTON:
THE CLOUD
CASTLE**

**THEA STILTON:
THE TREASURE
OF THE SEA**

**THE JOURNEY
THROUGH TIME**

BACK IN TIME:
THE SECOND JOURNEY
THROUGH TIME

**THE RACE
AGAINST TIME:**
THE THIRD JOURNEY
THROUGH TIME

LOST IN TIME:
THE FOURTH JOURNEY
THROUGH TIME

DON'T MISS ANY HEROMICE BOOKS!

#1 Mice to the Rescue!

#2 Robot Attack

#3 Flood Mission

#4 The Perilous Plants

#5 The Invisible Thief

#6 Dinosaur Danger

#7 Time Machine Trouble

#8 Charge of the Clones

#9 Insect Invasion

Meet
GERONIMO STILTONOOT

He is a cavemouse—Geronimo Stilton's
ancient ancestor! He runs the stone
newspaper in the prehistoric village
of Old Mouse City. From dealing with
dinosaurs to dodging meteorites,
his life in the Stone Age is full
of adventure!

#1 The Stone of Fire   #2 Watch Your Tail!   #3 Help, I'm in Hot Lava!   #4 The Fast and
the Frozen

#5 The Great Mouse   #6 Don't Wake the   #7 I'm a Scaredy-Mouse!   #8 Surfing for Secrets   #9 Get the Scoop,
Race   Dinosaur!   Geronimo!

#10 My Autosaurus   #11 Sea Monster   #12 Paws Off the Pearl!   #13 The Smelly Search
Will Win!   Surprise

MEET GERONIMO STILTONIX

He is a spacemouse — the Geronimo Stilton of a parallel universe! He is captain of the spaceship *MouseStar 1*. While flying through the cosmos, he visits distant planets and meets crazy aliens. His adventures are out of this world!

#1 Alien Escape

#2 You're Mine, Captain!

#3 Ice Planet Adventure

#4 The Galactic Goal

#5 Rescue Rebellion

#6 The Underwater Planet

#7 Beware! Space Junk!

#8 Away in a Star Sled

#9 Slurp Monster Showdown